Subcontractors of Guilt

Subcontractors of Guilt

Holocaust Memory and Muslim Belonging in Postwar Germany

ESRA ÖZYÜREK

STANFORD UNIVERSITY PRESS
Stanford, California

Stanford University Press
Stanford, California

Printed in the United States of America on acid-free, archival-quality paper

Library of Congress Cataloging-in-Publication Data
Names: Özyürek, Esra, author.
Title: Subcontractors of guilt : Holocaust memory and Muslim minority belonging in post-war Germany / Esra Özyürek.
Description: Stanford, California : Stanford University Press, [2023] | Includes bibliographical references and index.
Identifiers: LCCN 2022034042 (print) | LCCN 2022034043 (ebook) | ISBN 9781503634664 (cloth) | ISBN 9781503635562 (paperback) | ISBN 9781503635579 (ebook)
Subjects: LCSH: Holocaust, Jewish (1939-1945)—Study and teaching—Germany. | Antisemitism—Study and teaching—Germany. | Antisemitism—Germany—Prevention. | Muslims—Education—Germany. | Muslims—Germany—Attitudes. | Collective memory—Germany.
Classification: LCC D804.33 .O998 2023 (print) | LCC D804.33 (ebook) | DDC 305.6/970943076—dc23/eng/20220816
LC record available at https://lccn.loc.gov/2022034042
LC ebook record available at https://lccn.loc.gov/2022034043

Cover design: Jason Anscomb
Cover photo: Unsplash / Enxh Shehi
Typeset by Elliott Beard in Brill 10/15

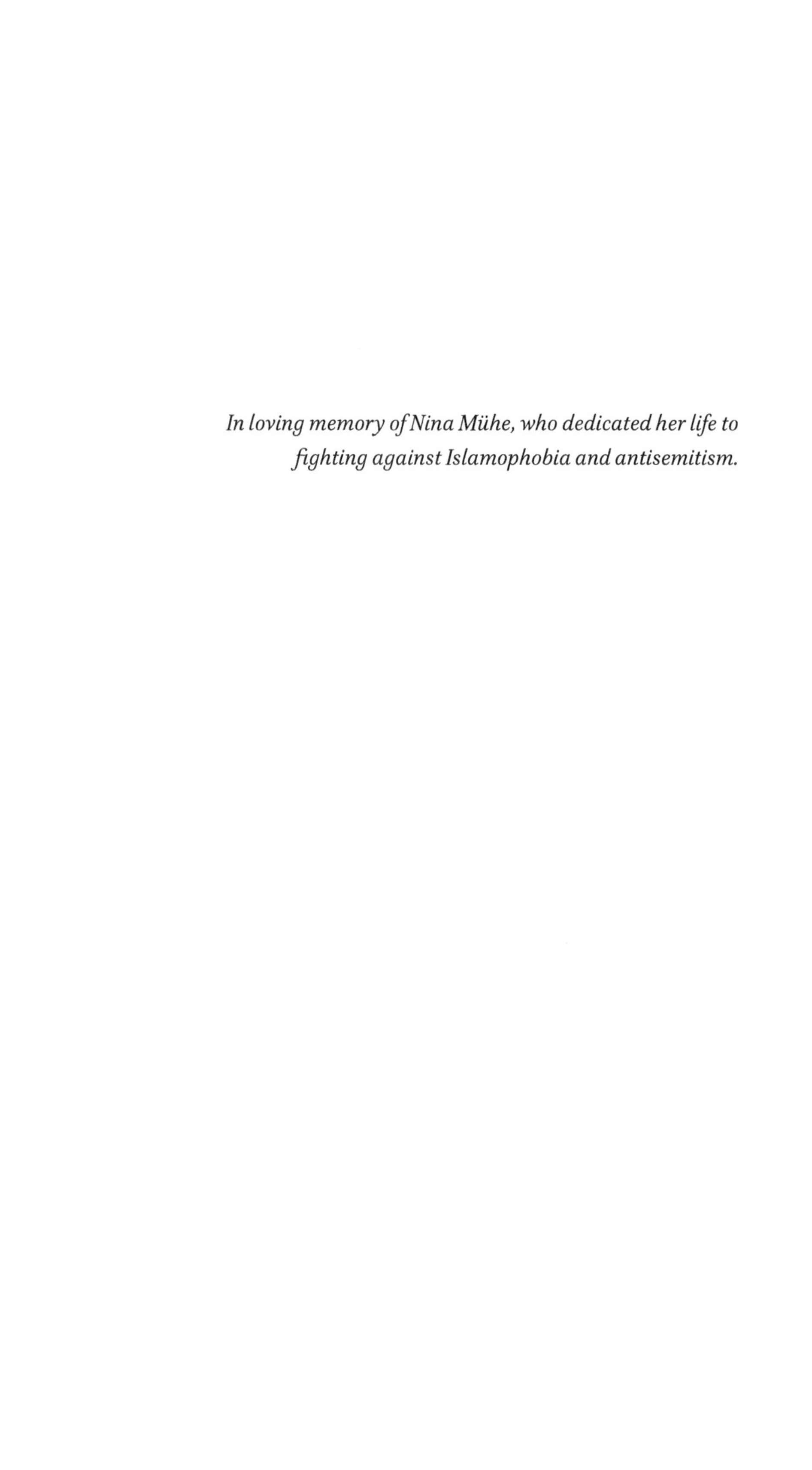

In loving memory of Nina Mühe, who dedicated her life to fighting against Islamophobia and antisemitism.

CONTENTS

PREFACE AND ACKNOWLEDGMENTS

When I first arrived in Germany in 2006, I was transfixed by the *Stolpersteine*, the brass-plated "stumbling stones" set in the sidewalks of Berlin and around Europe outside the last known homes of the many victims of National Socialism. My intellectual coming-of-age in the early 1990s in Istanbul intersected with the emergence of a critical mass of intellectuals in Turkey who believed that admitting to the genocidal crimes of the late Ottoman Empire was important for the prospects of peace and justice not only with Armenians but also with Kurds, Alevis, and other oppressed groups in Turkey. In these circles, Germany was perceived as a positive role model. I was then and remain now in awe of the time, energy, and commitment private German citizens and public institutions invest in coming to terms with the heinous crimes the Nazis and their supporters committed in the name of the German nation. Once in Berlin, I began to wonder how Istanbul, Van, Malatya, or Maraş would look with stumbling stones set in the sidewalks to mark the last known homes of Armenians and Assyrians forced on a death march through Ottoman lands during the genocide of 1915. I sat next to the memorial water fountain at the Hauptstrasse of Schoeneberg that lists the death camps under the slogan "We will never forget!" and thought about what it would be like were Turkey to admit to the destruction, genocide, and appropriation upon which the nation is built. I genuinely wanted to understand and learn from the German experience of looking back at grievous wrongdoings with the intent to draw lessons from them.

At the time I was a naturalized American citizen with a dozen years in the United States behind me. I was also the beneficiary of US investment in Germany, ongoing since the end of World War II, in that I received a residential fellowship at the American Academy in Berlin. With me was my Jewish American partner, whose ancestors had migrated to the US from the area that is today

Poland and Russia during the late nineteenth and early twentieth centuries. His family left Europe before the Holocaust. Despite our lack of previous connection to Germany, we both found ourselves absorbed into already existing categories in the country. Coming to Germany made me "a Turk" and "a Muslim" and my partner simply "a Jew," groups seen as categorically different and in opposition to each other in ways neither of us had ever experienced in the US or in Turkey. I routinely was met with surprise when I said I am a professor. "A Turkish professor!" some would exclaim. My partner, also a professor, never once received such a reaction, but instead found himself answering countless questions as to whether he was experiencing antisemitism, how he felt living as a Jewish man in Germany, whether he knew this or that Jewish person, regardless of whether they came from the US, Israel, or some other country. In my case, the many questions probed how it came about that my parents had allowed me to study, travel to the US, and marry a non-Muslim man, and what kind of identity our children would have. We could not help noticing again and again how people who could so reflexively and painstakingly think through the most subtly disguised manifestations of antisemitism could also be so blind to their own xenophobic prejudices. The sharp focus on our religious/ethnic identities, the differential treatment we received on a daily basis, and our immersion in the material signs and sensations of the German past led us both to think and eventually to write about the intersection of the Muslim and Jewish questions in past and present Germany.[1]

Yet another path led me to the study of Muslims and Holocaust memory in Germany: my earlier research on German converts to Islam, *Being German, Becoming Muslim: Race, Religion, and Conversion in the New Europe*. Given the racialization of religion in Germany, I asked: How are white Germans who embrace Islam able to reconcile their German and Muslim identities? Although Islam, as a major world religion, has a universalist appeal and message of peace and justice, it is also fashioned as a racialized identity in Europe, seen as belonging primarily to certain geographies and certain groups. To claim Islam as their own without giving up their privilege, white German Muslims promoted an Islam stripped of any and all qualities perceived as Middle Eastern, and the newly deculturalized version is considered a better fit with German/European Enlightenment values. As I was conducting my research, I would ask myself, and whoever else I was talking to: What would it take for a born Muslim, Turk, or Arab to become German? Although it was more difficult (and categorically ambiguous) for a nonwhite person to become German than for a German to become a Muslim, I quickly came to the conclusion—given that Holocaust memory has the qualities of a civil religion and is the foundation of postwar white German identity—that one of the most important ways of doing this would be to co-shoulder German guilt and responsibility for the Holocaust. This presented a challenging problem: With racialized Islam seen as "belonging" to the Middle East, and responsibility for the Holocaust viewed as the sole property of the ethnic Germans in whose name the crime was committed, how could Muslim-background immigrants claim the universalist message of Holocaust memory and become Germans so long as their racialized identity kept them from claiming it?

While I was conducting my research on German converts in the mid-2000s, the topics of "Muslim antisemitism" and "Holocaust education for Muslims" began to occupy considerable space in German public discussions. At the time I had the privilege of meeting Derviş Hızarcı and later Ufuk Topkara, who were among the first Muslim German activists dedicated to fighting antisemitism. They shared with me how their motivation for fighting antisemitism and keeping the memory of the Holocaust alive is deeply connected to their commitment to Islam and the experience of growing up as members of a religious minority in Germany. Muslim Youth in Germany (*Muslimische Jugend in Deutschland*), one of the groups I focused on during my research on German converts to Islam, was already promoting the idea that the fight against antisemitism is a Muslim German duty and also was organizing trips to Auschwitz. I started attending education programs organized by the Kreuzberg Initiative against Anti-Semitism (*Kreuzberger Initiative gegen Anti-Semitismus*), the Wannsee Conference House, and Amira: Anti-Semitism in the Context of Migration and Racism (*Anti-Semitismus im Kontext von Migration und Rassismus*), and attended countless training and information programs about Muslims, antisemitism, and Holocaust memory. Internet searches on the topic led me to organizations such as the Socialist Turkish Workers' Union or individual Turkish-background schoolteachers who organized Holocaust education and antisemitism prevention programs for Muslims. During the five years I lived in Berlin (at various times from 2006 to 2014), and later in frequent trips to Duisburg and three trips to the site of the Auschwitz death camp in Oświęcim,

Poland, I took part in five different Holocaust education programs designed for Muslims in Berlin, Duisburg, and Dortmund. For two months, I observed tenth-grade history classes in a mixed-track high school that caters mostly to non-German-background students in Berlin. I conducted semi-structured interviews with more than a dozen Holocaust educators who regularly teach Muslim minorities and with close to a hundred Turkish- and Arab-background German men and women from different socioeconomic backgrounds and age groups in Berlin, Aachen, Dortmund, Duisburg, and Frankfurt on their relationship to German history. I also followed closely the artistic and public intellectual engagements of Muslim-background Germans with Holocaust memory, reading voraciously and attending exhibitions and performances regularly. I collected and analyzed calls to fund Holocaust education projects directed toward Muslims made by organizations such as the Federal Ministry of Education and Research (*Bundesministerium für Bildung und Forschung*), the Federal Ministry of Family Affairs, Senior Citizens, Women and Youth (*Bundesministerium für Familie, Senioren, Frauen und Jugend*), and the Foundation Remembrance, Responsibility, and Future (*Stiftung "Erinnerung, Verantwortung und Zukunft"*).

In 2014, Rosa Fava, a trailblazing critical researcher on Holocaust education for Muslims, sent me an online link to an interview with Burak Yılmaz, a young Turkish- and Kurdish-background German educator who had co-founded an education program in Duisburg with the attention-grabbing title, Muslims in Auschwitz. As I happened to be on my way to Düsseldorf for a conference, I got in touch with Burak and asked if he would meet me. That meeting and Burak's generosity of mind opened new doors for me to a unique community of Turkish-, Kurdish-, and Arab-background young men searching for ways to transform their own communities and German society to make them more just and equal, especially in terms of gender- and race-based injustice. Shining a spotlight on the lives and activities of the young adolescent males who live in northern Duisburg opened a completely new window onto the realities of racialized young men in western Germany. Over the next five years, I traveled to Duisburg regularly and followed them on their retreats in Germany and on a trip to Auschwitz. I participated in and observed their project meetings and conducted individual interviews with the educators and participants. The youth generously allowed me to enter both their lives and their intense discussions about their role in German society. They introduced me to their families and continued communicating with me when I was no longer in the country. Without such intimate knowledge of the dedicated work that goes into the Heroes program in Duisburg and its Muslims in Auschwitz project, I would not now understand what it takes for a marginalized Muslim-background German to shoulder the weight of German Holocaust memory while bearing the brunt of racism in the country. Nor would I understand what the postwar German social contract looks like from the standpoint of Middle Eastern/Muslim-background young men. The story I tell in this book starts with the Germany into which their grandparents and parents stepped after the war and how they transformed it fundamentally, if invisibly. Grandchildren of these Middle Eastern/Muslim-background guest workers and children of other immigrants and refugees are now claiming the past, present, and future of Germany, making sure it is recognized that they belong to Germany and Germany to them.

My research and writing for this book was supported by the American Academy in Berlin, Humboldt Foundation, Fulbright Foundation, German Academic Exchange, and British Academy. Three different universities at which I worked since 2006—University of California–San Diego, London School of Economics, and University of Cambridge—have made it possible for me to do the research trips and take the time to write the book.

I would not have been able to think through this book without the generous help of friends and colleagues in Germany, Turkey, the United States, the United Kingdom, and Israel. People who thought with me through the duration of the project and read parts of the work include Lori Allen, Kimberly Arkin, Bilgin Ayata, Elisabeth Becker-Topkara, Michael Bodemann, Irit Dekel, Aycan Demirel, Fatima El-Tayeb, David Feldman, Sarah Gerwens, Julian Goepffarth, Amos Goldberg, Elke Gryglewski, Asena Günal, Derviş Hızarcı, Aslı Iğsız, Banu Karaca, Oliver Kontny, Kader Konuk, Jacob Lypp, Ruth Mandel, Dirk Moses, David Motadel, Nina Mühe, Yael Navaro, Anne Parkinson, Ayşe Parla, Damani Partridge, Michael Rothberg, Stefanie Schüler-Springorum, Yasemin Shooman, Ufuk Topkara, Theresa Truax-Gischler, Yasemin Yıldız, and Gökçe Yurdakul.

Above all, the writing of this book was made possible by the generosity of the Middle Eastern/Muslim-background youth, project leaders, and educators who commit themselves to learning about and from the Holocaust.

Parts of chapters 2 and 3 were drawn from two previously published articles: "Export-Import Theory and Racialization of Antisemitism: Turkish and Arab-Only Prevention Programs in Germany," *Comparative Studies in Society and History* 58, no. 1 (2016): 40–65; and "Rethinking Empathy: Emotions Triggered by the Holocaust among Muslim-Minority in Germany," *Anthropological Theory* 18, no. 4 (2018): 456–77.

Subcontractors of Guilt

INTRODUCTION

German Holocaust Memory and the Redemptive Path toward Democracy

Postwar German national identity is based on atoning for the high crimes of the Holocaust and learning the ethical lessons of empathy, tolerance, and democracy. The Holocaust has not been remembered uniformly throughout Germany, but German civil society (Wustenberg 2017) and the state heavily invested in establishing a shared cultural memory that would unify and define the present and future values of German society (Assmann 2011). Despite its commitment to antinationalism and antiracism, German memory culture failed to include members of society who are not ethnically German. Or, as Michael Rothberg and Yasemin Yıldız argue (2011, 35), the exclusion of racialized groups from the foundational narrative of postwar German society was not a failure but rather a calculated effort: that is, founders and defenders of German memory culture, believing that only an ethnically homogeneous German identity could ensure German responsibility for the Holocaust, regarded racialized groups, such as the Muslim-background Germans who helped to build postwar Germany, as both external and irrelevant to the postwar public German narrative of democratization.[1] As a result, Muslim-background Germans could not be included in the postwar German social contract, through which a new and free (West) German society was allowed by the Allies to emerge on condition of having learned the correct lessons from the Holocaust.

This long-lasting perceived irrelevance of nonethnic Germans to Holocaust memory underwent a radical and unexpected change beginning in the 2000s. Since then, Turkish- and Arab-background Germans have been central to the public narrative, but only as the prime obstacles to German national reconciliation with its Nazi past and its embrace of democracy now and into the future. This status as obstacle is shared only to a lesser degree by Germans from the formerly socialist East Germany, who are viewed as having insufficiently acknowledged and atoned for their part in the Nazi crimes (Shoshan 2017). Today, Middle Eastern/Muslim-background Germans are routinely accused of being unable to relate to Holocaust history, incapable of establishing empathy with its Jewish victims (chapter 3), and of importing new forms of antisemitism to a country that is assumed to have dealt with its own antisemitism more or less successfully (chapter 2). In a country where 90 percent of antisemitic crimes are committed by right-wing white Germans, fingers continue to be pointed at the Muslim minority for being the major carriers of antisemitism (Dekel and Özyürek, forthcoming). The federal and local governments as well as NGOs, having embraced this perspective around the turn of the twentieth century, began to organize an assortment of Holocaust education and antisemitism prevention programs designed specifically for Muslim-background immigrants and refugees.

Subcontractors of Guilt explores when, how, and why Middle Eastern/Muslim-background Germans moved from the periphery to the center of Holocaust memory discussions in Germany as potential perpetrators of antisemitic crimes, and what this development means for Holocaust commemoration on the one hand and for the place of immigrants in Germany and in an enlarged Europe on the other. By focusing on the recently formed but already sizable sector of Muslim-only antisemitism and Holocaust education programs, this book explores the paradoxes of postwar German national identity through the prism of Middle Eastern/Muslim-background Germans. Ostensibly these programs aim to ensure that Muslim Germans also finally learn the necessary lessons from the Holocaust and thereby embrace Germany's most important postwar political values. Providing remedial programs for a population who passes through the national curriculum like all others, however, posits them as less able to "learn the lessons of the Holocaust." In effect, these programs erase the more than sixty-year-long history of millions of postwar migrants who reconstructed Germany from the early 1960s to today. The logic behind the programs also depicts white Christian-background Germans as having reached their destination of redemption and redemocratization, or at least of having come far enough in terms of dealing with the Holocaust (Wilds 2013) to qualify themselves as judges and educators of others. A unique focus on Muslims in antisemitism prevention, thus, offloads the general German social problem of antisemitism onto the Middle Eastern–background minority and further stigmatizes them as the most unrepentant antisemites who need additional education and disciplining.

Subcontractors of Guilt explores Middle Eastern/Muslim-background responses to this unprecedented call to shoulder the responsibility of the German past from which they have thus far been excluded despite their full participation in building the postwar German society. It follows minority groups and individuals who eagerly take this weight onto their shoulders with a variety of motivations and expectations. In the German language, the word "guilt" (*Schuld*) also means "debt," a personal or national liability that can be handed down from generation to generation but also can be widely distributed or even canceled. What are the consequences of distributing the foundational German guilt and the inherited debt of the Holocaust to people who mostly arrived after the crime? What is the nature of this contractual relationship between the parties who exchange guilt and debt? What can non-German-background minorities who arrived after the war gain or lose if there is a new German social contract? And what of the white Christian-background German majority, in whose name the crime was committed but before they were born? Can just anyone, irrespective of their relationship to Germany or the German nation, take in this guilt or pay off this debt? What happens to the guilt or the debt itself once it is spread around or subcontracted?

Emotional Basis of Postwar German Democratization

Whether and under what conditions Germany should be part of the post–World War order has been a topic of intense debate since 1946. The Allies allowed Germany to regain its sovereignty only if it denazified, demilitarized, and divided into two nation-states (see Jarausch 2006; Schissler 2001; Poiger 2000; Fay 2008; Naimark 1995). West Germany was given Marshall Aid on condition that it re-democratized itself. In the new social contract, Germans, and especially West Germans, would no longer be united on the basis of their shared bloodline, as before, but through their civil commitment to a democratic constitution. An important precondition of this postwar social contract was German acceptance that they had committed egregiously immoral actions during the Third Reich and would agree to fundamentally transform themselves and the culture that had created the breeding grounds for Nazism. Hence, the postwar social contract that brought (West) Germans together does not date back to a hypothetical time when Germany was in a Lockian state of nature but to a recent time and place: the chaos at the end of World War II. After a regime that led to ruination based on fantasies of blood-based membership, a new social contract was not initially signed solely among Germans but between Germans and the Allied Forces: Germany could exist on condition of admitting guilt and promising a thorough transformation.

The Allied Forces, and especially the United States, monitored the emotional and cultural expressions of Germans to determine whether they were fulfilling their part of the contract. While doing so, Americans approached National Socialism as an expression of German exceptionalism, locating the sources of fascism in German culture and social psychology and promoting the idea that this culture and psychology could change (chapter 1). The victorious Americans, whose own society was segregated along racial lines, perceived democracy not simply as a matter of elections, legislation, and the workings of the German parliament but as "a type of behavior, a public attitude, and an affective relationship to the state, independent of those other political institutions" (Fay 2008, xiv). Reeducation was "conceptualized largely as a psychological and cultural task" that "demanded a well-tuned sense of public opinion of democratization" (6) to be successful. Sociologists, psychologists, and anthropologists came together in the United States under new schemes funded by the Department of War to figure out what had gone wrong with the emotional makeup of German culture and how it could be rehabilitated (Fay 2008). One might argue that the motivating factor behind the upsurge in the social sciences in the US of the 1950s was to understand and transform Germany and, later, other enemy nations.

The occupying Americans vigorously promoted the idea that inculcating certain emotions toward the Jewish victims of National Socialism was crucial for Germany's reeducation and normalization as "a measure of moral capacity or even a gauge of humanity" (Parkinson 2015, 9). To ensure that West Germans faced what they had done, they were forced to walk through death camps and look at pictures of suffering victims, as well as at posters that read "You are Guilty!" (Jarausch 2006). During these psycho-educational activities, the Americans closely scrutinized the Germans' emotional expressions. In her study of postwar Germany, Anne Parkinson demonstrates that a lack of emotion, and especially a lack of melancholia and sadness, both of which would be expected to naturally result from intense feelings of guilt, was often viewed as the root of the German problem and the element that made them seem unfit for democracy. According to Parkinson, both Americans and Germans characterized postwar Germany as "suffering from coldness, or *Gefühlskälte*, and emotional rigidity, or *Gefühlsstarke*, frozen affect and emotional inability" (Parkinson 2015, 5).

German philosopher Karl Jaspers answered the Allies' call by associating the postwar condition with the "correct" emotion, mainly guilt, in his short book, *The Question of German Guilt* (*Die Schuldfrage*) ([1947] 2001), written in the context of the Nuremberg trials. He argued that acceptance of collective guilt was the only hope for individual and national penance and renewal. In other words, he suggested a new social contract where criminal Germans would be able to create a new German identity and a new sense of social integration (74) on the basis that they admit and share their guilt, and relinquish their pride and arrogance in favor of humility and purification. He suggested that the root of this new affiliation among Germans would no longer be based on blood ties but on a sense of co-responsibility and empathy. Important to the discussion developed later in this book, the empathy to which he drew attention as the basis of the new social community in 1946 did not flow from German to Jewish victim but from German to German, all sharing the burden of bearing guilt.

German scholars exiled in the US, such as Theodor Adorno, also played a key role in formulating the emotional basis of the German postwar social contract. After being expelled from university by the Nazis, Adorno left Germany for Oxford, New York, and Los Angeles. While in exile, Adorno wrote about the German authoritarian personality, antisemitism, propaganda, and how to develop German democracy (Mariotti 2016). Adorno believed that only proper education would foster mature, self-critical, self-aware citizens resistant to authoritarian tendencies (French and Thomas 1999). He advocated a confrontational social-psychological approach toward the Nazi past (Meseth 2012) and critical self-reflection (Cho 2009). West German memory culture and Holocaust education was heavily shaped by Adorno and also motivated by West Germany's desire to be an equal partner in the Western alliance (Moeller 1996).

At every turn, however, tendencies inspired by Adorno and like-minded thinkers for the "institutionalization of a ritual shame" (Fulbrook 1999) or a "ritualized regret" (Olick 2007) competed with a desire to recognize Germans as victims of the war (Biess 2006; Moeller 2005) and to relativize the crimes of National Socialists (Bartov 1998; Moeller 1996; Niven 2006). In 1978, West German chancellor Helmut Schmidt (1974–82) became the first German leader to visit a synagogue and ask for reconciliation with Jews, while underlining the innocence of today's Germans (Wolfgram 2011, 66). In the 1980s, conservative German historians stated that it was time to embrace a positive nationalism and accept that Nazi crimes were cruel but comparable to those of other totalitarian regimes, especially the USSR (Kampe 1987). After reunification of the two Germanies in 1990, a memory culture that is unapologetic about German guilt and that conceives of the Holocaust as an unquestionable "negative myth of origin" and "a primal phantasmatic scene of guilt and shame around which German national identifications are organized" (Moses 2001, 94) became official and mainstream. Into the 2000s the Holocaust memory discourse became rigid and highly controlled to such an extent that Dirk Moses (2021) called it catechistic, where comparing it to other crimes became a taboo. As a victim-centered memory discourse established itself, unexpectedly more white Germans began to psychologically identify themselves with the Jewish victims of the Holocaust (Jureit and Schneider 2010).[2]

In the east, the former German Democratic Republic declared itself the successor to the war's resistance movement. Many West German and American scholars suggest that this attitude of defining themselves as the good Germans kept East Germans from going down the thorny path of soul-searching about their role during National Socialism (Fox 2001). Other scholars, however, argue that East Germans were better at confronting the National Socialist past. They suggest that the argument about East Germans having ignored the Holocaust is a post-unification West German fabrication (Clark 2018, 606). Jewish American moral philosopher Susan Neiman (2019, 108), for example, notes that despite its much smaller population compared to West Germany, East Germany convicted twice as many Nazis (almost 13,000), actually put them in prison, and executed over one hundred of them, whereas West Germany convicted far fewer (6,500), commuted most imprisonments, and did not execute any. Neiman adds that while the East German state defined the primary victims of the Third Reich as "victims of fascism" and as communists, it overlooked the fact that antisemitism was the driving force of German fascism.

Despite their differences in relating to National Socialism, East and West Germany also promoted similar myths into the 1980s that made ordinary Germans seem like innocent victims of the Nazis (Moeller 2006). Both versions of Holocaust memory discourse held that Germans and Nazis were two separate groups and that the Nazi state had terrorized everyone to the point that resistance was nearly impossible (Wolfgram 2010). As late as 1986, conservative historians from West Germany argued that it was time to view Germany's past as not distinctly evil and to consider the crimes of Nazism as akin in severity to those of Bolshevism (Kampe 1987). In the late 1980s a so-called "historians debate" took place among German public intellectuals. Conservative historian and philosopher Ernest Nolte contended that the crimes committed under socialism predated and predetermined the Holocaust and hence were essentially "Asiatic" and not German and were comparable to those of the Holocaust (Nolte 1986). Other conservative historians such as Andreas Hillgruber argued that socialism was such a huge threat to Germany that historians need to place more emphasis on the necessity of the German Army to protect their country and population from the Red Army (Hillgruber 1986). At the same time West German philosopher Jürgen Habermas strongly stood against these claims, arguing for the uniqueness of the Holocaust and the German responsibility in it (Habermas [1986] 1993). Helmut Kohl, the conservative chancellor (1982–98) who oversaw German unification, wanted to focus on the positive aspects of German history prior to World War II. He and other conservative politicians perceived Germany as the victim of Holocaust remembrance and representation, especially in the United States (Eder 2016).

The vision of Holocaust memory that saw Germans as the main victims of National Socialism lost the public debate in West Germany in the 1990s. Two important contributions to this process changed the way large numbers of Germans thought about the Holocaust: an exhibit about the active involvement of the Wehrmacht in the Holocaust that debuted in Hamburg in 1995 and toured the country for four years (Wolfgram 2010, 141), and the German-language publication of US scholar Daniel Goldhagen's *Hitler's Willing Executioners* in 1996, which debunked the myth that there had been a major difference between ordinary Germans and the Nazis (Eley 2000).

The years that followed the unification of the two Germanies consolidated Holocaust memory as the basis of a unified Germany and, several years later, of an expanded European Union. After unification, Habermas played a crucial role in the official embrace of a victim-centered and hence guilt-based commemoration where Germans were to take full responsibility for the Holocaust as proof of their responsible citizenship. Habermas saw himself as a "product of reeducation" made possible in the Federal Republic (Müller 2000, 104). In so doing, he relied on his professor Theodor Adorno's legacy in his strong opposition to those who wished to relativize and trivialize the Holocaust. He "translated Adorno's standpoint on the pedagogical aims of working through history as a model of critical remembrance into a protocol of ideal citizenship" (Ball 2009, 47) in Germany and also in Europe. German political philosopher Jan-Werner Müller points out that the Habermasian effort to turn Holocaust memory into the negative nationalism of a community of fate involves a deep paradox: "According to this view, Auschwitz was willingly recognized as a singular crime—but at the same time this crime was jealously guarded as a unique, almost metaphysical act which, yet again, had made the Germans a 'special people.' Also, there was a 'cunning' quasi-Hegelian drive inherent in the view that Auschwitz had enabled the Germans 'to know themselves' or rather, their mythical essence" (Müller 2000, 77). It is this inherent nationalistic particularism in the Holocaust memory, even when negative, that allowed center-right-wing politicians to shift the narrative from coming to terms with the Holocaust to an expression of subdued national pride.

Chancellor Gerhard Schröder (1998–2005) was influential in transforming the idea of confronting the past into a positive attribute of German society. He insisted that Germany could be more positive about its past precisely because it had faced it (Welch and Wittlinger 2011). In a 1999 interview, Schröder declared that the new generation's willingness to face their past was a source of empowerment that created "an opportunity to represent one's own interests in a more uninhibited manner" (47). Occurring at the turn of the twenty-first century, Germany's ability to accept its dark past came increasingly to be seen as the mark of a special kind of moral aptitude, which served to legitimize reunified Germany's reappearance on the world stage (Markovits 2006). Major post-unification projects, such as the Memorial to the Murdered Jews of Europe, which opened in the center of Berlin in 2005, and the establishment of the Foundation Remembrance, Responsibility, and Future (*Stiftung "Erinnerung, Verantwortung und Zukunft"*) in 2000 to compensate non-German slave workers during the Third Reich, are manifestations of Habermas's influence on a victim-centered Holocaust and National Socialism memory (Ball 2009, 12) and Schröder's declaration that a coming to terms with the past had, for the most part, been accomplished. Since German unification, a self-aware, self-critical, and victim-centered approach toward the Holocaust is considered "a core guarantor for the stability of Germany's liberal-democratic order" (von Bieberstein 2016, 909). Immigrants—that is, those latecomers to the scene of the crime who helped to rebuild war-torn Germany and became active participants in and contributors to the postwar German transformation—were left outside of the postwar German social contract that moved from admittance of collective guilt to collective pride at having come to terms with the past better than any other nation. Even if immigrants could gain German citizenship after 2000, they still could not become part of the emotional social contract of postwar German identity.

Gendered Nature of Postwar Democratization

After the defeat of the Nazis in 1945, not all Allies shared the opinion that German citizens could be easily rehabilitated. The Americans were influential in convincing others that Germans could be denazified and redemocratized if German culture—and in particular, German family relations—could be transformed. The US Department of War worked closely with psychologists, anthropologists, and sociologists to craft a narrative that would explain Nazism as a psychocultural problem specific to German culture and traceable to a core origin: German childrearing methods. In 1944, American psychologist Walter Langer submitted a report to the US Office of Strategic Services on Adolf Hitler's upbringing, which he later published in 1972 as *The Mind of Adolf Hitler*. Such ideas formed the basis of an approach to democratizing the Germans that by and large ignored contemporaneous social and economic explanations for the rise of National Socialism espoused by historians (Eichengreen 2018; James 1986; Strauman 2019) and reduced it to a matter of psychocultural socialization.

Ashis Nandy (2009) has demonstrated how both Orientalist and colonial discourses imagine others as children who need to be governed and controlled. What was unique in the social science produced around the time of the Allied occupation of Germany was the depiction of German difference as that of a *gifted but dangerous boy*—and here the emphasis was specifically on young men—who might be convinced via American-style childrearing techniques to change his bad behavior and grow up into a responsible adult (Fay 2008). A 1943 US government report titled *How to Treat the Germans* (Ludwig 1943) advised careful handling: "One of the leading nations within the framework of our civilization, Germany, has to be handled as a gifted but dangerous boy who must be watched and controlled by strict though well-meaning masters."[3] American occupiers and the social scientists who worked with them saw in Germany the potential for a bright future, leading the delayed and juvenile nation away from its *Sonderweg* (special path)[4] and toward the right path of adulthood and democratization.

In teaching democracy to Germans, Western occupiers approached them as children, and in turn Germans approached Nazis as naughty boys. Nazi criminality came to be seen as a case of juvenile delinquency. In his psychological bestseller *Childhood and Society,* the German American Jewish émigré Erik Erikson ([1963] 1993) dissects German identity through the heroic legend Hitler recounts of his own rebellion against his brutal father in *Mein Kampf.* According to Erikson, Hitler was "an adolescent who never gave in," "a glorified older brother, who took over the prerogatives of the fathers without overidentifying with them" (337). Because Hitler and Nazism had hypnotized Germans with black-and-white thinking, German youth were unable to go through the healthy stages of puberty. Instead, they became stuck in a protracted stage of adolescence and endless rebellion. Hitler's adolescent rebellion was popular among Germans, Erikson argued, because pre-Nazi German manhood had been wedged between harsh and authoritarian treatment of one's wife and children at home and submissive acquiescence to other men at work. It is telling that the most important findings published by those American social scientists who worked closely with Germany's American occupying forces appeared in the *American Journal of Orthopsychiatry. Mosby's Medical Dictionary* (Harris, Nagy, and Vardaxis 2014) defines the subdiscipline of orthopsychiatry as "the branch of psychiatry that specializes in correcting incipient and borderline mental and behavioral disorders, especially in children, and in developing preventive techniques to promote mental health and emotional growth and development" (1242).

In this evaluation of the problematic aspects of the German family, fathers were seen as guilty of having led their sons toward authoritarianism. This model was especially potent for redemocratization because it placed the guilt on the older generation and depicted younger Germans as innocent and changeable. Historian Till van Rahden suggests that a psychocultural understanding of democracy was embraced by many Germans, especially in Christian circles, as early as the late 1940s. By the 1950s, notions such as the "democratic family" and "democratic fatherhood" enjoyed wide circulation, proposed as a way out of the Nazi mindset (van Rahden 2011). It was suggested at the time that "only children who were raised to be mature members within [a democratic family] could later be expected to participate responsibly in social and political life" (68). When the occupation of Germany ended in 1955, a strong focus on fatherhood remained, even as fatherhood's content changed. Numerous publications and films encouraged fathers in their paternal and civic responsibilities, seen as necessary "for the future of the West German family and the nation" (120).

But by the end of the 1960s, a second wave of German democratization and denazification was underway. A new generation had emerged, and the entire family structure came under suspicion. The leaders of the 1968 student movement argued that in capitalistic societies the family was the root of repression, independent of the parents' wishes for their children and whether or not they were gentle with their children (van Rahden 2011, 109–10), leading to experiments with raising children without families.

With the student movement of 1968, a second German attempt to come to terms with its Nazi past was launched. This time, the focus was on a new generation of rebellious youth (students) who must reject their Nazi fathers. The 1968 movement has been characterized as an "anachronistic rebellion" and "a desperate attempt to correct history retroactively" (Schmidt 2010, 270). Student rebellion against authority aimed to destroy the culture and ideology that had led to the Holocaust. As German journalist Hans Kundnani asserted, a good portion of the '68 generation "spen[t] their entire lives attempting to escape their fathers' influence and to become the opposite of their fathers—and perhaps in doing so to atone for their fathers' sins" (Kundnani 2009, 11). Herbert Marcuse, a German Jewish émigré to the United States who came to be considered "the father of the new left," specifically instructed German youth to rebel against their fathers and to not take on their guilt (Marcuse 1971, 9). A number of '68ers subsequently published novels and memoirs about their struggles with their fathers, a prolific genre called *Vaterliteratur* (Schneider and Daniel 1984).

While the 1968 movement declared all family structures superfluous, their real enemy was Nazi ideology, which they believed promoted strict paternal authority and sexual repression. Inspired by the radical Austrian Jewish psychoanalyst Wilhelm Reich, who had died a decade earlier, a branch of '68ers led by activist Dieter Kunzelmann believed that to transform German society and break from the remnants of fascism, family arrangements and bourgeois sexual conventions needed to be demolished (Kundnani 2009, 52). Originally published in 1933, Reich (1970) argued in *The Mass Psychology of Fascism* that the masses had turned to authoritarianism as a result of sexual oppression implemented by their families, in the name of their fathers. "The moral inhibition of the child's natural sexuality . . . makes the child afraid, shy, fearful of authority, obedient, 'good,' and 'docile' in the authoritarian sense of the words. It has a crippling effect on man's rebellious forces. . . . Thus, the family is the authoritarian state in miniature" (30). To break with moral inhibitions and their authoritarian tendencies, Kunzelmann's Kommune 1 and subsequent German communes held daily collective psychoanalysis sessions, rejected monogamy, and experimented with drugs and sexuality. They believed that if young people could liberate themselves sexually, psychologically, and in relation to their family, they might then be able to resist the remnants of fascism in Germany and in so doing resolve social and political injustices (Herzog 1998).

American historian of German sexuality Dagmar Herzog (1998) argued that the sexually conservative attitudes which the '68ers insisted were the root cause of Nazi ideology were in fact not characteristic of Nazi culture but were rather a product of the Christian ideology that came to dominate postwar German society in the 1950s. Members of the student movement experienced multiple sediments of history simultaneously, one imposed atop the other. The '68ers aimed to transform their present experience with a past they remembered anachronistically, imagining their parents as sexually oppressed and as having been authoritatively controlled by their own parents. Both the first and second waves of German democratization were characterized by a strong desire to undo the past, coupled with a utopian belief in the potential of youth.

Entry of Middle Eastern/Muslim-Background Germans into Holocaust Memory

Middle Eastern/Muslim-background Germans who were left outside of the Holocaust memory debates as well as the redemptive democratization narrative suddenly found themselves at the center of it as both subjects and objects. This development was facilitated by a number of internal and external developments that, by the beginning of the twenty-first century, had transformed Germany. These included the unification of the two Germanies and the enlargement of Europe; the start of the Second Intifada, which brought mass protests against the Israeli government to the streets of Europe and Germany; the 9/11 and 7/7 attacks in New York and London by Muslim terrorists; the rise of Islamophobia and the rapid shift across the Western world and beyond toward the right end of the political spectrum; and the consolidation of right-wing settler politics in Israel. Emergent discussions within public Holocaust memory discourse about Muslims being the major obstacle to Germany's postwar recovery can be best understood as entangled within three webs of culturally significant meaning clusters that have been spun in German society since the end of World War II: guilt and responsibility concerning the massive crime of the Holocaust, committed in the name of a nation; democracy conceived not as a precondition but as a personal journey one must take; and the possibility of learning to empathize with past victims.

All three clusters of meaning are organized around a specific understanding of temporality and genealogy that positions contemporary ethnic Germans far along the path that leads from antisemitism to democracy, tolerance, and empathy. In this view, Germans are assumed to have already shouldered responsibility for Germany's Nazi past, matured personally and politically during this process, and learned to empathize with their former victims. This same understanding positions non-Germans in Germany and around the world at much earlier stages along this path. The complex and interconnected stories of how Germans came to confront and learn from the Holocaust, how ethnonationalism has been central to that confrontation, and how that story is publicly understood today are critical to comprehending the unexpectedly central place that Muslim-background Germans now hold in public Holocaust memory discourse.

To this day immigrants, their children, and grandchildren are commonly called *Ausländers*, literally, "outlanders," foreigners. Anthropologist Ruth Mandel (2008) notes that the word means much more: "It implies the unwanted foreigner who does not belong. It means unintegratable outsider, alien, rather than any neutral rendering of the English 'foreigner' " (80). She argues that the idea of the "non-German" as unchangeable has deep roots in German nationalism and dates back to the Reformation, when the church held to the doctrine of the nonconvertibility of Jews (216). Mandel reveals that remnants of this idea may be seen in the disparity in resources devoted to support the integration of *Aussiedlers*—ethnic Germans living in Eastern Europe and the Soviet Union who migrated to Germany en masse after 1993—versus those earmarked to helping immigrants from elsewhere. Only in January 2000 did German immigration law make it easier for individuals residing long term in Germany and their children to eventually claim German citizenship. The change in law brought new anxieties about who truly belongs in Germany. In that same moment the very group of people who would be called *Ausländers* or Turks (even when they are not Turkish) were now being called Muslims (Spielhaus 2011; Yıldız 2011). This religious label, which potentially might have made it easier to convert these "others" into the national identity—in the sense that it is more difficult to be a German if you are Turkish but easier if you are defined as Muslim—proved effective in connecting different Muslim groups with each other, such as Turks, Arabs, Afghans, Bosnians, etc., rather than integrating them into German society. Daunting questions remained for Muslim others. What does it take to be accepted as genuine members of German society? How can they prove their devotion and good intentions? How can Muslim-background immigrants make themselves fit for belonging in German society without irritating exclusionist stakeholders? What will make it possible for them to enter the postwar German social contract?

In addition to these long-standing internal processes, an external development helped to propel the Muslim-background minority into national discussions of Holocaust memory—namely, the consolidation of right-wing politics in and around Israel. Although Zionist groups have long likened Palestinians to Nazis and diverse Arab figures, including Saddam Hussein, Yasser Arafat, and Gamal Abdel Nasser, to Hitler (Ilan 2000), the mobilization of this narrative to an international level occurred in the 2000s. During this period, pro-Israel lobby groups emphasized reframing North African and Middle Eastern Jewish exile as equivalent to Palestinian exile in order to neutralize the Palestinian claims for land and property. Kimberly Arkin (2018) notes how, in 2002, Justice for Jews in Arab Countries was formed in order to lobby for the recognition of 850,000 Jewish refugees from Arab lands who had settled in Israel as compensation for Palestinian losses from 1948 and 1967 in a future peace settlement. In 2006, Justice for Jews in Arab Countries launched a worldwide campaign to register and recognize Arab states' human rights abuses against and dispossession of Arab Jews. In 2014, Israel observed its first-ever national remembrance of Jewish departure and expulsion from Arab and Iranian lands (984). Central to this teleological narrative was the extension of the Holocaust to North African and Middle Eastern Arab countries and Iran, insisting that Arabs were prepared to kill Jews during the war, and were only prevented from doing so because the war ended before they could carry out their plans. Arkin argues that "in this framework, North African [and Middle Eastern] Jewish experiences are not analogous variants of the Holocaust but part and parcel of its telos, a telos that was fortuitously and highly contingently, stopped prior to its full unfolding" (988).

This teleological narrative that sought, seventy-five years after the Holocaust, to include Arabs and Iranians as perpetrators and Sephardic Jews in North Africa and the Middle East as their victims went hand in hand with Benjamin Netanyahu's attempt to place responsibility for the Holocaust on Arabs. In October 2015, at a speech before the World Zionist Congress in Jerusalem, Netanyahu asserted that Hitler had not planned to exterminate German Jews but only to expel them—until, that is, the Mufti of Jerusalem convinced him to commit genocide (*Haaretz* 2015). Although this assertion was met with strong protests by the German government and Holocaust scholars in Israel and abroad, it set the stage for a new Holocaust narrative that would include Arabs and North African and Middle Eastern Jews. This Israel-specific assertion, made to further the political aims of Netanyahu's administration and the ruling right-wing populist Likud party, had a strong ripple effect in Germany, making it easier to include Arab- and even Turkish-background immigrants in the German Holocaust memory narrative as past and present perpetrators of violence toward Jews.

These internal and external developments facilitated the initial entry of Muslim-background immigrants into public discussions about German Holocaust memory practices through what I call an "export-import theory of antisemitism" (chapter 2). The theory suggests that German-originated antisemitism was initially exported to the Middle East via German missionaries in the nineteenth century and then by Nazis during the early twentieth century. This ideology during the postwar period was then carried back by Muslim-background immigrants into a Germany that had already overcome its antisemitism problem. Having worked hard to confront and overcome their antisemitism, this theory posits, the defeated Germans were now confronted with the antisemitism they had once exported, brought back into their midst by Middle Eastern immigrants. The theory in essence depicts Muslims as carriers of Germany's past problems into the present.[5] A second rendering of Muslim-background immigrants in Holocaust memory discourse suggests that because their antisemitism was imported, immigrants were incapable of empathizing with the Jewish victims of the Holocaust and of learning the necessary lessons from Germany history. Until they atoned for their antisemitism, the theory went, they would remain locked in (Germany's) shameful past (chapter 3).

Despite public unease around their engagement with the Holocaust, research has revealed the keen participation of Turkish- and other Muslim-background Germans in Holocaust memory discourse, but in a way that deviates from national expectations.[6] Instead of performances that symbolically transform German guilt and shame into responsibility and engagement (Dekel 2013), Turkish German artists and activists, until recently, routinely identified with the victims. Turkish German authors such as Emine Sevgi Özdamar (Konuk 2007) and Feridun Zaimoğlu (Margalit 2009), immigrant association leaders (Yurdakul and Bodemann 2006), and ordinary Turkish-background Germans (Georgi 2003; Mandel 2008) have drawn parallels between themselves and the Jews under National Socialism. Leslie Adelson (2000) suggests that this process of building connections involves not a simple equation but a complex of "touching tales" among Turks, Germans, and Jews. Yet the fact that half of the "Turkish" population in Germany prior to World War II was Jewish (Guttstadt 2013) unsettles the neat categories of victim, perpetrator, bystander, and outsider. Recent research by Marc David Baer (2020) shows that Turks, Arabs, and other Muslim groups were already present during the Holocaust in Germany but were later removed from its national memory. Baer argues that Muslim and Jewish Turks already have an insider share in this history, positioned multiply as victims, perpetrators, and bystanders. However, the ways Turkish, Black, and other minority artists engaged with the Holocaust memory in their work did not fit the necessary conditions to be included in the postwar German social contract.

The Muslim minority also entered into the sex- and gender-based aspects of German democratization narrative as a problem about twenty years earlier, starting in the 1980s, when Germany faced a turn toward nationalism after the liberal 1968 movement (Chin 2010). Rita Chin argues that as the New Left's view of fascism was inextricably bound up with sexual domination and oppression, Turkish gender relations posed a major concern for them (Chin 2007, 170). "Turks, the argument went, threatened to reintroduce reactionary behaviors into a country that had worked tirelessly to transform itself into a modern, firmly democratic society. . . . they potentially undermined West Germany's hard won emancipation from Nazi ideology, especially in terms of women's rights, marriage, and gender roles" (170). This view led to a myriad of social projects that aimed to protect and rescue Muslim women.

Public focus directed at Muslim women as victims slowly turned toward Muslim men as perpetrators (Ewing 2008). Even though this trend started to crystallize in the 2000s, it reached a climax following the arrival of mostly male Syrian and other Middle Eastern/Muslim refugees to Germany in the summer of 2015 and led to violence against Muslim men and refugees throughout the country (Frey 2020). In contrast to an earlier focus that promoted social projects aimed to help Muslim men, the later focus on men as perpetrators led to policies that aimed to punish, discipline, and exclude them. The Muslim man, according to Ewing, "is stigmatized in the name of freedom, democracy, and human rights and is abjected as the antithesis of these principles. He is recognized as seeking honor and respect primarily through violence and the oppression of women, means that are incompatible with the ethical subject of a democracy" (Ewing 2008, 4). Yasemin Yıldız argues that the recent focus on the victimized Muslim woman aims toward a transformation in European governmentality in that it facilitates "redefinitions of tolerance and the rejection of multiculturalism; revisions of responsibility for the European past encompassing colonialism and the Holocaust; and revisions to the model of the welfare state" (Yıldız 2011, 72–73).

Subcontracting Genealogical Guilt

If assuming a collective guilt forms the basis of the social contract that brought postwar Germans together, how can this sense of "we" be protected, since contemporary Germans are neither perpetrators of nor bystanders to the Holocaust? Four decades after the liberation of Auschwitz, German chancellor Helmut Kohl uttered the phrase "*die Gnade der spaeten Geburt*," the blessing of a late birth, during his 1984 visit to Israel to mark the innocence of Germans born after 1930, who cannot be considered guilty for the crimes of National Socialism because they could not have played a conscious role in it. The phrase has become an important catchphrase in discussions about the nature and extent of guilt and responsibility among succeeding generations of Germans. However, by the 1990s, Holocaust memory scholars and also the German public had an understanding that guilt and trauma did pass on through generations.

The genealogical understanding of Holocaust memory is powerfully revealed in a 2018 graphic novel, *Belonging: A German Reckons with History and Home*, by German American author Nora Klug. The book documents the author's journey back to Germany after settling abroad in New York for over a decade to figure out the exact nature of her family's relationship to the National Socialist crimes committed against Jews. For Klug, accepting this "German Original Sin" was a matter of bloodline: "We felt that history was in our blood, shame in our genes" (24). To detect the kind of guilt her genes carried, she felt obligated to trace her family history and find out what her immediate forefathers had done in World War II. As Klug traces the extent of her family's involvement with the crimes of the Third Reich, her emotions alternate between tension and release. Small bits of information, such as a great-uncle having worked as a driver for a Jewish man or the possibility of him being partly Jewish, are comforting to her (102). She goes to the Karlsruhe City Archive to look at US Army files on her grandfather, measuring his involvement with the Nazi regime and its crimes. Waiting in the archive to learn the outcome was particularly anxiety-producing, insomuch as it would finally reveal whether she had inherited the cancer-like disease of guilt or not: "My grandfather's name pops up on the screen like an alarming find on an x-ray image. . . . I have to wait to find out if it is malignant or not" (140). As she waits, Klug wants to know what her grandfather did during Kristallnacht, the 1938 pogrom carried out by paramilitary forces and civilians across Germany. "Was he in another part of the town? Ill at home? In his office? Or where it happened?" (151). The level of her grandfather's involvement has great consequences for how Klug will feel about herself today.

Klug confronts the criminal involvements of her own family unapologetically. This calm but unforgiving postmortem of her grandparents' actions makes Klug the kind of postwar postnationalist German that took generations of education and memory activism to achieve. Unlike ethnic Germans, immigrant-background Germans do not have such Nazi stories to discover in their family history. There are no archives they can visit to discover their grandparents' level of involvement with the crimes of National Socialism. Concomitantly, there is no path forward for them to demonstrate that they, too, are atoning for the crimes their ancestors committed in the name of the German nation. Or is there?

In her influential book *The Generation of Postmemory: Writing and Visual Culture after the Holocaust*, Marianne Hirsch (2012) shows that due to strong identification, victim memories are also transferred to future generations to the point where those who were not there to live the event "remember" it all the same. In *Haunting Legacies: Violent Histories and Transgenerational Trauma*, Gabriele Schwab demonstrates that the traumatic memories of Holocaust violence are also passed on to the descendants of perpetrators. Schwab argues that for everyone involved, "the damages of violent histories can hibernate in the unconscious, only to be transmitted to the next generation like an undetected disease" (2010, 3). Others insist that by the second generation, both victims and perpetrators inherit the trauma (McGlothlin 2006). Scholars of German history have also suggested that the crimes committed during the Holocaust are so severe that they create a special bond between the offspring of victims and perpetrators, leading to a lasting "negative symbiosis" creating a "communality of opposites" (Diner 1986) among the descendants of victims and perpetrators. All of this research into personal trauma and guilt, passing from parent to child, sits in tension with collective, abstract guilt and shame, leaving those Germans who are neither the descendants of victims nor of perpetrators outside of this generational and thus blood-based (post)memory.

Parallel discussions about the transmission of "guilt" by moving into a country that is in the midst of confronting it, or whether we can talk about "the blessing of an immigrant birth," have until recently been conspicuously absent. In the 1990s Turkish German author Zafer Şenocak provocatively asked, "Doesn't immigrating to Germany also mean immigrating to, entering into, the arena of Germany's recent past?" (Şenocak and Tülay 2000, 6). He wrote novels that brought together victims and perpetrators of the Jewish Holocaust and the Armenian Genocide. The main character of his novel *Perilous Kinship* is the son of a Turkish general who perpetrated the Armenian Genocide and a German Jewish mother who found refuge in Turkey. It took another decade for these ideas to move from the field of art and literature to political educational projects. However, this migrant travel to the German past did not bring migrant, Jewish, and German backgrounds together as Şenocak imagined in his novels. Few historians showed that Turks and Arabs were already part of the Holocaust narrative, some as Jewish victims, some as enablers of the Nazi regime, and that overall there were varied reactions toward the Nazis (Baer 2013a; Guttstat 2013; Achcar 2010; Boum and Stein 2018). Despite the complicated nature of the Holocaust history, Middle Eastern–background immigrants entered Holocaust history narrative without mixing with German nationals, and found themselves the recipients of parallel stories of implication in relation to the Holocaust.

Muslim-only Holocaust education and antisemitism prevention projects that I have observed teach Turkish and Arab youth about Arabs and Turks who collaborated with or inspired Nazis in their heinous crimes or who, in rare cases, saved Jews in the same way other "righteous" Germans and white Europeans did. This model incorporates Muslim-background Germans into Holocaust memory discourse as a parallel society of perpetrators, bystanders, and rescuers. Paradoxically, this narrative serves to first include non-German-background nationals in the German "community of fate" (*Schicksalgemeinschaft*) by emphasizing that they, too, have a share in Holocaust history, but then immediately excludes them, given that their share is one tainted by its own particular guilt and its own particular community of fate outside of Germany. Because Arabs and Turks have yet to atone for their contribution to the Holocaust, this narrative paints Arab-background, and to some extent Turkish-background, nationals as morally inferior to repentant white Germans.

In 2020, the seventy-fifth anniversary of the end of World War II, research conducted by the German weekly *Die Zeit* (Policy Matters 2020; Staas 2020) revealed that more than half (53 percent) of Germans believed that Germans should resolve to end further discussion of the history of National Socialism. Another 56 percent agreed that constant reference to National Socialism prevents

Germans from developing a healthy national consciousness that citizens of other countries enjoy, and 68 percent agreed that Germany had dealt with its Nazi past so well that they should serve as a role model for other countries. At the same time, 77 percent agreed that Germans have a responsibility to ensure that National Socialism and the Holocaust are never forgotten. It seems the majority of Germans want to have their cake—not to feel burdened by Holocaust memory—and eat it too—by continuing to commemorate the Holocaust as a special German responsibility.

This book suggests that focusing on Muslim antisemitism offers the German public a release from various tensions: between universalism and particularism; between the desire to embrace the specific German responsibility toward the Holocaust and the desire to feel proud of being German; and between including Middle Eastern/Muslim immigrants of three generations into the fold of German identity and yet keeping them apart. Designed to make good on Germany's promise to safeguard the memory of National Socialism and the Holocaust, Muslim-only education programs externalize antisemitism onto racialized and migrantized groups who have been living in Germany for generations, thus subcontracting part of the guilt onto them. By doing so it allows white Germans to move on, but not away, from their seventy-five-year-old guilt, to enjoy a more anodyne German nationalism, and to congratulate themselves for their continuous investment in fighting against antisemitism in Germany and around the world.

When migrantized groups and individuals take their first steps into the German social contract by accepting the responsibility of learning from the Holocaust, these latecomers to German society become subcontractors while lacking the privileges of the original contractors. Most importantly, their contractual relationship is not one that safely passes from generation to generation but rather one that is always conditional and precarious. For example, on June 6, 2021, Mathias Middleberg, policy spokesperson for the CDU/CSU (Christian Democratic Union / Christian Social Union) parliamentary group, called for a change in the naturalization law in Germany.[7] He asked that the German Citizenship Act include the following sentence: "Naturalization does not apply if the non-citizen (Auslaender) has committed an anti-Semitic act." He said, "Anyone who publicly agitates against Jews, questions the existence of the state of Israel or burns the Israeli flag must not become a German citizen." In addition to the required declaration of loyalty to Germany, he demanded that the law should make explicit that antisemitic acts are incompatible with the basic law's guarantee of human dignity. Even though the citizenship law, as of this writing, has not incorporated this change, should the change occur, it would place extra demands on immigrants, since German nationals who commit antisemitic acts would not lose their citizenship. It also shows how immigrants' inclusion into German society is conditional on their taking on the German guilt and responsibility for the Holocaust.

A number of Muslim-background Germans are nevertheless willing to enter into this subcontractual relationship, which they regard as a better option than not entering into it, and which leaves open the possibility of changing the terms of the contract. They talk about Muhammad Amin al-Hussaini, the notorious Mufti of Jerusalem who collaborated with the Nazis and then worked in the pay of the Third Reich. They discuss the rampant antisemitism in Turkey and Iran or the antisemitic propaganda distributed by Hamas.[8] Locating antisemitic forebears in their own genealogy gives them an unexpected opportunity to include themselves in the German narrative and moral order. As they publicly and sincerely perform guilt and responsibility, the Muslim minority demand to be properly accepted members of German society. They also use the rare public attention accorded them when they talk about antisemitism to also shed light on other forms of racism rampant in German society. By displaying their empathy for Jewish victims of the Holocaust and also for younger Germans who carry the burden of this past crime on their shoulders, Middle Eastern/Muslim-background Germans aim to cultivate empathy for their own racialization and for the heavy work of taking this genealogically conceptualized guilt upon themselves.

Empathy as a Political Project

Holocaust education programs implemented in 193 countries around the world emphasize building tolerance and empathy as their central goals (Carrier et al. 2015). The United States Holocaust Memorial Museum's web page (2019) states that through Holocaust education students learn how "silence and indifference to the suffering of others, or the infringement of civil rights in any society, can—however unintentionally—perpetuate these problems." Dutch Holocaust educators claim that "of all the educational objectives of Holocaust education, the ability and willingness to empathize with others is perhaps the most valuable. Empathy allows individuals to find the universal within the particular, to respect that which makes people different but to recognize their common humanity" (Boersema and Schimmel 2008, 69). Dutch educators also believe that empathy leads to desirable forms of political action. Rescuers during the Holocaust are seen to be people who "recognized their common humanity with the Jews or another oppressed people," and from whom "this empathy spurred them to action" (69).

In today's Germany, of all places, the home of the perpetrators of the Holocaust, a moral emphasis on empathy and good citizenship is the norm. State schools are given the duty to educate generations of Germans morally and politically through teaching the Holocaust (Meseth 2012), stressing "empathy-building, a focus on rescue and resistance and the bystander response, building a knowledge base about the Holocaust, stories of individual experiences, and opportunities to make personal connections" (Jennings 2010, 35). In addition to the goal of learning historical facts, during history lessons about the Nazi era teachers are expected to disseminate moral positions, including identification with victims of the Holocaust and empathy for persecuted minorities (Meseth and Proske 2010).

Throughout this book, I demonstrate that the empathy which these Holocaust education programs for Middle Eastern/Muslim-background Germans attempt to inculcate assumes a certain subject position as a given—namely, that of a past, now-repentant perpetrator who embraces the qualities of a rescuer. Holocaust education was first developed to be delivered to the defeated Germans, whom the victorious Allies suspected were not taking responsibility for their atrocities. Today, Holocaust education throughout Europe is designed first and foremost for people who are descendants of perpetrators, collaborators, or bystanders, not rescuers, outsiders, or victims. The programs help people who stand in ethnic German perpetrator or bystander shoes to step into a different pair—the shoes of their forefathers' Jewish victims—thereby shifting their subject position from (potential) perpetrator/bystander to (potential) rescuer.

In this sense, in today's Germany, the concept of empathy has come to denote the highly valued and sociopolitically desirable characteristic of ethnic Germans who are momentarily able to imagine what it might have been like to have been victimized by their parents and grandparents. When they step back into their own contemporary shoes, it is hoped, they will have developed the characteristics of yet another set of shoes: rescuers, who may also have been resisters; that is, those Germans who possessed empathetic qualities from the start. But what of other subject positions and shoes Germans might step out of and back into? What happens when the hoped-for empathizers are not the ethnically German grandchildren of ethnically German perpetrators, bystanders, and rescuers? What happens during Holocaust education when non-German empathizers are not thinking from within past German positionalities but from within present non-German ones and do not therefore perceive themselves in relation to past Nazi perpetrators? How can we develop a nuanced understanding of empathy that can account for the many and varied experiences and structurally fixed subject positions empathizers undergo as they confront Holocaust memory?

I attempt to map these various past and present subject positions and how they play out in contemporary Holocaust education in Germany through the prism of empathy, understood as a complex, nuanced, highly situated experience of intersubjective connection. My critique of German Holocaust education, and of the conceptualization of empathy that constitutes it, flips the inquiry: rather than putting the emotional reactions of Muslim-minority Germans to the Holocaust on trial for their inadequacies, I interrogate reigning assumptions of German national belonging that offer a single historical perspective as a moral standard. Building on Husserl's concept of the intersubjective nature of empathy (chapter 3), we see that it is the previous experiences and positionality of the empathizer and not their moral qualities that shape the character of the empathetic process.

My ethnographic observations on Muslim-background encounters with the Holocaust reveal that the strong identification of German Muslims with the Jewish victims of the Holocaust, without assuming they are one and the same with them, is common and forms the basis of a strong empathy. Chapter 3 discusses the difficult tension between the radical empathy Muslim-minority Germans feel with Jewish victims, and the strong negative reactions these emotions generate in Holocaust educators. Because the emotional connections that the Muslim minority in Germany establish with the Jewish victims of the Holocaust will inevitably be different from those established by ethnic Germans, public Holocaust memory discourse in Germany, as well as the emotionally based

German social contract, needs to expand to allow for the many and differing identifications of its citizens.

When Muslim-minority German youth identify with the Jewish victims of the Holocaust, not only because of the current visibility of their persecution but also due to their racialization, they appear to ethnic Germans to be competing with Jews for victim status, and face accusations of being antisemitic, thus losing their opportunity to be legitimately heard in Germany. When Muslim Germans express fear, they are judged to be lacking in the cognitive skills required to understand how different today's Germany is from that of the 1930s. When they demand empathy for their own racialization, they are judged as too immature for full participation in German democracy and acceptance into the German social contract. Political legitimacy in postwar German national identity politics derives from adopting the repentant perpetrator position. As anthropologist Sultan Doughan (2022) asserts: "Historical perpetratorship is an inclusive concept in Germany and it includes the figure of the Jew as a sacrificial victim. Once one submits to perpetratorship, it enables and empowers them to act and be recognized as a rightful citizen." Some Muslim Germans, hence, find the solution in assuming the repentant perpetrator position and the guilt that comes with it in order to enter into the German social contract and claim they are also deserving citizens. This book suggests that before Muslim-background Germans can empathically step into the shoes of the Holocaust's Jewish victims, they are first asked to step into the shoes of the Nazi perpetrator/bystanders or their grandchildren in order to repent, which is the necessary condition for entering the German social contract. In that sense, in order to legitimately ask to be accepted as a member of German society, Muslim-minority Germans are expected to empathize and sympathize with contemporary white Germans in whose name the Holocaust was committed, and that they too now have to live with this guilt. This kind of empathy, which brings together people who have to live with guilt, is exactly what Karl Jaspers had hoped would define the basis of the new German society.

This book provides an analysis and critique of German postwar national belonging. Its more ambitious aim is to show how racialized groups attempt to make space for themselves in a powerful narrative that excludes them by performing the script of the narrative better than anyone else. It goes against the suggestion that Muslim groups engage with the Holocaust narrative cynically, for the sole purpose of finding a way into the German social contract. My years-long fieldwork shows that scores of Middle East/Muslim-background Germans do relate to the Holocaust passionately, genuinely, and with radical empathy, and that the space for empathic connection and emotional engagement with the victims of the Holocaust is much wider than assumed by the national script. Racialized groups in Germany hold the key for a more inclusive public Holocaust memory discourse that can be organically carried to new Germans, who are new because they are young or new because they recently arrived.

CHAPTER 1

Rebelling against the Father, Democratizing the Family

In May 2019 I was invited to join a Heroes meeting in a youth club in the industrial town of Duisburg in North West Westphalia, a safe space for young people to talk about issues relating to gender inequality in their culture. As we waited for everyone to arrive, two of the boys shared a long gummy snake, each eating one end of it and giggling. A few of us had our eyes turned in their direction, watching to see whether they would brave it to the point of coming lip to lip. They broke off in laughter before meeting in the middle, letting the uneaten part of the snake drop to the floor. Sandra, the female director of the boys youth club, then started the meeting by letting us know about a queer party that the municipality of the city was organizing and urging the group to attend.[1] The invitation led to further giggles by the gummy-sharing duo, but others were taking it calmly, and all quickly agreed to go. Heroes spend a lot of time socializing together outside their weekly meetings and regularly represent their organization in such social activities.

That day Burak and Sirri, Turkish- and Kurdish-background social workers, were prepared to bring up the topic of gender stereotypes for group discussion. They began the session with a role-play: "Christian" wants to play volleyball, but "Burak" says the game is for girls, and he doesn't want to play. He warns his friend that if they play, everyone will think they're gay. At that point, Burak and Sirri stopped their playacting and asked the group what they thought about the scene. Sirri asked specifically whether they thought the role-play was a good representation of reality. The youth agreed enthusiastically. Bahadir, one of the boys who had been chewing on the long gummy snake, said that you don't even have to play a girls' game; all two men need do is to talk together politely, and they will immediately be accused of being gay. One of the group confessed that he had found it disturbing to see a man wearing a long black skirt at a festival.

Sirri then asked the group why they think men have such strong reactions whenever other men step outside traditional gender roles. As he often does, Burak took a provocative position. "Well, if I spend a lot of time with Christian, and everyone will think I'm gay, then it's easier for me to leave Christian alone. It's less stressful for me. I want to be a respectable member of society." The young people began to challenge Burak's take. Cemal, a recently arrived Kurdish-origin Syrian, said, "I love playing volleyball. And I drink wine. Why shouldn't I?" Erol gave him a high five, and they smiled triumphantly.

Then a few of the boys started acting as though they were gay, hugging each other and nervously laughing out loud. Bahadir turned to the boy next to him and said that he wanted to marry him: they could have a simple wedding, only it had to be in the mosque, and his friend could wear a simple white dress; that would be enough for him, so he wouldn't have to pay for an expensive wedding. Some of the youth laughed at this joke, but others, ones who had already gone through the entire Heroes training program, were neither laughing nor smiling, indicating that they did not approve. Later, while discussing the meeting with Burak, I shared my perception that talking about gender stereotypes heightened Bahadir's anxiety about being taken as gay, and prompted him to crack jokes that made fun of gays, even to the extent of placing himself in the equation as the so-called active partner in a homosexual relationship for laughs. I was reminded that the young men who made and laughed at these jokes were not yet certified as heroes and had only recently begun thinking about gender equality.

After the meeting was over, I asked Burak whether they would have done something different had I not been there. His original plan had been to discuss culture: what it is, if it is genetic, whether it changes over time, what happens when someone disagrees with their own culture. He had thought about asking the group to imagine the life of an ethnic German baby adopted by a Syrian family. I was disappointed that there had not been enough time to have this discussion while I was there. Remarkably, these are the same kinds of questions American social scientists supported by the Department of War asked in relation to German culture immediately after World War II. American anthropologists like Margaret Mead and social psychologists like Erik Erikson, a German

Jewish émigré, asserted vehemently that there is nothing genetic about culture and that cultural traits can change through reeducation. Taking as their example Germans who had emigrated to the United States and become democratic citizens, they reasoned that, with the proper methods, formerly Nazi Germans could transform themselves and adopt a democratic culture without having to leave Germany. Seven decades later and several generations after their forebears migrated to Germany, Muslim-background youth who attend extracurricular programs like Heroes are trying to transform their own cultures. They promote the idea that, just as a German baby adopted by a Syrian family would keep his German looks but assume his adopted family's Syrian culture, heroes are Muslim-background youth who have been adopted not by ethnically German families but by the culture and nation-state of Germany—and who act like it. The problem, however, is that in this formulation the youth are "adoptees," when in reality they have never been orphans, potentially calling their commitment to their families, and especially their fathers, into question.

Erol, Mehmet, Fatih, Adnan, Metin, and Bahadir, who I return to throughout the book, are young people of Turkish, Kurdish, and Arab background. Varying in age from sixteen to twenty-eight, they are the children and grandchildren of guest workers or refugees who came to Duisburg one to three generations ago. All are involved in two programs: the first, Heroes Against Oppression in the Name of Honor,[2] is devoted to fighting gender inequality among people who belong to "honor cultures"; the second, Muslims in Auschwitz, fights antisemitism. Burak and Serkan, among the social workers who work on these projects, share a similar background with the youth, even though they are ten to fifteen years older than most of them. They meet weekly in the basement of a modest youth center in northern Duisburg, a significantly poorer and mostly nonwhite part of the city. Situated at the intersection of the Rhine and Ruhr rivers in western Germany, Duisburg is a major center of Germany's iron, steel, and chemical industries and was heavily bombed by the Allies during World War II. After the war, the city was rebuilt by the grandfathers of the likes of these minority-background young people, guest workers who came to postwar Germany in search of jobs and opportunities. Now their young grandsons want to be heroes, graduates of the Heroes program, and help change what they consider to be the negative aspects of their cultures.

Many grew up in the Duisburg neighborhood of Marxloh, an industrial area that has not recovered from the economic downturn and white flight of the

1990s, when thousands of local industry jobs were lost due to economic restructuring in the Ruhr area. As unemployment soared, thousands of white German businesses and residents left the area, and residents of Turkish origin and Turkish passport-holders grew to 25 percent of the overall population (Ehrkamp 2006). By the time I started doing my research in the 2010s, Turkish-background families had been replaced by newer arrivals from Lebanon, Bulgaria, Romania, and Syria. Several heroes in the making told me with a wry grin that their neighborhood was the Gaza of Germany. Indeed, Marxloh's most notorious resident is Muhammad Atta of the 9/11 attacks. Although as home to a large assortment of Turkish restaurants, bakeries, and wedding dress stores geared toward a Middle Eastern clientele, Marxloh's principal commercial thoroughfare presents a lively facade, its back streets are occupied by some of Germany poorest residents. An internet search on Marxloh brings up news items warning that it "stinks of garbage" and noting its "no-go areas" and "motorcycle gang fights" (*Deutsche Welle* 2013; Wüllenweber 2018; Virtue 2018).[3]

The youth center is located a few tram stops from Marxloh. Heroes-to-be go there once a week, descending the narrow steps that lead into a low-ceilinged basement room decorated with freshly painted bright orange walls, posters promoting gender equality, paintings about forced marriages drawn by girls in Turkey, and comfortable black leather sofas. The coffee table at the room's center often has plates piled high with store-bought cookies, gummy bears, pretzels, and bottles of Coke. The group is led by three people: Serkan, the son of a Turkish teacher who educates the children of guest workers; Burak, a teacher and youth worker, who is the grandson of a Turkish man who arrived to work in the Duisburg factories after World War II; and Sandra, a middle-aged German-background social worker.

The German Social Contract: Fathers, Sons, Sisters

The youth club for boys and its young male patrons came to national attention through its Holocaust education and antisemitism prevention program, Muslims in Auschwitz, a program aimed at young Muslims initiated by the social workers of the club. Observing and following the program closely as I did for three years, it became clear to me that many of the ideas behind Muslims in Auschwitz were based on Heroes, a social program for immigrant and second- and third-generation Muslim male youth that encourages them to fight the oppression of women carried out in the name of honor. By acknowledging their own responsibility in this oppression, leaving behind aspects of what they define as their "honor culture," and rebelling against their fathers in order to set themselves free, they are in effect declaring themselves ready to integrate into German society. Theirs is the story of a group of Middle Eastern/Muslim-minority youth in Germany who respond to their own stigmatization (Ewing 2008) by accepting the stigma and committing to transform themselves. Central to the stigma removal work of these minorities is an all-important offer to position themselves at the starting point of the path Germans have walked since the end of World War II: by shouldering the burden of German history that does not belong to them, they hope to enter into the German social contract and be included in the German "us."

In making a case for their belonging in German society, a group of contemporary Muslim-background public intellectuals and youth rely on narratives of German re-democratization from the 1950s and 1960s. Importantly, just like many postwar American and German psychologists, social psychologists, and anthropologists who attempted to explain Nazism as a problem of child socialization (Schaffner 1948; Dicks 1950; Karr and Wesley 1966) and sexual oppression (Herzog 2005), Muslim-background social workers and public intellectuals of the postmillennial era blame Muslim fathers. Similar to the postwar Christian- and Jewish-background German social scientists, this group of Muslim-background German public figures suggests that rebelling against fathers and embracing sexual freedom is the only way out of family structures that promote authoritarianism. In the same way that German social scientists of the 1950s practiced the "science of democracy and reeducation with the double task of research and public pedagogy" (Müller 2000, 36), German Muslim public intellectuals of today comment on a so-called democracy deficit among Muslims and promote democracy education geared toward Muslims as the remedy. But although this specific group of Muslim public intellectuals model their demands on the postwar German transformation and the making of the new German social contract, their project is different in the sense that Muslim intellectuals want to transform who constitutes the "us" in the German identity.

Liberated sons writing a new social contract is a common theme running throughout the work of twentieth-century European social theorists. In *Totem and Taboo* ([1913] 2001) and later *Moses and Monotheism* ([1939] 2001), the Austrian founder of psychoanalysis, Sigmund Freud, argued that civilization begins when sons kill their primal, authoritarian father, who controls his wife and daughters and blocks access to them by his sons. It is only at the stage when those sons, in rebellion against their father, agree to give up control over their sisters and daughters (Freud [1913] 2001, 141–44), that the democratic redistribution of power, moral restrictions including exogamy, and religion become possible and necessary.

Another psychoanalytical approach to the meaning of the rebellion against the father's authority as a precursor to a new collective identity is gleaned from a Lacanian perspective on the symbolic order and the child's relationship to the father. In his influential lectures on the Psychosis (1955–56), French psychiatrist Jacques Lacan developed the concept of the Name of the Father, in which he locates the starting point of the child's conceptualization of society not in the death of the father but in the establishment of the father's authority (Lacan 2015). He argues that the "name" of the father—in French, *nom*, a word phonetically identical to the word for "no," *non*—is the mediator between the child and the mother. In opposition to the exclusive relationship between the mother and child posited within object relations theory, for Lacan the father becomes the symbolic word (*nom*) of prohibitionary law (*non*) that denies access of the child to the mother as he or she grows older. Rebelling against the authority of the Lacanian father also involves leaving his realm of rule and law, allowing children, especially sons, to enter into a new realm of law or a new contract with other men as equals.

Although Germans did not kill their own metaphorical father—Hitler's death, while a suicide, was brought about by Germany's enemies, the Allies—they nevertheless embraced the necessity of life after war in a democracy without an authoritarian father figure (Borneman and Senders 2000; Borneman 2004). Postwar Germans forswear allegiance to Hitler, whom they had seen as the father of the nation, as well as to their own fathers, who had been Nazis. Once they were metaphorically and literally orphaned, Germans invested their energy in developing a new and abstract concept of fatherhood that rejected authoritarianism and allowed ample freedom to the sons (van Rahden 2019). Only after having cut their ties with the nation's father were they given permission to establish a new government and a country that found space in the world order.

In his work on child abusers and their rehabilitation in Germany, John Borneman (2015) argues from a Lacanian perspective on psychosexual development that for immigrant children, there are two fathers in competition with one another: the imaginary father (either as an "ideal" or a "bad" construct the individual has built up in fantasy) and the symbolic father (as embodied in the regulation of desire by society and the law). For Borneman, the German symbolic order is different from the symbolic order that migrant fathers impose on their sons. "In the case of migrants in Germany, the question is what the inheritance of the name of the father means for them, and to what extent they must distance themselves from the father in order to enter the symbolic order of desire of Germany" (177–78). Given that migrant fathers do not belong to and cannot therefore impose on their sons the German symbolic order, Muslim youth who want to become part of German society have no choice but to rebel against their non-German fathers—not only to mirror the German sons who rebelled against their Nazi fathers but also to repudiate the power of their fathers' non-German symbolic order over them and enter the German symbolic order. To do this, their imaginary father must be "bad" or at least "wrong." In the Heroes immigrant youth group, heroes imagine their liberation from their father's authority as a condition for entry into the German symbolic order.

French anthropologist Claude Lévi-Strauss, however, saw another central point in the social contract that helps us further understand the Heroes project. He argued in his study of the structure of family relations, *The Elementary Structures of Kinship* (1949), that society is made possible by the incest taboo, which ensures that men exchange their sisters and daughters with each other rather than keeping the women to themselves. The incest taboo then imposes a rule of reciprocity on such exchanges, thereby creating a set of obligations about the exchange. According to Lévi-Strauss, it is these rules of exchange that allow men to build new alliances which reach across generations and enable the structural conversion from the state of nature to society. Lévi-Strauss disagreed with earlier anthropologists in that he emphasized exchange, not descent, as the basis of kinship structures.

Feminist British political theorist Carole Pateman argued some thirty years ago that even though the rebellion against patrilineality was the basis of the social contract, the new order it created was still patriarchal because it was about freedom for men and the new kinds of relationships they could establish with each other. In Pateman's (1988) words, "the men who defeat their father, claim their natural liberty and, victorious, make the original contract, are acting as brothers; that is to say, as fraternal kin or the sons of a father, and by contracting together, they constitute themselves as a civil fraternity" (78).

In that sense, it is the Lévi-Straussian emphasis on the necessity of the exchange of sisters and the definition of kinship not as bloodline but as a network of exchange that opens up space for Muslim-minority intellectuals and activists to enter into the social contract. In other words, 1950s Christian and then later 1960s leftist demands to move from patrilineality (a blood-based understanding of German identity) to patriarchal fraternity (an anti-authoritarian German identity) parallels the demands for the sexual liberation of Muslim women and men in programs like Heroes. Muslim-background intellectuals promoting sexual liberation emphasize the establishment of a new "we," a new basis for social solidarity in which young women as well as men are not the objects but rather the subjects of their own sexual choices. By placing disproportional emphasis on the authority of their Muslim fathers and their own willingness to rebel against them and show their readiness to release control over their sisters, the young men in programs like Heroes demonstrate their eagerness to enter into a social contract with fellow German men as free equals.

As a way of demonstrating their readiness to enter into a social pact with their fellow German men, the Middle Eastern/Muslim-background German public actors and youth I focus on in this chapter—public intellectuals such as Necla Kelek, Seyran Ateş, Ahmad Mansour, and Hamed Abdel-Samed; the Heroes-attending youth I mentioned earlier—emphasize the need and willingness of migrantized sons to rebel against their fathers and, more importantly, to stop controlling their sisters. It is striking that nowhere in the popular Middle Eastern/Muslim-background German ponderings about the evils of Muslim patriarchy is there discussion about what women should do beyond the "evidently self-evident" fact that daughters and sisters be free to love and sexually engage with whomever they like. Unlike Muslim fathers who need to be fought against and metaphorically killed to free the daughters, there is no mention of Muslim mothers. This is the extent of Middle Eastern women's (non)entry into the new German social contract. The willingness of Muslim men to rebel against their fathers is thus demanded exclusively as a token of their readiness to loosen control over their own sisters and exchange them with German men. Whether through education or public debate, Muslim men who choose to take on this task offer to locate themselves in a past that white Christian-background German men have already passed through, to take up the mantle as determined travelers, and to tread the sole path that leads to democracy and postwar German identity. In so doing, they emphasize the point that migrantized Muslims are neither essentially different nor unable to undergo a conversion; rather, they are positioned in the same "bad place" in which Germans found themselves at the end of the World War II. They seem to say: if Germans once caught in the vice of the Third Reich can change, so can they.

Walking in the Footsteps of Postwar Germans

By the turn of the twenty-first century, a new cohort of Middle Eastern/Muslim-background German public intellectuals, many of them appreciated by the German center and far right, entered and quickly became well represented in the public debate on the Muslim question in Germany (Göpffarth and Özyürek 2020). What is common to the members of this group is their embrace of the idea that migrantized Muslim Germans differ fundamentally from mainstream German society. Yet at the same time and to varying degrees they promote the idea that, under certain conditions, these people can radically transform themselves and become part of mainstream German society. Similar to West German leftist and liberal intellectuals of the postwar period who were committed to being "watchful about continuities with the pre-1945 past and re-orient[ing] Germany toward the political and cultural traditions of the West" (Müller 2000, 56), Muslim intellectuals constantly emphasize the similarities between contemporary Muslims and pre-1945 Germans and try to direct Muslims toward contemporary German values. Although in the first decade of the twenty-first century members of this cohort were Turkish and Kurdish women, such as Necla Kelek, Seyran Ateş, and Serap Çileli, in the next decade Arab men such as Ahmad Mansour and Abdel Samed became highly visible. Their arguments fluctuate between being highly critical of Muslim beliefs and cultures to being promoters of reforming them. Even in the most radical cases of Hamed Abdel-Samed and Necla Kelek, who call for leaving Islam completely, they use their own examples as proof of the concept that (former) Muslims can transform themselves and become deserving members of a German society based on shared values instead of shared blood.

Muslim-background intellectuals who serve the interests not of their own communities but of those who oppress them have been conceptualized by Edward Said (2003) as "native informants" and by Hamid Dabashi (2011) as "native informers." Literary critic Graham Huggan (2001) called ethnic-background cultural producers in the West "postcolonial exotics," who market an authenticity they usually do not have. Yasemin Shooman (2014) has argued that such claims to insider status allow ethnic-background intellectuals in the West to depict themselves as firsthand victims of Islamic oppression (100). What is unique to the intellectuals I analyze here is that, informed by the essentialized "-nesses" produced by national character studies of authoritarian nation-states, they posit their "Muslimness" as being identical to that of "Germanness" during and immediately following World War II. In their depictions, Muslimness needs to be transformed; but like Germanness after the war, it is also able to transform itself. This particular group of public intellectuals, who self-identify both as Muslims and critics of Islam as a religion, build heavily on the theories of "authoritarian national character" originally developed to explain Nazism to argue that the authoritarian fathering practices of Muslim families result in violent, paranoid, and antisemitic adolescents fit only for, and therefore uniquely vulnerable to, authoritarian ideologies. They frequently describe in vivid and dramatic detail a generic Muslim family likened either overtly or covertly to the generic Nazi family that the American occupiers, and later the German 1968 student movement, set out to demolish.

Ahmad Mansour is a Palestinian-background Israeli who migrated to Germany in 2006 to finish his studies in psychology and has become well known for his work in the Heroes program. Affiliated with the Green Party, he has written several op-eds with the party's Turkish-background leader, Cem Özdemir.[4] Despite his formal disengagement, Mansour is also appreciated by the center and the far right (Göpffarth and Özyürek 2020). He frequently appears on mainstream TV news shows and is interviewed regularly in the newspapers. He has received numerous prestigious awards, including the Moses Mendelssohn Prize from the Berlin Senate in 2014, the Josef Neuberger Medal from the Jewish community of Düsseldorf in 2015, the Human Rights Award from the Gerhart and

Renate Baum Stiftung, and the Theodor Lessing Prize from the German-Israeli Society of Hanover in 2019.[5] In 2016, he was named Ambassador for Democracy and Tolerance Award by the German Federal Agency for Civic Education (*Bundeszentrale für politische Bildung*). In his first bestseller, *Generation Allah*, Mansour (2014) combines his personal experiences growing up in a Palestinian village in Israel and his encounters over the past ten years with Muslims in Germany from his vantage point as a social worker with pseudoscientific statements about how a homogenized Muslim "psychoculture" works across time and place. The Muslim family he depicts is a cruel one that aims to break the will of their children, inflicts verbal and emotional violence, and allows no space for independence. Mansour itemizes the damage children suffer within this collectively traumatized Muslim family and warns his readers how such bad childrearing practices can lead to dangerous results for both for Muslim communities themselves and the whole of German society. Because this state of affairs is, according to him, a general psychocultural problem for all Muslims, the threat Germany faces comes not from a few hundred fanatic Islamists but from an entire generation of young Muslims—"*Generation Allah*"—who are all under threat of Islamic radicalization (Mansour 2014, 32). By calling Muslim youth "Generation Allah" and generalizing from his focus on a specific group of Muslim youth, Mansour depicts all Muslims as troubled youth who need, on the one hand, to be brought to heel and governed, but who, on the other hand, are innocent and thus transformable through the proper methods.

The dynamics of the Muslim family Mansour depicts and the end results he warns against are strikingly similar to the authoritarian family models developed by émigré scholars such as Erik Erikson ([1963] 1993) in the postwar period that were later picked up by intellectuals of the German 1968 movement. Developed in the 1950s as American social scientists collaborated with the US Department of War to understand the mindsets of authoritarian American enemies—Germany, Japan, Russia—in order to change them, this genre of national character studies sought to explain and cure Germany's authoritarian "character" by explaining and curing German "authoritarian" family structure. But Mansour's *Generation Allah* also picks up on a similar national character approach espoused in a 1973 book, *The Arab Mind* (Patai [1973] 2002), that would later inspire the abuse and torture of prisoners at Abu Ghraib Prison in Iraq (Whitaker 2004). Written in the tradition of the American national character studies of authoritarian nation-states, the book fits in well with its 1950s and 1960s predecessors. Its author, Raphael Patai, was a German-speaking Israeli born in Hungary who moved to the United States in 1947 to teach anthropology of the Middle East. With doctorates in rabbinical studies and Jewish studies, Patai owed his success in the US to his ability to fit in with the newly emerging field of anthropology (Schrire 2010). *The Arab Mind* depicts a simplified, essentialized view of Arabs, paying disproportionate attention to childrearing practices and the place of sex in Arab culture. The way the book depicts Arab culture as being based on fundamental tensions between authoritarian fathers and overindulgent mothers, sexual repression and obsession about sexuality, unity, and conflict, parallels how Ruth Benedict depicted Japanese childrearing practices, hierarchical relations, and shame in *The Chrysanthemum and the Sword* ([1946] 2019) as unchanging, undifferentiated, and the antipode of its Western counterparts. Despite Patai being both a German speaker and an Israeli, the book has not been translated into German or Hebrew, suggesting that it was written primarily with a popular American audience in mind. Reprinted in 2002 by Hatherleigh Press during the American occupation of Iraq, *The Arab Mind* includes a new introduction by former US army colonel Norvell B. de Atkine, head of the Middle East studies program at Fort Bragg. "At the institution where I teach military officers, *The Arab Mind* forms the basis of my cultural instruction" (Patai [1973] 2002, x). Investigative journalist Seymour M. Hersh (2004) brought further public attention to the book when he wrote that the sexualized torture to which prisoners in Abu Ghraib Prison were subjected was inspired by Patai's observations on the sex taboo and its purported association with shame and repression in Arab culture.

Similar to Benedict and Erikson, Patai depicts a timeless, undifferentiated, and unitary Arab society and culture, an "Arab mind" he aims to decode by starting with an examination of their childrearing practices, honor culture, and sexuality. What he discerns is a stern, authoritarian father, a strict separation of gender that shapes Arab individuals, especially as boys enter the world of men, and the central role of honor and sexual repression in Arab culture. Patai's emphasis on the centrality of suppression of female sexuality to a man's honor, the fact that women may lose their honor but not regain it, and the sex taboo as centrally occupying the Arab mind are all repeated in Mansour's *Generation Allah*.[6] Another central element in Patai's book repeated by Mansour is the idea that Arab men are defined by the "sexual repression-frustration-aggression syndrome of the Arab personality" (Patai [1973] 2002, 137), a notion that then serves as the basis for a number of education programs directed toward Muslims throughout Germany. Again, in the tradition of the national character studies genre, another important element in Patai's book is Arab hatred of the West. Mansour follows Patai's view that Islam runs so deep in the Arab mind that "[it] permeates the totality of life" (329).

Like Mansour's book, Heroes, the social program he popularized in Germany for sexual equality, uses "honor culture" and Islam interchangeably. According to Mansour, it is the sexual control of women by men that prevents Muslims from adopting the democratic culture of Germany. He builds a model of a catastrophic Muslim child development that oppresses not only sexual drives but also the development of a healthy and mature personality. According to Mansour, sexual oppression is the root of honor culture and the main source of radicalization among Muslim youth:

In a shame culture where modesty is a positive value, genders are segregated, and sex is taboo, neither men nor women can develop their individuality. This produces suffering, anger, anxiety, a feeling of being torn, depression, and violence. Especially for young men, it creates a considerable and often dangerous potential for violence. (Mansour 2014, 129)

Following the postwar scholars of national character studies, Mansour argues that in patriarchal families with authoritarian fathers, boys develop a strict, zealous, intolerant superego; black-and-white conceptions of right and wrong; respect and submission to authority; a negative view of people; and become preoccupied with violence and sex (Adorno et al. 1950; Mansour 2014). Strictly patriarchal families prevent children from experiencing a healthy adolescence from which they should be able to grow into mature adults fit for democracy. According to Mansour, this dynamic becomes especially problematic for Muslims, because they have a correspondingly strict patriarchal image of God, which strengthens the authority of the father (Mansour 2014, 106). As Muslims become stalled in adolescence, he argues, they turn toward Islamic radicalization, which places them in rigid authority relations with clear rules.

Mansour also posits an alternative Muslim father model experienced especially in Western Europe: the dysfunctional father. According to him, this is equally if not more dangerous for the development of children. He discusses

> a disempowered father who is to some extent a phantom, whether because he has lost his job, his self-esteem, his ability to be a role model, or because he shows weakness for other reasons. Let's look at a father who speaks broken German, while his son and daughter speak the language fluently. The more the father tries to regain his authority, the more he loses it. Often such children look for other authority figures, role models, and idols that can act as a substitute for the idealized father fantasy. (106–17)

According to Mansour, this dysfunctional dynamic is especially problematic for Muslim children, because the search for a replacement father figure leads them to Allah and his representatives. Children who grow up in such families, he contends, will inevitably find Salafism, a puritanical approach to Islam: "The Salafistic God-phantom correlates with a longing resulting from dysfunctional and often traumatic experience in early childhood. Its promise of paradise and rigidity is enormously complementary to the damaged psyche" (108). In other words, if the Muslim father is authoritarian, his children will become radicals because they are comfortable only in frameworks of authority; if he is a disengaged or absent father, his sons will become radicals by looking for authoritarian substitutes. Like prewar German fathers whose display of simultaneous "aloofness and harshness" (Erikson [1963] 1993, 332) led their children to Nazism, Mansour argues that the Muslim fathers' simultaneous strictness and absence leads their sons to Islamic radicalization. In this model, unchanging and undifferentiated Muslim children live completely cut off from a mainstream German society depicted as their antipode, and their radicalization is exclusively the result of the wrong (Islamic) family values.

Seyran Ateş is a Turkish- and Kurdish-background lawyer and feminist activist for immigrant women's rights formerly on the radical left who, with the encouragement of former interior minister Wolfgang Schäuble, recently became a liberal imam and established the reformed, gender-neutral Ibn Rushd-Goethe mosque in Berlin (Ateş 2017). She has since come under attack by conservative Muslims and been highly appreciated and supported by the German far right as a model for German Islam (AfD Potsdam 2017; Breitbart London 2017). She, too, argues in her book *Islam Needs a Sexual Revolution* (Ateş 2011) that Islamic emphasis on obedience to parents is what keeps Muslims from becoming mature adults and citizens suitable for a democratic regime. "The rebellion against authority, whether it be the state or family members, but especially the father and mother, has no political character in the Islamic world. Submission and obedience thus remain with a great many Muslims for a lifetime" (92). According to Ateş, the sexual revolution helped people in the world, above all Germans, to rid themselves of the sexual oppression that was the cause of National Socialism in the first place. According to her, having learned from Austrian psychoanalyst Wilhelm Reich (1970) that the rise of the Nazis was directly tied to the repression of sexual desire, the German 1968 movement fought for sexual liberation because they knew that "an inhibited sexuality leads to aggression and frustration and encourages empathy for dictatorial systems" (Ateş 2011, 87). For Ateş, the Muslim world today closely mimics pre-sexually liberated and pre-denazified Germany:

> When I look at the Muslim world, I see those same Western youth of the 1960s. I myself grew up with the ideas of honoring older people, paying them respect (even when they make mistakes) and obeying them, because they did everything better and made all the decisions. In the Muslim world, children understand nothing and have no rights. Those who do not follow the rules and instructions, those who are open-minded or who stand up, receive a thrashing. My childhood is not so long ago, but the majority of Muslim children growing up today are being raised exactly the same way. (92)

As a European Muslim, Ateş believes that it is her duty to encourage rebellion first among European Muslims and then among the Muslim population at large so that they can be democratized.

What the writings of Mansour (2014) and Ateş (2011) share is the European trope that views both colonial subjects and minorities as troubled children who need to be monitored and disciplined (Nandy 2009) and asserts that the colonial distinctions between colonizers and the colonized are secured through sexual control and middle-class notions of respectability (Stoler 1989). The way in which Mansour and Ateş turn the Muslim problem into the figure of the unruly male adolescent whose sexuality and violence is out of control because of his authoritarian and/or absent father is unique in its connections to Germany-specific discourses about the Nazis as they were conceptualized under American occupation in the postwar German democratization project. And because the terms of that German democratization project were complicated by the postwar partition of Germany into East and West, the Muslim problem in reunified Germany today—something we might conceptualize as a fourth wave of German democratization—is closely related to Germany's third-wave democratization project focused on its East German problem following reunification in 1990.

This new Muslim German intellectual trend of likening Muslims today to Germans at the end of World War II who stood at *Stunde Null* ("zero hour") at midnight on May 8, 1945, ready to begin efforts to democratize themselves, shares parallels with the discourse that conceptualizes the German Democratic Republic as frozen in time (Borneman 1993; Glaeser 2000). Anthropologist Nitzan Shoshan (2017) has argued that "the contrast with East Germany allowed the West to corroborate and reaffirm its liberal-democratic credentials and hence to fortify its claim to a radical difference with the Third Reich. After 1989, however, the East has continued to serve the same purpose, casting Germany's liberal-democratic society as mature enough to crusade for what it once had to be taught" (41). By likening the Muslim problem to that of the East German problem and indicating that Muslims are capable of following (first) West and (later) East Germans in their pursuit of democratization, Muslim-background Islam critics appeal to German nationalists at both ends of the political spectrum. Importantly, a large number of West German intellectuals viewed the Muslim and East German problems in relation to unsatisfied men: unsatisfied sexually in the case of Muslim Germans and economically in the case of East Germans. This unsatisfied male desire is commonly seen as the reason behind the turn of Muslim men toward Islamic radicalism and East German men toward the far right (Bernhold 2018; Spierings and Zaslove 2015).

Muslim Men as Barriers to Democracy

In *Stolen Honor: Stigmatizing Muslim Men*, Katherine Ewing (2008) examines how ideas that view Muslim men as perpetrators are founded in the commonly held view that conceptualizes Muslim women as victims of patriarchy (also see Farris 2017; Korteweg and Yurdakul 2009). She argues that this discourse is based on the stigmatization of Muslim masculinity as a form of abjection "in which Muslim men's sense of self and honor are represented in European national discourses as an uninhabitable way of being" (Ewing 2008, 2). In her ethnographic study carried out among Turkish Muslim immigrants in Berlin, Ewing demonstrates how publicly circulated images of Turkish immigrants such as those seen in German cinema and literature work hand in hand with discourses in the social sciences and social work to highlight the putatively essentialized differences of Turkish culture, in particular Turkey's oppressive gender regime. She notes that as early as the late 1970s there were sociological studies of Turkish families in Germany that pointed out the oppressive conditions in which Turkish women and girls lived. German social policies in the 1980s and 1990s thus focused on liberating Turkish youth, especially girls. Women's shelters dedicated to Turkish women and girls were established with the aim not to transform women but more basically to protect them from their families. The trends Ewing observed during her research in late 1990s and early 2000s intensified in the ensuing years. Ewing documents a paradigmatic shift in the focus of public debates and policies on Muslim Germans, from protecting Muslim women (seen as victims) to transforming Muslim men (conceived of as perpetrators), which plays out in the story told here.

This turn away from Muslim women as victims and toward Muslim men as perpetrators was marked by the increasing popularity in the German market of books like Güner Balci's *Arabboy: A Youth in Germany or the Short Life of Rashid A.* (2008), a novel written by an Alevi Turkish-background female journalist and social worker about the dismal culture of young Muslim Germans, especially Arab Germans. Balci later became a founding member of the reformist German Muslim Forum led by Ahmad Mansour and made a documentary about Seyran Ateş's liberal mosque. Upon publication, *Arabboy* was reviewed widely in the German newspapers, eventually adapted for the theater, and Balci was invited for TV and radio interviews across the political spectrum. In the hype around the book, *Arabboy* was treated as a true account of Muslim German life in the Berlin borough of Neukölln rather than the fictional account that it is: the story of a Palestinian-Lebanese youth caught up in drug cartels who loses his life to drug addiction. The synopsis on the back cover gives a good idea as what is to be found in the book's pages:

> Violence is nothing special for Rashid and his gang. At home or on the streets, it is part of everyday life. Former social worker and journalist Güner Balci tells the moving and shocking story of Rashid—a story of hate, destruction, and failed integration. An intense, hard-hitting report from the oft cited but as yet unknown parallel world that is the bitter reality for many young people in Germany.

Reading the novel, it is difficult to feel pity for Rashid. He is an antisemitic, sexist bully who tortures the boys and girls around him, records his cruelty on video, and uploads it to the internet. His first sexual experience is the rape of his own brother. The only possible reason to feel any compassion for Rashid is the knowledge that he was physically abused by his father in endless beatings. Rashid's fictional story stands in contrast to the autobiographical one Balci tells in the introduction of her own Alevi Turkish German family. Unlike the Sunni Arab families she depicts in the novel, hers was both attentive and liberal: although her parents were not educated, they paid careful attention to their children's success at school, and her brother never sought to limit her freedoms the way the Arab families in *Arabboy* did.[7] Placed together, the fictional novel and biographical framing serve to document how seemingly impossible it is to integrate a certain group of Muslim-background boys and young men into German society, whereas another, smaller group waits in the wings, ready to be included into the German fold.

While Ewing's insight into the stigmatization of Muslim men as exemplified in German media representation, cinema, and social work is accurate, I would add that Muslim male abjection in Germany is viewed not only within the frame of Germany's relationship with the Middle East but also with respect to its own history. The stigmatization of Muslim men depends therefore not only on their representation as the embodiment of Middle Eastern tradition but also on their resemblance to Germans who were Nazis, supported Nazis, or adopted the Nazi worldview. Ewing states that the Muslim man "is stigmatized in the name of freedom, democracy, and human rights and is abjected as the antithesis of these principles. He is recognized as seeking honor and respect primarily through violence and the oppression of women, means that are incompatible with the ethical subject of a democracy" (Ewing 2008, 4). But specificity makes all the difference here. In German discourses, Muslim German men are not set in opposition to the idea of democracy; they are set in opposition to the historically distinct German democracy that was achieved by negating Nazism after its defeat in World War II.

Gender Equality: The New Heroism Available for Muslim Men

In 2007, German sociologist Dagmar Riedel-Breidenstein imported to Germany a Swedish program that aimed to transform Muslim views on issues regarding family relations and sexual oppression: Heroes. Ahmad Mansour was one of the program's first group leaders, while Turkish-background dramaturge Yılmaz Atmaca worked to ensure the program's mediatization and popularization. Beginning first in Berlin, the program then spread to eight cities in Germany. Each of these projects runs with an annual budget of 100,000 euros, funded by prize monies as well as through public and private sources (Lueter and Bergert 2015). The prestigious awards include the Otto-Weiss Prize for Democracy in 2018 given by the Social Democratic Party; Theodor-Haecker Prize in 2017, an international human rights award; Act Now Youth Award in 2015; Hatun Sürücü Prize in 2014 given by the Green Party; Widmung Bambi Award for integration in 2012; and Prize for Democracy and Tolerance in 2012. The Heroes program also has been visited by numerous top-level German politicians.[8]

In interviews, Mansour stated that Heroes began as a reaction to an increasing number of honor killings in Germany. Established after the sensational murder of Hatun Sürücü in 2005, the program received much attention in the media. Sürücü was a Kurdish-background woman from Turkey who divorced the cousin with whom she was in an arranged marriage and was killed by her youngest brother, allegedly for living a free divorcée life and taking a German lover. This tragic event had already received wide media attention and precipitated the publication of Necla Kelek's *Foreign Brides* (2005), Serap Çileli's *We Are Your Daughters, Not Your Honor* (2006), and Seyran Ateş's *Islam Needs a Sexual Revolution* (2011). Ateş states in her book that her first intention was to name her book *I Fuck Whomever I Want*, in reference to Hatun Sürücü, but was convinced otherwise by her editor. The Hatun Sürücü case attracted so much attention precisely because it represented the classic stereotype of an honor killing committed by a male member of the woman's family of origin, one that could be clearly distinguished from the high rate of femicides committed by white German men. In Germany annually there are more than three hundred attempted murders of women by men, one third of which are successful and two thirds of such murders are committed by non-immigrant German men (*Deutsche Welle* 2020). It is nevertheless rare that German women are killed by their brothers or other non-partner male family members, and hence killings like that of Hatun Sürücü are marked as foreign.

To this day, the Hatun Sürücü case is a key touchpoint for the Heroes program. Heroes visit Hatun Sürücü's grave each year on the anniversary of her murder. The program's role-plays modeling problematic aspects of Muslim family culture are based on Sürücü's murder. Heroes act out the roles of young men like Sürücü's three brothers, two of whom were later acquitted, emphasizing how they view themselves as representatives of patriarchal authority, exerting control over their sisters and even killing them if deemed necessary, under pressure from their fathers. The larger aim of the program is to encourage Muslim boys to free their sisters, and in the process free themselves from the authority of their fathers. In exchange for relinquishing their loyalty to their fathers—or, from a Freudian perspective, symbolically killing their fathers—the Heroes program offers young Muslim males a Lévi-Straussian model of social contract maintained through the exchange of women. By relinquishing control over the sexuality of their sisters, Heroes allow them to be available to German men and simultaneously express a willingness to partner with German women, and hence show that they want to be full members of German society.

In a telling interview about the newly established Heroes program, Ahmad Mansour noted that while there had been a number of organizations over the previous decade that had worked with young immigrant-background women, none had been organized for young immigrant-background men, even though, he emphasized, boys are the ones who may become perpetrators. On its website, Heroes defines itself as a program aimed at male adolescents from honor cultures, one that seeks to avoid oppression in the name of honor to enable men and women to live together without violence and with equal rights.[9] Although the assumption of oppression of Muslim women by Muslim men is long-standing in Germany in the modern German debate on immigration, Heroes came to being as public German attention shifted away from women as victims to be protected and toward men as perpetrators to be transformed.

In earlier iterations of the project concept on their website, Heroes emphasized how they saw themselves as central to resolving a culture conflict they believe troubles young male immigrants. They explained how young men with a migration background often find themselves caught in a complex space where the traditions and ideas of their community as well as family ordinances meet the values and requirements of German society. Due to patriarchal and collectivist structures as well as an archaic role distribution, Heroes suggests, possibilities of a free development of personalities and a self-determined life of young male immigrants are limited. Undergoing a comprehensive reeducation program for one to two years, heroes learn to resolve this conflict by setting aside the teachings of the so-called honor culture. Through intensive engagement with issues such as equal rights, honor, human rights, and masculinity, young men are persuaded to reflect on their own position on these issues and take a stand, to question existing patterns of thought, and to distance themselves from patriarchal structures that lead them to control their sisters.

Conversations with social workers who work with Heroes, however, revealed that not all of them shared the same view of what the program stands or aims for. Sirri a social worker who is the son of a Turkish-background teacher in Duisburg, sees in Heroes a sexual liberation project that is fit for all men, regardless of ethnic and religious background. He sees the concept of honor as having some connection to Islam, but also as having preceded Islam and to be found in many cultures, including German culture. He envisions the program as creating heroes for every community to remind German youth that they already believe in human rights and gender equality, and that it is not only acceptable but desirable to do so. For him, the Heroes program aims to offer positive and gender egalitarian models of masculinity for all men.

Sirri told me that the sexist positions migrant-background youth assume are not always the ones they bring with them from their family's countries of origin, but are in fact imagined traditions, versions of an honor culture created in Germany based on a fantasy of their culture of origin. Throughout his work he observed that young people are constantly in search of their identities and their positions on social issues of import, and that they often say things they do not necessarily believe. They play the role of an authoritarian father in relation to their sisters, even when it is not necessarily how their fathers behave. Even when they have never seen certain behaviors at home, they have no trouble proclaiming "how it is" in their culture. Serkan explained that acknowledging sexism is a common problem; the idea that it works differently in different cultures and communities is a "fine and difficult line to walk." He believes it is helpful to first construct these cultural stereotypes that mainstream German society and migrant youth hold onto, so that they can be deconstructed later.

Hero is originally a Greek word meaning "protector" or "defender." Seth L. Schein (1984) defines the classical hero as a "warrior who lives and dies in the pursuit of honor" (69). The English word "hero," which the group uses in place of its German equivalent, *Held*, is conceptually connected to the concept of honor. The connection becomes more obvious when one uses the German word for honor, *Ehre*. In her book on Muslim men, *Stolen Honor* (2008), Katherine Ewing argued that Muslim men have had their honor taken away from them by the social stigmatization of practices they consider to be heroic and honorable, such as taking care of their family and protecting women. Heroes bravely take on all stigmas directed at them, including that they are sexist, potential honor-murderers, homophobic, antisemitic, inherently violent members of society, and potential threats to German democracy. They suggest that there is a new type of heroism and honor available for Muslim men: the struggle against honor cultures, the promotion of gender equality, and the fight against antisemitism. As they become heroes, young men systematically work through the issues surrounding those undesirable aspects of their "culture" and embrace a new model where fighting against these negative aspects of their culture becomes an issue of honor. Tellingly, in Burak's book, *A Matter of Honor: Fighting Antisemitism* (Yılmaz 2021), as the title makes clear, he considers it an honor to join the fight against antisemitism. Heroes learn that protecting women, homosexuals, and Jews is something to be proud of. Paradoxically, the self-criticism and self-transformation they embrace inevitably contributes to the further stigmatization of Turkish and Arab communities and what is imagined about their culture.

Heroes School Workshops: Imagining Patriarchy in the Single-Mother Muslim German Family

Heroes reach out to other Middle Eastern/Muslim-background young men and women through school workshops on the topic of "Oppression in the Name of Honor." Some of the male participants join the Heroes program and go through a one-year training consisting of weekly meetings where they talk about gender relations within families and family life. Meetings function almost like group therapy sessions and have as their end goals the embrace of new values, such as equality of the sexes, and transformational practices, such as going out dancing, accepting premarital sex, and being tolerant of drinking alcohol. Outreach programs at schools are important not only for recruitment purposes but also for reinforcing heroes' commitment to the new value system. At schools, the youth talk over the role-play scenes, identify gender-related problems in their group, and develop solutions for them. The idea is that the heroes serve as role models for the students in finding ways out of situations common to their "honor cultures." While one-off school Heroes workshops cannot by themselves effect major social transformation, they are opportunities to advertise the Heroes program to new recruits and solidify what they have learned by acting as role models for the student population.

On a chilly autumn day, I met several heroes in Duisburg at the gate of a large, academic-track middle and high school with close to a thousand students. Built in the 1970s, the school was not particularly attractive, but it was functional, with ample indoor and outdoor space. Ninety percent of the school's students had an immigration background, mostly Turkish but also Bulgarian, Romanian, and Syrian. Despite being an academic-track school, in each cohort of approximately one hundred and thirty students, only thirty would go on to take the Abitur exam for entry to university, about half the average for all of Germany.[10] We learned from the school counselor that the majority of the students who take the Abitur exam are girls. As a consequence, they find the better jobs and end up making more money. A significant number of boys mix with and are recruited by motorcycle gangs, orthodox Salafi religious groups, or Kurdish guerrilla groups who are active in the area. The same counselor estimates that 15 percent of the students are "unreachable" and that the only hope for them is that they do not create major disruptions in school.

When we met at the school entrance, the heroes were dressed in their usual outfits of dark colored jeans, white or black T-shirts, dark hoodies, and sneakers. We were greeted enthusiastically at the door by the school administration. Mr. Bilmez, a personable Turkish-background school counselor in his late thirties, took us to his office. He was happy about the prospect of a program on gender inequality and explained to us that student views on gender relations are highly problematic: "While the students believe that men should work, and women should stay at home, at least half of them come from families with single mothers who have no choice but to work." He then shared his observations about different ethnic groups in the school. "Broken families are especially difficult for students with Turkish backgrounds. When Turkish parents separate, they say bad things to their children about their ex-partner. Arab students experience families with one husband and multiple wives. Youngsters from both groups marry at a very young age with large, expensive weddings, but then most of the marriages dissolve within months. Bulgarian and Romanian students are in an even more difficult situation in that they marry at the age of fourteen and fifteen, and the girls end up leaving school." The further the lived reality of their own families is from the student's ideal of what a family should be, the school counselor noted, the more embarrassed the young people are about them. "They fantasize about family relations based on an idealized picture of traditional family structures which, given the realities of their lives, cannot be realized. Boys then begin to pressure their sisters and girlfriends to conform to their ideal family relations fantasies."

The heroes nodded knowingly as they listen to Mr. Bilmez. The stories he related were familiar to them. Although many of the heroes present were graduates of this school, I could not help noticing how different their stories are from the majority of the students now at the school. All the heroes in the room were university students. None of them came from the kind of challenging, "unreachable" families Mr. Bilmez told us about. They all had families who were more or less supportive of their education, were able to provide them with a quiet room in which to study, did not require them to work to support the family, and allowed them to keep any money they did earn. They were, however, brought up with similar gender stereotypes in the family, and these stereotypes were further strengthened during adolescence in their friendship group. Like Mr. Bilmez, they wanted to help migration-background youth aim for the kind of independent, success-oriented life that would make it more possible for them to realize their full potential in Germany.

There is one major difference in how the school counselor and the heroes talk about the immigrant-background youth and their families. Mr. Bilmez thinks that the biggest problem the youth face is the clash between the facts of their family life—that they come from broken families headed by single mothers—and their patriarchal family ideals. As we will see in the role-plays they organized for the workshop that day, because the heroes assume the patriarchal Muslim family to be intact, they see the relentless authority of the father as the source of the students' gender-inequality problems. From his vantage point, witnessing the everyday lives of his Duisburg students, Mr. Bilmez recognizes that women are the new leaders of immigrant-background families—as breadwinners and as single parents. Yet in Heroes role-plays, mothers are imagined as silenced subjects who are strictly controlled by male family members.

Three Role-Plays about Perpetrator Fathers and Victim Sons

Role-plays about Muslim masculinity are at the heart of the Heroes program. Every Heroes' role-play and subsequent pedagogical discussion is about the oppressive nature of the father-son and, to a lesser degree, brother-sister, relationship. Surrounded by other male peers, fathers, and to a lesser extent brothers, are seen to be the source of the problem. The Muslim families displayed on the Heroes stage are headed exclusively by authoritarian fathers who victimize their sons and daughters. Male friends who pressure brothers or fathers into becoming honor-culture perpetrators against their sisters and daughters also make their appearance. While the role-plays portray fathers and male family members or peers as perpetrators, they also portray sons as victims, a role that allows them the opportunity to become different kinds of fathers. In Heroes role-plays, the path to liberty and self-transformation inevitably runs through sons rebelling against their fathers. While this liberty and transformation may benefit daughters and sisters, they are not portrayed in the role-plays. Nor do the role-plays suggest that daughters and sisters can effect change; they are at the mercy of their fathers and brothers. Mothers also do not appear on stage. Basically, women are victims, without the potential to become heroes themselves or to transform relationships for the better.

In her analysis of the roles, scripts, and styles used in theater plays where Germans and immigrants stage stories about immigrants, Katrin Sieg (2010) leverages Edward Said's insight that for the West, the Orient is a theater. While Heroes role-plays differ in kind from theater productions, as instances where immigrants portray a vision of themselves to other immigrants and non-immigrants, they build on earlier representations, including those depicted in the German guestworker literature of the 1970s and 1980s. Whereas the guestworker literature was typically built around the "captivity narratives" of female migrants that "predicate revaluating ethnic difference on recognizing prior victimization" (150), Heroes role-plays recast male migrants as victims. As with the oppression of females in the guestworker literature, the oppression of male protagonists in Heroes narratives is located in the Turkish/Muslim gender system. Yet responsibility for this system rests solely with authoritarian fathers. Similar to the sexually prohibited, victimized, and segregated Muslim women depicted in *The Caged Virgin*, a collection of essays by Somali-born Dutch American author Ayaan Hirsi Ali (2006), young Muslim men are depicted in Heroes role-plays as caged male virgins who are oppressed by their fathers and then sexually limited through peer pressure from friends who, like them, have been taught to control their sisters. Because they are given the job to control their sisters, they cannot enjoy sexual relations with the sisters of others either, as their tyranny over their sisters leads to the oppression of their own sexuality. The Heroes program, however, motivates sons to rebel against their fathers so they can transform from victims to heroes and save themselves and their sisters.

Act I: The Father Who Forces His Son to Oppress *His Sister*

We enter a ninth-grade class where some twenty fourteen- and fifteen-year-old students have already arranged their chairs in a circle. Two male teachers in their late twenties wearing jeans and T-shirts that reveal their tattoos and piercings look more interested in us than the students do, who are also wearing jeans, T-shirts, and sweaters but mostly without the tattoos and piercings. The heroes start things off by introducing themselves. Mahdi is a twenty-two-year-old born in Marxloh, currently studying philosophy and biology at university. Hamid is a twenty-year-old studying medicine and has been with Heroes for three years. Orhan is twenty-three, also from Marxloh. Burak, the Duisburg-born program leader I already know, is also here. The students state their names and ages. The names are mostly Turkish-, Arabic-, and German-sounding, with a few I cannot place. They look neither overenthusiastic nor disinterested. It seems that they don't yet have a clear idea of what to expect.

The first role-play begins with a loud mock blow struck by a father across the face of his son. The son almost falls over. Cradling his cheek in one hand, he looks surprised and distraught. The father yells at his son, "Where is your sister? Where is your sister? It's 8:00 p.m. already!" "I do not know," the son responds sheepishly, making the father even angrier. "You don't know where your sister is? Aren't you the man of this house when I'm not here? Go get her!" Still holding his cheek, the son calls a friend and learns where his sister is. Together, he and his friend go to fetch her and bring her back. When they find the sister, she says, "I'm hanging out with my friends. I don't want to go home right now. I'll be back in half an hour." The friend needles the brother. "Look at how she talks back at you! If this were my sister, I would have slapped her already!" Aggravated, the son pulls his sister by the arm harshly and drags her home to the angry father.

By now the students have been drawn in by the exercise. While only a handful of them are being vocal about it, I can see that most are following the role-play and, once it starts, the discussion closely. Mahdi begins by asking what kinds of violence they can identify in the scene they have just witnessed. A number of the girls seem eager to list them, while a number of the boys want to talk about the father's good intentions. As I listen to the boys admiring the authoritarian father, I remember Mr. Bilmez's words about how many of them have no father at home.

Salih (*male student*): He intervened because he didn't want his daughter to have bad friends.

Teo (*male student*): The father wanted to show that he's the boss.

Mehmet (*male student*): Maybe the girl will do something wrong, you know. Maybe she would be raped, maybe she would drink alcohol. Girls are weak. Her brother needs to make sure that she's doing the right things.

During the discussion, the heroes alternate between prompting the youth to express their own ideas about the role-play, as a teacher would; vocalizing the motivations and thoughts of the characters they have just played; and modeling the right kind of thinking in this situation by speaking as themselves. All the while, they draw the students' attention to the gender inequality in the scene, and how it does not make much sense for the son to pressure his sister, even when his father has expressly commanded him to do so under threat of violence. Asking the students challenging questions meant to elicit responses, heroes make a particular point of highlighting the built-in gender bias, expressed in the scene in the way female bodies are controlled.

Mahdi (*hero*): What do you think about this? Is this fair? When boys brag about having sex, it's like they've won a trophy. But when girls do it, they're sluts. Is that fair? Is the only important thing about a girl what lies between her legs?

One of the girls who had not yet spoken suddenly challenges Mahdi with a daring smile.

Zeynep (*female student*): Mahdi, how would he feel if he learned his sister isn't a virgin?

Mahdi (*hero*): I don't think it's any of my business to judge. Think about it. People kill their own children because of this, and then they blame religion for what they do.

Zeynep (*female student*): Okay, then. How would you feel if a friend of yours told you that he had had sex with your wife before you met her?

What she proposes is the logical outcome of the Levi-Straussian model of men exchanging their sisters and not controlling their sexuality: there will be men whose wives had sex with their male friends. Mahdi remains calm, speaking again for himself.

Mahdi (*hero*): There are contradictions in what you're saying. First, someone who comes and tries to hurt you by saying something like this is not your friend. Second, I love my girlfriend and I want her to be happy with me, but I don't care about what she might have done before she met me. It's her life.

Burak chimes in with his own perspective, but steers the topic away from the relationship between husbands and wives to the main focus of the workshop, namely the way brothers should treat their sisters.

Burak (*hero*): If someone came to me and said, "I saw your sister with a boy," I would say, "What's it to you?" That's my family. She's my sister. If I try to control her behavior, will she ever tell me about her boyfriends? How could I ever have a good relationship with my sister?

The heroes move on to the final scene of the first act, where they encourage the youth to imagine another kind of interaction between the family members. In the now improved scene, the father calmly asks his son to help him by reaching out to his daughter, and the brother rejects his friends meddling in his sister's whereabouts. The problem is solved peacefully when the brother asks his sister nicely and she promptly agrees to return home.

I have watched heroes stage this role-play in a number of school workshops. This is the role-play that provokes the most engagement among the audience. Although they do not appreciate the father's violence, both boys and girls easily identify with the authoritarian father portrayed in this play. They often agree with the principle that the girls' sexuality needs to be controlled and that protecting it falls on the shoulders of the father and the brother. In the improved version, neither the son nor the daughter rebels against their father. Instead, both the father and the brother fulfill their female-controlling urges, only without violence.

The parallels between this contemporary nonviolent, nonauthoritarian version of immigrant-background family relations and the democratic father model promoted in Germany in the 1950s is striking. Both imagine "good" ideal fathers who are present and lovingly involved in the raising of their children and "bad" wrong fathers who are violent and callously authoritarian toward their sons and daughters. Similar to German families of the 1950s, many immigrant families today do not have sole breadwinning fathers who can assert any kind of patriarchal authority, whether it be loving or violent. Imagining a "wrong" patriarchal family where authoritarian fathers pressure their sons to control their daughters, Heroes encourages youth to resist these "bad" relations between fathers and their children in exchange for "good" relations between brothers and sisters. Act I thus necessarily entails equal sexual freedoms for brothers and sisters alike and potential premarital sex within the friend group with the children of other families in the community as well as with the non-immigrant German society.

Act II: The Father Who Prevents His Son from Marrying the One He Loves

In the workshop's second act, the father is absorbed in a soccer game on TV. His son comes and sits next to him and tells him that he has graduated from school and received his diploma. The father barely reacts. With his eyes on the screen, he says, "Yes, son. I'm proud of you." The son tells his father that he's planning on getting married. Now the father is interested. He turns toward his son and gives him a congratulatory slap on the leg. "That's wonderful!" The son breaks the news that he will marry Michelle. The father immediately becomes angry, forbidding the marriage. "This is impossible. You will marry Gamze [typical Turkish woman's name]," a girl whose parents have long promised her to the son. "You owe everything you have to me—your education, your car, your clothes. I paid for it all. Go away and never come back."

Although this role-play does not engage the students like the first one did, I was curious about how it would be received. Several days before, I had spent an afternoon at the youth club observing the practice run-throughs. On that day, the young man who played the role of the father was an especially shy person. While he could easily radiate being disinterested in his son, he could not dramatize anger toward him. A discussion ensued about whether the father looked realistic enough. The social workers and heroes repeatedly directed the young man to show more emotion, to really get angry at his son. At that moment, I joined the conversation and said that in my opinion, the fathers in the role-plays are so bad that they come off as unrealistic. I asked the group whether they thought that fathers might be acting in the interests of their children, even when they did things to limit their children's freedoms. In trying to protect them, could they at least have good intentions? The group leader, Serkan, shook his head as I was talking. "Quite the opposite. I think the father should look even meaner." He explained that because most students in the workshops are conditioned to agree with the fathers, it's important for heroes to depict them as unlikable. Although the violent father of the role-play of Act I was sympathetic enough to be defended by some of the students, in this second role-play not one student sided with the father.

Mahdi started off the group discussion by pointing out how the son told his father that he was planning on marrying Michelle. "Would you do the same?" he asked. The students all had the same perspective on this scene.

Melis (*female student*): I would fight to the death for my love.

Mahdi (*hero*): I would do the same. My marriage is about me. I should be happy in it, not my father. Who worked hard here to be successful, the son or the father?

The students agreed that the son had worked hard, and that he had done so for himself, not for his father. Mahdi then asked whether the boy felt loved. The students agreed that he did not. Burak asked if the father was paying sufficient attention to his son, and the students agreed that he was not. Burak declared that the father was afraid of losing his honor and did not really care about his son.

Mahdi (*hero*): What kind of a father suggests that his son consider someone else after he has told him that he wants to get married? What is this? A TV show? How can you have sex with someone you don't want to have sex with?

> It's the duty of the father to feed the son, support his education, give him a comfortable home. These are not things to bring up later to elicit feelings of guilt.

The students were in complete agreement with the heroes that the father was in the wrong. But they were also not as moved by Act II as they had been by Act I. They didn't find it realistic. Ilkay, who had vigorously defended the father from Act I, said, "I don't think such things happen in this day and age. At least not in Duisburg. If the father wanted to control who his son marries, he should have stayed in Turkey and not come to Germany." Another girl agreed. "No one would marry like this, by force." Mahdi disagreed with her and explained that every year some three thousand forced marriages take place in Germany, half of them between underaged people. Everyone in the room became silent.

When I discussed it later with the heroes, they told me that they had wanted to stage this role-play in this school because there were a number of fourteen- and fifteen-year-old students in attendance who are already married. According to German law, when someone gets married at that age, it is classified by definition as a forced marriage. Although the students must have been aware of such marriages in their school, they still found the role-play unrealistic. Perhaps this is because the role-play depicted a working-class Turkish family where the son receives a good education, finds a job, and then wants to marry a German woman. But in the case of the Romanian and Bulgarian underage pairs mentioned by Mr. Bilmez, a considerable number of whom are of Roma background, the dynamics are likely quite different than depicted in this act.

The tension displayed here between students and heroes is a reflection of the expansion of the legal definition of forced marriage that occurred in Germany during the first decade of the 2000s. It was Necla Kelek's 2005 book, *Imported Brides*, that prompted the change in the legal definition of arranged marriages as forced marriages. In the book, Kelek argues that generation after generation of Muslim-background immigrants fail to integrate because Muslim men bring in brides from Turkey. Arriving at a very young age without education or knowledge of German, these young brides suffer, Kelek argues, a modern form of slavery. The author of multiple books that have won multiple awards, Kelek eventually became a government advisor on immigration issues. In this second Heroes role-play, arranged marriages are seen as a major obstacle to the liberation of Muslim-background men and thus to their integration into German society in the figure of the German bride-to-be. The figure of the disinterested or absent father portrayed in this role-play appears as a major figure in Necla Kelek's follow-up book, *The Lost Sons* (2006), where she explores what is wrong with Muslim men and why their sons become criminals.

Over the years I have seen many different iterations of this scenario as performed by Heroes. In each case, the Muslim/Turkish-background boy wishes to marry a girl with a recognizably Christian/German name, most often Michelle. The scenario sends an unambiguous message about the oppression of the young Muslim man, the obstacles he faces in marrying the Christian/German girl he loves, and his subsequent inability to become fully integrated into German society via marriage. The only thing standing in the way of his emotional and sexual fulfillment and integration into German society is his unloving, despotic father who cares more about his own reputation than he does about the hopes and dreams of his son. The German girlfriend is completely absent; how it affects her, or even her family, does not enter into the act. Absent, too, is the idea that the son might choose other unwanted marriage partners, for example, members of other minority groups or sexual orientations. The unchanging pairing of a Muslim man with a German woman sends the message that young Muslim men would be marrying white German women all the time, if only their Muslim fathers would not stop them from doing so. The implicit assumption that Act II makes about the relationship between marriage and integration is clear: were they allowed to marry German women, young Muslim men would be able to fully integrate into German society and be happy and fulfilled, which would mean that they would no longer be bringing young brides from abroad, who, as Necla Kelek contends, are the reason these communities in Germany never integrate.

Act III: The Father Who Prevents His Daughter from Studying

Two men are talking together. One of them says that he's decided to send his daughter away to another city to study. The other is surprised. "Why are you allowing this? That's not right. You shouldn't send your daughter away to study."

Mahdi begins the discussion by asking whether the education of girls is important and who in the family the students think has the primary responsibility to look after the children. The students seem more engaged by this role-play than the previous one. A heated debate quickly breaks out, but not about whether girls should attend university. This one's about whether they should continue to work once they are married. Unlike Act I, where the boys and girls were more or less in agreement about fathers and brothers exerting control over their daughters and sisters staying out late, this time they disagree. Ilkay, who has taken the most conservative and sexist positions throughout the workshop, says that if a man makes 3,000 euros per month, slightly higher than the average net salary in Germany, his wife would not need to work, and therefore she should not work. The few girls who speak up in the discussion say that the men should share the housework, no matter what. Ilkay protests.

> *Ilkay* (*male student*): This is ridiculous! I should both make the money and then come home and clean the floors?
>
> *Female student*: You know what? No one will marry you! With those horrible thoughts you will never find anyone willing to marry you!

Having been challenged, Ilkay tries to explain his position from another perspective.

> *Ilkay* (*male student*): Most of the jobs aren't suitable for women. That's why. Maybe being a teacher. But compared to most other jobs, sitting at home is much better. Why should a woman go and clean someone else's house? I think it's better to sit at home and clean your own house.

Mahdi interjects with his own thoughts.

> *Mahdi* (*hero*): If my wife ends up making more money than me, than maybe it's better for me to stay at home and take care of the children. But it's something we can decide together.

When the students act out a more enlightened version of the play, the father defends his daughter against the pressure of his friend, saying, "If my daughter wants to study, I will of course support her."

This final role-play articulates the socioeconomic conditions that produce what Sara Farris (2017) calls "femonationalism," the instrumentalization of immigrant women by right-wing European nationalists. Farris argues that one of the main drivers of right-wing political support for immigrant women's rights and their liberation from immigrant men is the great need in European economies for women immigrants to perform the care work that used to be done by local European women at home. As German women began to enter the workforce in the postwar period, their domestic duties of child and elderly care fell to immigrant women. Given the increasing demand for care work in a rapidly aging population and the better educational track record of immigrant girls over boys, the mythical patriarchal family Ilkay so vehemently defends no longer functions in the real world of today's Germany. In many immigrant families, fathers are not the main income earners and women do not stay at home to take care of the house and the children. On the contrary, women are now often the main income earners.

While Act III suggests that in order for immigrant women to realize their economic potential, their fathers—and their father's male peers—must get out of their way, its message to the young males who are its audience suggests that sons, too, must learn to accept the new status quo and resist the instincts of fathers who try to control their sisters. While Act III itself features no imaginary son, the flesh and blood sons in the room are invited by the heroes to flip the script and transform this "bad" father's control over their sisters into a "good" father's support for her socioeconomic success.

Freedom from the Father

Targeting the flesh-and-blood sons in the room, the Heroes role-plays send the message that freeing oneself from the "bad" father's authority will allow the son to make autonomous decisions about his own body and life, self-knowledge, sexual, marital, and socioeconomic satisfaction, and that these liberties will produce happier individuals, a more democratic society, and perhaps even prevent radicalization. For these things to happen in Muslim-minority families, Heroes suggests, the father-son relationship urgently needs to be transformed. Unlike German Christian organizations of the 1950s that gave direct messages to German fathers on how to become democratic fathers who can raise democratic children, heroes do not talk to fathers. They instead talk only to sons. In the role-plays, fathers are authoritarian figures who do little more than scold, insult, threaten, and even strike their sons. Outside of flip-the-script reinventions where very different imaginary "good" fathers are portrayed, these imaginary "bad" fathers do not appear as characters that can possibly be transformed. By showing fathers at their worst, sons are invited not to transform their fathers but to rebel against them. In fact, the Heroes program does virtually no work with parents. It is only by recognizing the victimhood of the son and opening up space for his possible rebellion against the father that the hapless sister may be rescued, and thus her abuse will cease.

The message in the role-plays is that Muslim fathers may physically and psychologically abuse their sons and daughters in order to prevent them from realizing themselves socially and sexually. The primary aim of the Heroes program is to make adolescent sons realize that by being forced to control their sisters and by not being allowed to love and marry the (German) girl they are assumed to desire, they, too, are being victimized by their authoritarian fathers. The role-plays tell their viewers that if Muslim men victimize Muslim women, it is because they are victimized by their fathers and pressured by their male friends. If they rebel against their fathers and resist the pressure of their peers, they will no longer need to victimize Muslim women.

Heroes promises young Muslim males freedom from the burden of controlling their sisters. The hapless sisters will in turn become grateful for the camaraderie of their brothers, who will now help them hide their boyfriends from their fathers. Furthermore, were Muslim brothers to relinquish control over their sisters, they would themselves be allowed to enter into an exchange of female partners with ethnic Germans, building alliances and gaining the rewards of integration through relationships and marriage. Were their sisters free, they would be able to marry someone with a name like Michelle.

The message of Heroes is crafted exclusively for young men. Muslim mothers and daughters are not given any messages about what they can do to take an active role in this process. Young women appear only in relation to the men: as daughters, sisters, sisters of friends, potential girlfriends and wives. They are talked about but not talked to and they do not have any voice in the project. Their liberation depends entirely on their brothers' rebellion against their fathers. Unlike their brothers, there is nothing sisters can do to improve themselves so as to better integrate into German society, nothing they can do to work toward a better future self. In Act I there is a sister who is controlled by his brother. Gamze, the daughter of a family in the community, is promised as a future bride in Act II. In Act III, an unnamed daughter plans to go to another city to study. There is no discussion of how or if the sister or Gamze will rebel against their fathers. Will Gamze agree to the marriage? How does the sister feel about being summoned by her brother? How does the daughter feel about studying in another city: Did she work hard or argue persuasively to be given this opportunity? Does she feel guilty about leaving? Is she concerned that no one will want to marry her? Would she consider running away were she not allowed?

Mothers are completely absent from Heroes role-plays and public messaging. They are neither objects nor subjects in any of the discussions. In none of the role-plays are they shown to be of any value to immigrants seeking entry into the German social contract, possibly because as women past the age of childbirth they are no longer valuable for a Levi-Straussian society-making exchange. As Carole Pateman has argued in the *Sexual Contract*, the revised social contract suggested by Muslim public intellectuals as a way to include themselves in German society aims to challenge patriliny but not necessarily patriarchy. This is not because Middle Eastern/Muslim men are inherently patriarchal, but because social contracts are.

We Can Be Heroes: Mehmet and Fatih

Over the years, I have met dozens of heroes and have had the chance to observe them as they traveled from late adolescence into early adulthood. Mehmet and Fatih, both young men of Turkish background, were among those heroes with whom I developed the most comfortable rapport. During one visit, they offered to give me a tour of Duisburg as they experienced it. We sat down at a fancy café frequented by the Hells Angels, one of two warring criminal motorcycle gangs in the city known to engage in human trafficking, extortion, and drug sales. A significant percentage of the Duisburg Hells Angels members are of Turkish background. The characters Mehmet and Fatih discreetly pointed out to me as gang members had a menacing look about them, with plucked eyebrows, buff bodies covered in tattoos, some in tight T-shirts, others in three-piece suits with cloth handkerchiefs folded neatly into the breast pocket, clothing and appearance that were out of place in this immigrant café and working-class town. I could tell that Mehmet and Fatih didn't approve of these people but were nevertheless impressed by them. As we drank our lattes, our conversation shifted back and forth between their interactions with the gang members and Mehmet's attempts to enter the police force, two common fascinations and possible futures for Duisburg youth. As our conversation delved deeper, I appreciated the sincerity with which they reflected on their life journeys, the care they have for their fellow heroes, and the rich vocabulary they leverage when speaking about emotional tensions that mark their lives as young Turkish-background men in western Germany.

Fatih is a second-generation immigrant, the son of successful parents who own a company that maintains industrial machines. He is a charming young man with artistic flare. He heard about Heroes for the first time when he was fourteen via the internet and was immediately intrigued. Upon turning sixteen, he joined the group, but then left after six months. At the time, he was constantly fighting with his family, had become embroiled with the notorious gangs, and had to repeat tenth grade twice. At one point he left his parents' home and lived with the family of his girlfriend for three months. Heroes came to the rescue at this difficult time in his life by talking to him regularly and sending a social worker to mediate the conversations between him and his family. He eventually returned home and now studies at university while working part-time for his father's company.

Despite the role-plays and discussions he leads concerning authoritarian fathers, Fatih told me that Heroes made him appreciate the value of his own family and helped improve relations with them. When I visited Fatih's family, it was clear that the children were the center of his parents' lives and that they did everything to please them. His mother recounted how she had more than once waited in long lines to buy the newest release of expensive sneakers for Fatih. At the time of my visit, Fatih's older brother had recently gotten divorced and was living with them. Their youngest daughter, whom they referred to as "the princess," was studying law in another city. Fatih's parents' faces lit up when her name was mentioned, and they proceeded to brag about her success, her beauty, and her commitment to her parents. Fatih's parents were proud of the public attention Fatih was receiving and that he was doing good things for society. They were grateful that Fatih had found Heroes, in that it had clearly helped him put his life back on track.

I get the sense that issues of honor and sexual freedom did not play an important role in Fatih's life. Over the few years I knew him, he had a number of Turkish- and German-background girlfriends. I cannot imagine that he ever had to control his sister. Unlike the parents of the sisters who featured in Act III of the Heroes high school workshop, Fatih's parents were completely comfortable with his sister living and studying law in another city. What Fatih needed (and received) from Heroes was a network of devoted friends, a peer group that could offer him the right kind of advice and positive reinforcement as he passed through the difficult years of adolescence.

Mehmet comes from a different kind of family. His family is loving, close-knit, pious, and working-class. His mother and sisters all wear headscarves, and he tells me that he practically grew up in the mosque located a mere fifty meters from their house. Unlike many other Turks in Germany, one thing he never cared about, he told me, was nationalism. As he grew up, his father said to him that what matters most is to be a Muslim; being a Turk comes second.

Mehmet found Heroes in 2011 as a high school student deep in an existential crisis. He told me several times that he had wasted too much time thinking through identity questions.

> Thanks to Heroes I found the courage to call myself German. I don't know when and how exactly. Maybe in my eyes, anyone who defends human rights and equality is a German, and that's what I struggle to be, so that's how it happened. But today I can easily say I'm a German, or more likely, I'm a German with a Turkish background. Before Heroes, I could never say this. I would only say I'm a Turk and would feel very proud of it.

When he found Heroes, Mehmet was about to finish school without taking his Abitur exam, but with an option to finish the required courses in preparation for the exam. He started the Heroes program in search of an answer to one question: whether he should get his Abitur and consider going to university or graduate and get a job. After joining Heroes, he passed his Abitur and began studying political science at the university in Duisburg. He ended up not finishing and got a well-paid job as an electrician at a factory, the profession he had studied in high school.

Mehmet attributes his belated success at school to the self-esteem given to him, and the new intellectual horizons opened up for him, by Heroes.

> They always told me, "You're the best. You know it best. You will do it the best." They told me things I had never heard from my parents. It gave me so

> much motivation. I started talking at school about the things I had learned at Heroes. Like what the Enlightenment is, what Goethe argued, and such. I started talking with such confidence. My teachers were very impressed with me. I suddenly became the best student in my history and political science classes. It was such a great feeling!

Mehmet said that Heroes also encouraged him to talk to journalists and TV stations when they came to observe their activities.

> When they said, "Go ahead, talk to them," I felt like turning around to see if there were someone else they were talking to. I eventually believed them and did things I would never have done otherwise.

Although Mehmet appreciates everything he gained through Heroes, including the transformation he underwent, he sometimes lingers over the question of whether every piece of his new belief system is right. With a bemused smile, he confessed to me that one of the main reasons he joined Heroes was that he didn't like how some of his friends in Heroes talked about honor and father-son relations, and he was determined to change them and show them that their thinking was wrong. The first meetings he attended lasted for hours, and they would have huge fights. "I saw people break doors, punch the walls. Sometimes we would have screaming fights until midnight. It was really difficult and intense."

Mehmet readily admits that he still finds some topics difficult, such as antisemitism, jealousy, and especially homosexuality. He thinks he has come a long way on these issues, but he still finds them challenging. None of them is a problem when he is with other heroes, but he finds them particularly challenging when he hangs out with his other friends, especially the ones from the mosque.

> I tell them I fight for the rights of homosexuals and Jews because it's an issue of human rights. They give me examples from the Qur'an about how bad Jews and homosexuals are, and I generally don't have good answers from the religious point of view. They really push every single one of my buttons to drive me crazy. Not long ago I made a video with a gay German guy. It's a really nice video. We exchange T-shirts. I say, "Now I am gay," and he says, "Now I am a Turk." We're trying to say that now we'll try to understand the world from the other's perspective. But my other friends say, "See. You said

> with your own mouth that you are now gay. Tell us the truth, so we know how to behave toward you." These friends know me for a long time. In the old days we made fun of gays together, said antisemitic things together. They tell me that I'm being ridiculous. And I find it difficult to answer back. It's easiest for me to just not spend time with them.

Perhaps bringing up the topic of how his older friends challenge him called to mind the lingering question of whether it was the best idea to transform his outlook so radically. That day, he and Fatih were giving me a tour of "their" Marxloh. We had been to the neighborhood where Mehmet grew up, where his school is located as well as the mosque he used to attend. As we sat down to drink tea at the mosque's tea shop, Mehmet looked at me with a serious expression and said that he wanted to talk over a question that occupies him a lot. He wanted to hear what I think because he appreciated that I think differently both from his old friends and from Heroes, that it gives him a new perspective.

> Once a former radical Muslim came to the group to talk about his experiences. He told us how in the radical group he joined they supported each other and made each other feel special. Listening to him, I said to myself, "Well I've had very similar experiences since I joined Heroes, and I have the exact same feelings now, but I'm not a radical. Or at least I don't think I'm a radical."

Later he talked about this to Sandra, a social worker at the youth club.

> I told her that when I first joined Heroes, especially, I felt that I was special. I thought I was on the right path, and I still feel that way. I have this strong sense of a path, just like the ex-Muslim radical described it. I asked her, "What if tomorrow I become a radical feminist? Or a radical human rights defender? What's the difference between me and this guy?"

Mehmet tells me that at that point Sandra's cheeks turned red. She explained to him that the main difference between heroes and other radicals is that heroes are against violence. When he asked me what I thought, I told him about the parallels I observed with young men of his age and background from my earlier research who had joined orthodox Salafi religious groups (Özyürek 2014). It was mostly young men who felt they had no clear purpose, were high school dropouts, did drugs, or became involved in petty crime who experienced a major transformation once they started attending Salafi mosques regularly. Many of them found a new self-confidence in themselves: they finished school, started businesses, got married, had children, maintained stable lives. I told him that most young people benefit from the support of a group of people they can relate to. These groups give them a structure that can help them aspire to be the best versions of themselves. I added that I thought that subscribing to a new set of values and making a new set of friends could provide a person with a sense of a fresh beginning that could be very powerful. "As long as you find your new path meaningful and beneficial to both you and others and you don't feel pressured to stay with the group," I told him, "in my own view, it's okay to change your worldview. And it's not in fact uncommon." Mehmet thought about it for a few minutes, and then told me that over the years a few people had left the group when they felt it was no longer right for them.

After listening to us attentively, Fatih ventured that there was indeed some pressure in the group, but something more akin to internalized pressure. "People who receive their Heroes certificates are too embarrassed to share a view that doesn't reflect one hundred percent the Heroes perspective on each and every topic. It's usually to do with homosexuality. They're afraid that people will say, 'What kind of hero are you?' " Mehmet disagreed. "But Sandra sees this as a problem. She always tells us that we are not machines. She encourages us to talk about whatever we're struggling with so that we can keep working on these issues."

Most of the young men I met in this program come from working-class families who buy into everyday sexism. But their everyday lives do not resemble the scenarios they enact in their role-plays or the pictures painted in the books of self-proclaimed Islam critics such as Necla Kelek, Seyran Ateş, and Heroes founder Ahmad Mansour. They all admit that talking about sexism, and especially about homosexuality, had been challenging for them and that doing so had changed their worldviews. At the same time, the most important transformation they experienced in their lives was finding a supportive group of friends and social workers who made them believe in their potential and encouraged them to take important steps such as continuing their education and staying in contact with their families.

Most likely the biggest paradox of a project like Heroes is that while it is dedicated to inculcating a world outlook that is believed to fit German society, in practice it encourages young Muslim men, who are seen to be a problem for German society, to solve their problems in social isolation. The young men who participate in Heroes are typically second- or third-generation immigrants. In Heroes they learn about "Muslim" traditions and outlooks they do not learn from their families, even if only to overcome them. In the name of making them better Germans, the project makes them better Muslims, who in the company only of other Muslim young men walk the path toward self-transformation.

Muslim Men at *Stunde Null*

Muslim-background German critics of Islam and Muslim society establish a linear German national temporality leading to democracy and suggest that Muslims can also begin moving toward it from their own "zero hour" (*Stunde Null*), the same place where defeated Germans began in 1945. Depicting a timeless Muslim family that suffers from the most troubling aspects of an equally timeless German family that birthed individuals who would become Nazis, these critics reason that, just like postwar Germans before them, if Muslims are treated as children who have been incorrectly parented and as adolescents who are unable to free themselves from their fathers' authority on sexual and social matters, they, too, can be democratized. With this parallel argument in hand, Muslim-background German critics of Islam insist that the German experience of having learned from the mistakes of 1933 can be repeated. Indeed, it will be liberating. Rehashing many of the arguments produced by postwar German intellectuals about German society, they promote the idea that together with Germany they can lead Muslim communities out of their inbred authoritarianism toward democratization.

In making this historiographic claim, their aim is clear: at the expense of equating racialized Muslim minorities with defeated Germans, they seek to include Muslim minorities in the German fold by placing them at "zero hour" on the timeline of contemporary German national temporality: 1945. With this rhetorical move, Muslim public intellectuals send the message that the ethnic Germans of today have reached the final destination of their seventy-five-year journey toward democratization and may at last unburden themselves of the sins of their Nazi fathers: now Muslim minority groups are ready to take up the democratization mantle and walk in their shoes by rebelling against their own fathers. As they liberate themselves from the authority of their fathers and relinquish control over their sisters, they will be able to enter into the postwar German social contract. Envisioned as a linear evolutionary historicity with Muslims at the starting point and Germans having reached the destination, this narrative then becomes a historical rulebook for learning from the Holocaust. It is key to how the center-right German temporal outlook relates to the past, the present, and the future in Germany today.

The suggestion that Muslim Germans should retrace the steps taken by postwar Germans so as to unshackle themselves from the grip of their authoritarian fathers in order to finally become part of German society creates a puzzling reordering of disconnected temporalities and makes establishing a social contract on an equal basis difficult to conceive. One important aspect of equating contemporary Muslims with defeated Nazis of generations ago is that it contradicts the more essentialist and racializing view that Muslims are a completely different people residing in their own national time, a time that can never connect up with the Germans of today. Instead, Islam critics on the left/liberal end of the spectrum suggest that Muslims are just a few decades behind Germans and can catch up if the right policies are applied to them. This discourse assigns contemporary Muslims to Germany's "past future" (Koselleck 2018, 102), a past future that the Allied victors once wished upon the defeated Nazis, a past future later wished for by Germans themselves. This emphasis on hope for a better future makes itself clear in the way that various Germans have been depicted as children in need of reform: the American occupiers of 1945 saw German Nazis as naughty boys; mainstream German society saw '68ers as rebellious and angry youth; Muslim-background German critics of Islam regard Muslim German minorities as adolescents who must rebel against their fathers to grow up and be accepted as full members of society. By declaring that Germans have realized their potential as mature adults who live in a democratic "future present" (102), a way of being that will last into the future, these critics erase Muslim minorities from the "present" (102) they cohabit together with the German majority.

The idea that the process of German democratization is a formula that different nationalities can repeat is enabled by a historicity prevalent since the end of WWII whereby different sediments of time are set in motion simultaneously and in tension with each other. In postwar Germany of the 1950s and 1960s, a conservative trajectory that prioritized family values; a left-liberal trajectory that promoted sexual freedom; a process of coming to terms with the crimes of the Third Reich; an immigration history that made Germany plural but also resurfaced racializing tendencies—all flowed and mixed in relation to one another. These sediments then encountered other social processes: an aging population, economic success, a refugee crisis that forced to the surface the underlying challenges of the European Union, ever-shifting global political alliances. The defeat of the Third Reich, the potential its occupiers saw in Germans despite the horrors they perpetrated, how German re-democratization is remembered today—all serve as triggers generating trajectories into a future where all flows coevally but at different speeds. A German social contract that accepts all members of society as equal partners requires an acceptance that they live at the same moment, even if different historical processes simultaneously or separately animate events and interactions at any given time.

CHAPTER 2

Export-Import Theory of Muslim Antisemitism in Germany

In Germany, researchers consistently find about a quarter of the population hold antisemitic prejudices.[1] Studies differentiating among types of antisemitism find that traditional antisemitism, the belief that Jews hold too much (usually financial) power and have brought their persecution upon themselves, is on the decline. Routine Bielefeld University polls on this type of antisemitism have charted a consistent decrease from 12.7 percent in 2002 to 8.4 percent in 2006 and 5.8 percent in 2016 (Zick et al. 2016, 50). "Secondary anti-Semitism" (Berek 2018, 23), a more recent type of anti-Jewish sentiment since the Holocaust that is based on the idea that Jews benefit from the Holocaust and unfairly make Germans pay for it, is also on the decline but is still supported by 39.5 percent of the population (Zick and Küpper 2011, 22). "Israel-related anti-Semitism" (Berek 2018, 24), a type of antisemitism that demonizes Israeli state as an absolute evil, equates Israel with Jews and Israeli policy in the Occupied Palestinian Territories with the Holocaust, and uses antisemitic stereotypes in critiques of Israeli government policy, also enjoys wide support of around 40 percent. The prevalence of these two newer types of antisemitism appears to be independent of age, gender, income, or education (50). Although the number of Germans who hold antisemitic views is declining, antisemitic crimes continue unabated, with more than one thousand violent antisemitic crimes per year that ebb and flow in parallel with tensions over the Israeli-Palestinian conflict. According to annual police reports, right-wing white Christian-background Germans commit more than 90 percent of the hundreds of antisemitic crimes in Germany, most of them directed against Jewish cemeteries and buildings (Bundesministerium des Innern und für Heimat 2020).

In contrast to wide-scale and repeated polls designed to measure the prevalence of antisemitism across the German population as a whole, representative studies designed to measure antisemitism among Muslim populations have been scarce, and those that have been conducted have produced widely varying results. Indeed, the latest *Anti-Semitismus in Deutschland* report (Bundesministerium des Innern 2017), prepared for the German Ministry of Internal Affairs by an independent commission of experts, notes that no systematic study has yet demonstrated that Muslim-background Germans are significantly more antisemitic than non-Muslim Germans (79). The report further notes that the few qualitative studies that have been conducted on Muslim-background Germans to date focus on anti-Israeli sentiments and generalize these sentiments as feelings toward all Jews (80). Another ministry-funded study cited in the report found that when controlled for education and duration of stay in Germany, differences between Muslim- and non-Muslim-background Germans disappear (Brettfeld and Wetzels 2007). Yet another study based on qualitative interviews and group discussions (Mansel and Spaiser 2013) found that while young Germans without a migration background are more inclined toward secondary antisemitism, Germans with a migration background lean toward anti-Israeli antisemitism.

Despite the lack of representative sampling, margins of error, data generalization problems, and marked differences in subgroup results that underpin the research on the antisemitic attitudes of Muslim Germans, two major reports on antisemitism produced by the German government single out Muslim Germans as a focus of concern (Bundesministerium des Innern 2011, 2017). Since the first time Muslims were counted or estimated by the Ministry of Interior Affairs at four million people in 2009, how this group has been categorized is full of problematic assumptions (Haug, Mussig, and Stichs 2009). The number was based not on religious affiliation but on which countries the individuals came from since the 1960s and on an estimate of how many children they had. The estimate thus includes Christian or Jewish individuals and their offspring coming from the Middle East as Muslim. Similarly, it considers many atheist Iranians who escaped the Iranian revolution in 1983 as Muslim. On the other hand, significant numbers of converts to Islam are not included in the number. Hence, this estimate considers Muslims as an ethnic rather than a religious group (Özyürek 2014). Regardless of the fuzziness around the concept "Muslim" and lack of reliable data on their antisemitism, an increasing number of millions of euros in German government funds are allocated each year to address Muslim antisemitism. It is important to highlight that no other ethnic, religious, or migration-background group is given such attention or dedicated special funds.

An important background to this government-wide policy emphasizing the fight against Middle Eastern/Muslim antisemitism is that the overwhelming majority of antisemitic hate crimes are committed by right-leaning white Germans (Bundesverband der Recherce- und informationsstellen Antisemitismus e.V. 2022), a population also responsible for the disproportionately large number of hate crimes targeting refugees, Muslim Germans, social workers who work for refugees, and politicians who defend the rights of refugees (Younes 2020, 257). Given these statistics, the biggest threat to German democracy today seems to lie not in Muslim-background Germans and refugees but in the two-pronged antisemitism and anti-Muslim racism of right-wing white Germans.

Yet despite the statistics, Muslims have been singled out over the course of the past two decades as the main carriers of antisemitism in Germany and throughout Europe by way of a discourse that seeks to define antisemitism as unique and wholly separate from anti-Muslim racism. As drivers of this discourse, German government-issued reports on antisemitism and education depict Muslims and their antisemitic attitudes as external to German society. Evaluating "their" antisemitism as more dangerous than that of local right-wing white Christian-background German nationals, they attribute to Muslim German populations a putative set of culturally transmitted psychopathologies that render their nations of origin as prone to antisemitism. In this depiction, this new struggle against antisemitism imagines an equally new Europe, and in particular a new Germany, that has liberated itself from any antidemocratic tendencies that had survived from its antisemitic Nazi past. It instead locates antisemitism outside of Europe, obscuring the connections between antisemitism and anti-Muslim racism, both active forces throughout German society.

Old Wine in New Bottles: "Muslim Antisemitism" and Holocaust Education

While Germany has been a core locus and actor in the campaign to define a new antisemitism, the campaign's activity has been transnational, with various European and regional nations and intergovernmental organizations as incubators. As Esther Romeyn (2020) argues, this new discourse is "a transnational field of governance and particularly . . . a transnational field of racial governance" (199) that targets specific Muslim-background populations originating from the Middle East and North Africa so as to set in place a "regime that performatively enacts boundaries of belonging" (200). Over the past two decades, two interconnected discourses on Muslim antisemitism and Muslim disinterest in and denial of the Holocaust have become the foci of pan-European attention. A concatenation of events contributed to their co-development: the expansion of the European Union and its transformation from an economic collaboration to a supranational political union in need of a common identity; the failure of the Oslo Peace Accords at the 2000 Camp David Summit, the resultant Second Intifada in the Occupied Palestinian Territory, and protests against the Israeli government; rising Islamophobia following the 9/11 attacks; and ongoing anti-Jewish attacks in North America and Europe. In January 2000, forty-six European nations signed the Declaration of the Stockholm International Forum on the Holocaust, promising to "uphold the terrible truth of the Holocaust against those who deny it" (International Holocaust Remembrance Alliance 2000) through Holocaust education, remembrance, and research. But by 2003, the Organization for Security and Cooperation in Europe (OSCE) had identified a new threat to democracy, civilized values, and security in the OSCE region: a "new" version of antisemitism that they determined to be "coming out of the Arab and Islamic world."[2] As a result, one of the primary foci for OSCE policy and programming during this period was Muslims' failure to have learned the right lessons from the Holocaust and their refusal to engage in the Europe-wide commitment to its remembrance. Teaching Muslims the right way to relate to contemporary Europe's foundational crime was seen to be paramount.

By 2004, the inadequacy of standard Holocaust education and the urgent need for educators to confront antisemitism and antisemitic critiques of Israel among Muslim communities had trickled down into practice. Organizations of varying sizes in Germany and across Europe developed special extracurricular Holocaust education modules designed specifically for Muslims, the largest of which include UNESCO, which partnered with the Aladdin Project in France, the Anne Frank House in Amsterdam, and the Wannsee Conference House in Berlin. Like the Muslims in Auschwitz program, which I focus on in the last three chapters of the book, dozens of smaller organizations throughout Europe have also been involved, mixing methods developed by larger organizations with their own models.

Common to these extracurricular, Muslim-only educational programs is the use of educators from the target communities and an emphasis on Arab and Turkish connections to the Holocaust. Muslim minorities are taught "help, survival, civil courage, and resistance to authoritarian structures" (Doughan 2013) in order to assure their integration into German society as democratic citizenry. Yet in challenging the national approach to Holocaust education, these programs ended up reproducing the idea that Turkish- and Arab-background Germans have been unable to properly learn from the Holocaust. To understand how this old wine was placed in new bottles, a genealogy of the emergence of this discourse and how it works on the ground as a field of governance is needed.

A Brief History of the New Trope of "Muslim Antisemitism"

With the failure of the Oslo Peace Accords at Camp David in 2000 and the outbreak of the Second Intifada in the Occupied Palestinian Territories, protests against the Israeli government's response erupted throughout Europe, many with antisemitic overtones (EUMC 2003). One reaction was an alarmist discourse that accused Muslims of a new antisemitism (Taguieff 2004).[3] In 2003, more than 450 OSCE representatives came together in Vienna at the Conference on Anti-Semitism, the first in a series, to determine how best to fight what they determined to be a unique form of antisemitism that was "surging in the world to an extent unprecedented since the end of World War II."[4] The participants stressed both that this antisemitism was new—"Anti-Semitism in Europe today is not a history lesson, but a current event"—and that it had a new source—"At the root of anti-Jewish efforts is the same kind of extremist thinking that lies behind the international terrorism that is threatening our civilization."[5] Stating it bluntly, their concern was "anti-Semitism coming out of the Arab and Islamic world."[6] Followed up by a conference in Berlin in 2004 and another in Cordoba in 2005, participants agreed to allocate funds to combat this imported form of antisemitism.

By 2003, two major developments had split political actors on which stance to take regarding the Second Intifada and the concomitant rise in anti-Zionism. These formed the background to the three OSCE conferences on antisemitism held in Vienna (2003), Berlin (2004), and Cordoba (2005). The first was the failure of the 2001 United Nations World Conference against Racism, Racial Discrimination, Xenophobia and Related Intolerance in Durban, South Africa, due to disagreements over how to approach the escalating Israeli-Palestinian conflict. The Arab League drafted a resolution criticizing Israel and likening Zionism to racism, accusing Israel of being a "racist apartheid state" and committing "crimes against humanity" including "genocide and ethnic cleansing" of Palestinians.[7] In response, Israeli and US representatives walked out of the meetings, and European leaders refused to sign the resolution.[8] A second controversy at the UN conference surrounded the issue of slavery. Based on the same model with which payments were given to Jewish survivors and offspring of victims of the Holocaust, a group of African countries demanded an apology and reparations from all countries that had been involved in slavery. The United States had from the start signaled its reluctance to engage in this topic by minimizing its conference representation and contributions (Maran 2002). European countries agreed to increase aid to Africa but refused to consider reparations. Both developments led to a widening rift in approach to the issues of racism and justice between the affluent, white, Western countries of the global North and the poor, brown and black, Middle Eastern and African countries of the global South.

It is this widening gap between the approaches to equality and justice prevalent in the global North and South that prompted the OSCE's follow-up meetings and conference to Durban to focus specifically on antisemitism. These discussions are significant in that it is the first time North-South tensions on the understanding of racism were revealed so clearly in a major international forum. Esther Romeyn argues that "Durban was the catalyst for Jewish NGOs (backed by the newly established Israeli Monitoring Forum on Antisemitism) to push the new antisemitism thesis forward in new forums, such as the OSCE, the European Monitoring Centre against Racism and Xenophobia (EUMC), later relaunched as the Fundamental Rights Agency (FRA), and the European Commission (EC)" (Romeyn 2020, 209). But it was the OSCE—itself the end-product of a drawn-out history that began with the 1973–75 Helsinki Process, which aimed to promote human rights and democracy in Cold War Europe—that came in the post–Cold War period to play a leading role in the fight against antisemitism in unified Europe: first in the Baltic countries and Central Europe, and then in Western Europe. Jewish delegates to a 2003 Warsaw meeting of the OSCE held in preparation for the Vienna Conference later that year argued that European states had only recently grasped that antisemitism was a "mutating virus that comes from different and new directions" (in Whine 2004). Defining the distinguishable qualities of antisemitism as consisting of conspiracy theories, Holocaust denial, anti-Zionism, and the belief in the imagined power of the Jews (Bundesministerium des Innern 2011, 137), conference participants argued that some Jewish communities felt threatened less by the racist far right than by the "spillover of tensions from the Middle East" (in Whine 2004).

By 2003, fighting antisemitism had been defined as a central value not only within Western Europe but also in the then-recent Eastern European entries to the European Union. In his opening speech to the 2003 Conference on Anti-Semitism in Vienna, the Bulgarian foreign minister and future chairman of the OSCE, Solomon Isaac Passy, said, "We understand that 'zero tolerance' to any form of intolerance, including antisemitism, is a key part of our role in international relations and of our share in the [European] integration processes."[9] He added that it was through international institutions such as the OSCE that the "strong common will of mankind [worked to] bring an end, once and for all, to the tragic and powerful legacy of World War II and the Cold War. The common commitment is the basis of integration in the Euro-Atlantic area and its only possible future. Anti-Semitism is not part of this future."[10]

In April 2004, a workshop on education to combat antisemitism was organized by the American Jewish Committee Berlin. Workshop participants asserted that existing Holocaust education was not fit for the purpose of confronting antisemitism among Muslim communities and antisemitic forms of Israel critique, and that education would need to focus on different events (Whine 2004). At the 2004 OSCE Conference on Anti-Semitism hosted by the German government in Berlin, the opening speakers pointed the finger directly at Muslim immigrants. The American Anti-Defamation League's director,

Abraham Foxman, stated that "Islamist campaigns within the Muslim world and Europe have moved the anti-Jewish beliefs within Islam from the fringes, where they historically resided, closer to the center" (Anti-Defamation League 2004). By declaring the new version of antisemitism as antithetical to democracy, civilized values, and security within the OSCE region (Bundesministerium des Innern 2011, 136–37), the OSCE Berlin Declaration (2004) framed the problem of antisemitism as being located outside Western civilization, a civilization to which most OSCE countries lay claim.

It is perhaps an ironic twist of fate that it is in the birthplaces of the most virulent strain of antisemitism, Vienna and Berlin, that immigrants were first accused of bringing antisemitism to a Europe imagined to be otherwise free of it. Antisemitism was now seen as the mindset of an external enemy that threatened European civilization and security. This "new" mindset attributed to immigrants was distinguished from all other forms of xenophobia, racism, and discrimination common to contemporary Europe, which were made to seem less significant as threats to democracy, civilization, and security. Concurrent with the Berlin Declaration, a plea to combat this "new" Muslim antisemitic wave was launched. Already in 2002 and 2003, the German Ministry of Family Affairs, Senior Citizens, Women, and Youth had commissioned the Center for Democratic Culture in Berlin to write a report on antisemitism, homophobia, and gender discrimination among Muslim immigrants. In 2002, the Taskforce on Education on Anti-Semitism was formed as a network of experts "due to the insight that previous educational approaches regarding topics like racism and methods in the tradition of general human rights education do not do justice to the specific challenges of anti-Semitism in the field and the development of possible educational actions against it."[11]

In 2004, the Anti-Semitism Research Center in Berlin published a report naming German residents of Muslim background as being centrally responsible for current expressions of antisemitism in Germany (Bunzl 2005). Consequently, between 2002 and 2005, the German federal government's Entimon action program[12] designed to strengthen democracy and civil society and prevent right-wing extremism and violence funded an organization called Educational Building Blocks against Anti-Semitism (*Bildungs Bausteine gegen Anti-Semitismus*) to develop material to combat antisemitism among Muslims. In 2003, the Kreuzberger Initiative against Anti-Semitism (KIgA), a civil society initiative, was established for the purpose of carrying out "pedagogical work with Arabic, Turkish, and Moslem youth" and to develop models for curricular and extracurricular education, including afterschool programs.[13] In 2004, Amira, the moniker for Anti-Semitism in the Context of Migration and Racism (*Anti-Semitismus im Kontext von Migration und Rassismus*), was initiated specifically to combat "the anti-Semitism of youth migrants whose families come from Muslim countries"[14] by developing programs that engage youth outside school. Other organizations such as the Amadeu Antonio Foundation, the American Jewish Committee Berlin, and many smaller groups also began implementing programs to combat antisemitism among Muslims, receiving funding from international, federal, and local sources newly earmarked for the set of educational and political measures. In an analysis of public funding for programs against antisemitism, Frank Greuel (2012) found that in the 2000s, antisemitism training for mainstream German youth was reduced dramatically and replaced by programs for Muslims. Tellingly, the organization that established Amira, the Association for Democratic Culture in Berlin, was originally set up to combat right-wing extremism among East German youth. But by 2007, it had narrowed its activities to Muslim youth only. Representatives of numerous smaller, youth-based social work organizations told me that following shifting funding sources, they, too, had switched from working with East Germans in the 1990s to Muslims in the 2000s.

In 2006, the German Ministry of Family Affairs, Senior Citizens, Women, and Youth established the Diversity Does Good: Youth for Diversity, Tolerance, and Democracy action program[15] with an annual budget of nineteen million euros, tendering applications for model projects to develop educational programs for "children and youth in danger of right extremism" and "migrants" designed to strengthen democracy and address "historical" and "contemporary" forms of antisemitism.[16] The language used by the Diversity Does Good program makes it clear that the children and youth in danger of right extremism are East German youth who are seen as prone to "historical" antisemitism, while Muslim migrants are seen to be already predisposed to "contemporary" antisemitism.[17] By differentiating between the antisemitism of locals and immigrants in temporal but not quantitative terms, the ministry in effect accorded different levels of urgency to the threat each group's antisemitism posed to society. Bewilderingly, temporalizing the antisemitism of right-wing non-immigrant residents of

Germany as "historical" meant that the antisemitic and anti-immigrant crimes carried out by this group in Germany at the time were suddenly deemed anachronistic and outmoded historical errors, which decline and eventually fade away if left alone. Concomitantly, temporalizing antisemitism among immigrants as "contemporary" made them the primary and most present and future danger.

The new focus on the uniqueness of antisemitism and its independence from all other forms of racism has also had ramifications for antisemitism and anti-Muslim hatred scholarship. It is particularly telling that during this period more German scholarship was directed at separating antisemitism from anti-Muslim hatred (Islamophobia) than from other forms of racism and hatred. Two German scholars from the Moses Mendelssohn Center for European Jewish Studies in Potsdam argue that Islamophobia and antisemitism are not suitable for comparison because "anti-Semitism has motivated mass movements, declared Jews to be the 'enemies of mankind,' and in its past and present forms, attributes to Jews global conspiracies, including hidden power, control over media and politics, the subterranean global destructions of societies . . . none of which [exist] even in the most radical forms of public anti-Muslim resentments" (Rensmann and Schoeps 2010, 52). Such a view promoting the idea that antisemitism depicts Jews as more powerful than other groups, while all other racisms depict their racialized subjects as less powerful, is widespread among antisemitism experts in Germany.

The desire to separate antisemitism from Islamophobia and any other racism began intensifying again in 2019 when the political atmosphere changed. The constitutional resolution declared the Palestinian-led Boycott, Divestment, Sanctions movement to hold Israel accountable under international law to be antisemitic. In the years preceding this political watershed, Germany witnessed a number of high-profile cases in which Arab-, Turkish-, African-, and Jewish-background Germans and non-Germans, a significant number of them women, were accused of antisemitism or of promoting antisemitic sentiments simply for having emphasized or stood against Islamophobia (Dekel and Özyürek 2020). These prominent scholars, experts, and cultural figures were uniformly denounced because of their nonadherence to the exceptionalist rules of Holocaust memory: they espoused neither the singularity of the Holocaust as distinct from other genocides nor the singularity of antisemitism as distinct from other forms of racism.

A public debate, quickly dubbed Historikerstreit 2.0, took place at the beginning of the 2020s at the end of conservative Angela Merkel's twenty-year rule, the rise of the Black Lives Matter movement, the criminalization of the Boycott Divestment and Sanctions movement, and seventy-five years after the liberation of Auschwitz. During this second historians debate, comparison or relationality was not between the Holocaust and Stalinist violence, but rather the Holocaust and colonialism. Unlike the first historians debate, public intellectuals who argued for the uniqueness of the Holocaust in 2020s ended up being the conservatives and the comparativists the progressives. Several simultaneous events sparked a public interest on the topic: the disinvitation of Cameroonian philosopher Achille Mbembe to a festival in Germany due to the accusation that he is an antisemite (Dekel and Özyürek 2020b); the translation into German, twelve years after its publication, of Jewish American literary scholar Michael Rothberg's *Multidimensional Memory* (2009), a book that explores connections between memories of colonialism, slavery, and the Holocaust; Jürgen Zimmerer's (2011) book on colonialism and the Holocaust; and a much-read blog piece by Australian scholar Dirk Moses (2021), who argues that German Holocaust memory culture has turned into an authoritarian civil religion, with its catechism declaring the uniqueness of the Holocaust, the Holocaust as a break in civilization, Germany's special responsibility to Jews and Israel, antisemitism as different from racism, and anti-Zionism as antisemitism (Moses 2021). A number of German public intellectuals accused these scholars and others for reducing the Holocaust to an act of colonialism (Schmidt 2021) or even trying to unburden German of their responsibility for the Holocaust, just as right-wing scholars aimed to do during the first Historikerstreit (Seidel 2021). However, unlike Nolte, Hillbruger, and others who tried to argue that socialism was a bigger and predecessor crime to National Socialism and that that the Third Reich should be appreciated for fighting against it, scholars such as Zimmerer, Moses, and Rothberg argue that both colonialism and the Holocaust as well as racism and antisemitism are connected but one does not justify or minimize the significance of the other.

The Export-Import Theory of Antisemitism

Despite having come to the conclusion by the end of the first decade of the twenty-first century that there is no antisemitism distinctive to Muslims (Bundesministerium des Innern 2011), German government policy makers and experts continued to identify Muslim immigrants as the main disseminators of antisemitism in Germany. The German Ministry of the Interior's 2011 and 2017 *Anti-Semitismus in Deutschland* reports differentiate seven forms of antisemitism: religious (Christian); social (defines Jews as usurers); political (attributes to Jews a special power and a desire to rule the world); nationalist (does not recognize the Jewish minority as part of the nation, but sees it as a disloyal enemy); racist (believes that Jews belong to another group due to racial characteristics and not to belief); secondary (sees Jews as guilty of what happened to them during the Shoah and confusing victims with perpetrators); and anti-Zionist (conceals classic antisemitic stereotypes behind criticism of Israel). In the 2011 report, the authors specifically concluded that there was no separate "new" Islamic antisemitism: "What were previously seen as new elements [in Muslim antisemitism] were actually already known" (Bundesministerium des Innern 2011, 12).

Such a conclusion about the lack of a distinctive "Muslim antisemitism" is the product of what I call the *export-import theory of antisemitism*, a theory that is widely embraced among antisemitism specialists in Germany and elsewhere in Europe. Another trend that seeks to identify the roots of a distinct Muslim antisemitism in Islamic texts, embraced for the most part by right-wing figures, is also becoming increasingly popular in Germany. These right-wing figures argue hyperbolically that Jihad and Jew-hatred belong together (Küntzel 2007) and talk about "an almost innate enmity the Prophet of Islam taught and practiced toward the Jews he encountered" (Israeli 2009, ix). Promoters of this view typically ignore the historical context in which such statements in the Qur'an and the Hadith were made, the fact that contrary statements can be easily found in the same sources, and, more importantly, that anti-Judaism has to this date never become the official policy of any Muslim polity, and that Jews had relatively better prospects in Muslim empires for hundreds of years (Barkey 2008; Cohen 2008). Instead, the government experts who authored the 2011 and 2017 *Anti-Semitismus in Deutschland* reports echoed the views of many German scholars who argue that antisemitism originated in Europe and was then exported to the Middle East, either through Christians, in the case of the Ottoman Empire, or, particularly in the Palestinian case, through Nazis seeking to collaborate with Muslim Arabs. In this European timeline, so this historical narrative goes, Europeans developed antisemitism into Nazism in the 1930s and exported it to the Middle East, then committed an antisemitic genocide in the 1940s, and ultimately got busy, after the defeat of the Axis Powers in World War II, coming to terms with and recovering from their own antisemitism. But in the Middle East timeline, this European- and especially Nazi German–branded antisemitism was preserved intact from the 1930s through to the 1970s, when it was imported back into a then antisemitism-free Europe by post–World War II Muslim immigrants to Europe.

The export-import theory is most clearly expressed early on by Klaus Holz and Michael Kiefer (2010) in one of their frequently quoted articles: "Anti-Semitism in the Arab world, and in the Muslim world in general, is a European import in all its essential aspects. Modern European antisemitism was simply adapted to Islamic semantics and required no fundamental change. As Muslim populations were partially re-Islamized, with the associated worsening of religious fundamentalism in Europe, this variant of modern antisemitism was imported back to Europe" (109). The influential journalist and Islam expert Claudia Dantschke (2009) makes a parallel claim that it was European Christian missionaries who originally infected Muslims with antisemitism, and that their ideas were brought back to Europe after being incorporated by Islamists into their ideology: "The classic Islamist view sees the Jew as denying God and wanting to separate humans from God [so as] to rule them. Such stereotypes, formed by nineteenth-century anti-modern European clerical anti-Judaism, were transported by Christian communities to the Ottoman Empire, where they entered Muslim and Islamist discourse. [In this Muslim view,] having disempowered Christianity, Jews are [now] ready to do the same to Islam" (16).

The export-import theory of antisemitism burdens Europeans, particularly Germans, with the invention of antisemitic ideas that now circumnavigate the globe. At the same time, it implies that in the period between antisemitism's exportation to the Middle East and its re-importation into Europe, Germans, and by extension Europeans, had eradicated it in Europe. In this way, antisemitism can be portrayed as a "new," "foreign" phenomenon in contemporary Europe and Germany. The belief in the current absence of antisemitic sources indigenous to Europe, and in particular to Germany, is so strong in this narrative that any report on antisemitism in Germany includes antisemitic writings in Turkish, Arabic, and Persian, irrespective of whether the texts are available in Germany. It is argued that Muslim-background Germans who are not recent immigrants but were in fact born and raised in Germany contract antisemitism from print media and satellite television broadcasting from the Middle East. The underlying assumption is that it is otherwise impossible to be socialized into antisemitic thinking in Germany. It is for this reason that more than half of the first *Anti-Semitismus in Deutschland* report's two hundred pages are devoted to antisemitism in the Turkish, Arabic (especially *al-Manar*, the official television channel of Hezbollah and Hamas, both banned in Germany), and Iranian media. It is noteworthy that the report does not discuss immigration to Germany from other countries with high levels of antisemitic prejudice, including Greece (67%), Poland (48%), Romania (47%), Ukraine (46%), Bulgaria (44%), Serbia (42%), and Hungary (42%) (Anti-Defamation League 2019).[18] More important, perhaps, than these egregious assumptions and omissions is the fact that the first *Anti-Semitismus in Deutschland* report (Bundesministerium des Innern 2011), which set the tone for much of German government policy and funding for the coming decade, does not address the most significant source of antisemitism in Germany—extreme-right-wing white Christian-background Germans.

The second such report prepared in 2017 amends some of the first's shortcomings but reproduces others. There are sections devoted to an analysis of antisemitism in the right-wing populist movement Pegida and the right-wing party Alternative für Deutschland. Yet despite documenting some 644 reported antisemitic crimes committed overwhelmingly by right-wing white Christian-background individuals and groups in Germany, the emphasis is again on antisemitic crimes committed by Middle Eastern/Muslim-background immigrants. As with the first report, the second report again included only one Middle Eastern/Muslim-background expert: Aycan Demirel, an education activist who is not a researcher but rather the founder of KIgA, a major recipient of government funding. Importantly for the *Anti-Semitismus in Deutschland* reports' claims to authorship by independent experts, the Anne Frank Zentrum and KIgA both receive government monies to run educational and civil society programs to fight antisemitism, the very kinds of programs that are recommended in the reports.

Revealingly, the first antisemitism report, which contradicts itself multiple times, repeatedly emphasizes that the children of Middle Eastern/Muslim-background immigrants do not actually follow the Turkish- or Arabic-language media of their parents' homelands. Rather, they follow German media and watch the same entertainment programs that non-immigrant youth do. There is even a discussion of how the Turkish media is no longer relevant to German Turks. It is admitted that sales of Turkish-language newspapers in Germany have decreased over the past few decades and currently total no more than sixty thousand copies. This is probably because "the readers have no direct connection to Turkey. Furthermore, the younger generations do not know the Turkish language well enough to read the newspapers, which in any case lack a connection to the reality of migrants in Europe" (Bundesministerium des Innern 2011, 110). Nonetheless, the report argues, the parents and grandparents of these young people do follow the media from their homelands and then pass on the antisemitic ideas they acquire in this way to their children and grandchildren, a questionable supposition supported by no evidence. This statement in fact seems counterintuitive since antisemitism among Muslims was never an issue of public concern in the 1960s, 1970s, 1980s, or even the 1990s, when, according to this line of thinking, antisemitic tendencies should have been strongest among immigrants newly arrived from the Middle East. Rather, the kind of anti-Israeli attitudes that are commonly also antisemitic that concern German authorities are not inherited from grandparents but developed here and now in relation to contemporary political developments in the Middle East and in Europe.

What is more, the cumulative argument laid out in the two reports denying that a distinct Muslim antisemitism exists but nonetheless holding Muslims responsible for antisemitism in Europe in general and in Germany in particular further equates anti-Zionism, opposition to the ideology of Zionism, itself originally constructed (in part) on the idea that Jews lacked a nation-state of their own, with classic modern antisemitism. In an influential essay discussing antisemitism and Islamophobia, Matti Bunzl (2005) stresses a crucial difference between the old antisemitism and the new, anti-Zionist version: "When young, disenfranchised Muslims attack French Jews, they do not do so in the interest of creating an ethnically pure France. Nor are they asserting that French Jews do not belong in Europe. On the contrary, they are attacking Jews precisely because they see them as part of a European hegemony that not only marginalizes Muslims in France but from their point of view, also accounts for the suffering of Palestinians" (504). Bunzl points to the irony that the success of the Zionist ideal of Israel as a place where European Jews could have a safe haven is what puts European Jews under attack now. But in arguing this, he inadvertently reveals that the contemporary antisemitism Muslims are accused of holding onto is not a hermetically sealed Nazi ideology that today's Arabs have inherited from Germans and now dutifully take with them wherever they go. Rather, the antisemitic prejudices and anti-Zionist stances of European Muslims are closely related to today's political developments in the Middle East and European social and political life. Holding Islam or Muslims responsible for passing on antisemitic Nazi ideology from generation to generation turns a blind eye to the contemporary political dynamics in Israel/Palestine that pour fuel on the kind of antisemitism the government reports and programs are aiming to understand and keep under control.

Producing Nationality-Specific Antisemitisms

Although antisemitism experts in Germany often discuss Arabs and Turks as co-carriers of the new wave of antisemitism, a careful analysis of their reports and programs demonstrates that different causes of and cures for antisemitism are ascribed to each group. While most of the antisemitism prevention trainings I observed in Berlin were aimed at Arabs, specifically at Palestinian refugees, I also participated in trainings for Turkish immigrants, the largest group of Muslims in Germany. The training discourses, prevention methods, and trainer attitudes differed significantly for each ethnic group. The trainers I talked with noted that the groups were so different that it did not always make sense to keep them together in one program.

It may come as no surprise that the descriptions of nationality-specific antisemitisms and the cures suggested specifically for them read very much like the national character studies produced by postwar American psychologists, sociologists, and anthropologists trying to figure out what had gone wrong with the German nation and how best to cure it. In training document after training document, Turks are assumed to be suffering from a false "myth of tolerance," a collective sense that Turks have a history of good relations with Jews. Arabs are assumed to be suffering from a collective pathology of "self-victimization" and "desire for pride." Both groups are believed to have brought these hereditary ethnopathologies from their homelands and now are passing them uninterrupted from generation to generation. German social workers and educators try to cleanse these immigrants of these perceived pathologies by providing evidence to young people of Turkish background that the Ottomans and the Turks have been intolerant toward Turkish Jews and by convincing young people of Arab and specifically Palestinian background that they are not victims of the Israeli-Palestine conflict.

Interestingly, antisemitism specialists and educators regard Kurds as non-antisemitic. Some specialists recommend that Kurds be included in the antisemitism prevention program as positive role models who may exert a constructive influence on Arabs (Klose and Verein für Demokratische Kultur 2008, 6). Needless to say, Kurds in Germany share religious beliefs, cultural traits, and migration experiences with those of Turks and Arabs. What is distinct about them, however, is how many Kurdish groups see their interests in the Middle East affiliated with Israel. The attributed lack of antisemitism among Kurds, hence, is yet further proof of the neglected political dimension of so-called Muslim antisemitism, which is branded as a distinctly religious and cultural problem.

Fighting Turkish Antisemitism, Demolishing Unknown Myths

Amira was one of the first organizations in Germany dedicated to fighting antisemitism among Muslim immigrants. In line with the notion that immigrants bring their antisemitism with them, the Amira team started off not by talking to young Germans with an immigration background but by sending a team of researchers to Turkey. Their aim was to study Turkish antisemitism at its roots. Published as a slick booklet with the title of *Anti-Semitismus in der Türkei* (Anti-Semitism in Turkey), the team's report begins with the following statement: "This brochure has been prepared for all educators who during their work confront Turkish-background youth or adults who make anti-Semitic statements. It gives a perspective on the background and context of anti-Semitism in Turkey" (Amira 2009, 1). The booklet is distributed at events on antisemitism organized for trainers and educators who work regularly with young Germans with Muslim backgrounds.

Because they assume the transmission of Turkish antisemitism to be strictly genealogical, passed down from guilty predecessors to their children, the Amira team argues that it is crucial for educators who work with Turkish-background youth in Germany to be familiar with historical and contemporary manifestations of antisemitism in Turkey. The implication is that Turkish Germans carry a

Turkish antisemitism passed on to them from their grandparents and also under the thrall of contemporary antisemitic trends in Turkey via their social group. "The hypothesis is that contemporary antisemitism in Turkey influences the Turkish migrant community in Germany through mass media, the internet, and transnational social contacts" (Amira 2009, 1). Such reports on Turkish German antisemitism rarely, if ever, discuss the social worlds in which Turkish Germans live in Germany. They are imagined instead as being wholly uninfluenced by current social and ideological forces in German society. Indeed, they are not viewed as part of German society, or the German social contract.

Among other observers who write about an essentialized "Turkish antisemitism" is journalist and Islam expert Claudia Dantschke (2010), who also makes no distinction between antisemitism in Turkey and among Turkish-background Germans. Dantschke argues that Turkish antisemitism is influenced both by Islam through Turkish nationalists and their "Turkish-Islamic Synthesis" ideology and by leftist discourses popular among secularists, all carried intact from Turkey to Germany.[19] The only evidence she offers to substantiate this seamless connection between Turkey and Germany is the sale of several antisemitic Turkish-language publications, one at a traveling Turkish book exhibit that visited a Turkish German mosque and the other in a small Turkish-language bookstore in the Kreuzberg district of Berlin. Antisemitic publications are abundant in Turkey, but it is hard to imagine that a traveling Turkish book exhibit and the small Kreuzberg bookstore are influential enough to dominate the ideas of the three million Germans of Turkish background.

Despite the problems with this model of ideological transmission, much of the recent wave of antisemitism prevention trainings in Germany is built on the assumption of a seamless connection between antisemitism in Turkey and Turkish Germans in Germany. In 2006, the Kreuzberg Initiative against Antisemitism (KIgA) developed a workshop for German educators working with Turkish-background youth. The handbook, prepared for teachers, offers up the unsubstantiated generalization that "paranoia, anti-Western resentments that hold the Western world and especially Americans and Jews responsible, are very influential in the Turkish community. Conspiracy theories are popular not among the most radical, as with extreme nationalists or Islamists; they are popular overall" (KIgA 2006, 57). But later the handbook confesses that "just a very small percentage of teenagers follow this debate" (57). The text continues in this same contradictory and inferential manner, saying that although young Germans of Turkish background do not believe such conspiracy theories, "these ideas are still very important to them. Their parents and representatives from nationalist and Islamist immigrant organizations receive their political arguments from their homeland . . . and pass them on to the younger generations" (57).

KIgA proposes that although Turkish German teenagers do not accept Turkish-origin antisemitic ideas, it is nevertheless important that ethnically German teachers who teach Turkish-background students be aware of them. Understanding the arguments of "the Turks," teachers can deconstruct them for their students and replace them with rational patterns of thought. KIgA especially encourages teachers to learn about and then shatter the myth of Turkish tolerance toward Jews: "What is of utmost importance when dealing with [antisemitism among Turks] is questioning the myth that Jews were fully accepted and lived without discrimination under Islamic rule and especially under the Ottoman rulers. Such a perception of history poses challenges for the serious treatment of contemporary anti-Semitism and the fight against it" (57–58). Following this reasoning, teachers are presented with extreme examples of antisemitic statements found in Turkey, despite the fact that German Turks are not typically exposed to them.

The workshop begins by giving the teachers a chance to discuss their experiences with their Turkish students and friends. This immediate singling out of Turkish Germans as different from other Germans, regardless of how long they have lived in Germany, sets the tone and the nature of the relationships. I attended a KIgA workshop for teachers who work with students of Turkish and Arab background that was meant to prepare them in the fight against Islamism. When the workshop opened with a question asking teachers to share their experiences of Islam and Muslims, the mostly ethnically German-background teachers spent considerable time enthusiastically swapping stories that must have been fueled by either their imaginations or their lack of understanding of the lives of their students. One teacher claimed that many of the Muslim girls in her school were traditionally married off at the age of eight and that boys commonly travel to Syria to fight for al-Qaeda—phenomena she would need to have reported to the police. When the workshop leader, who was of Turkish background, offered to tell them about Islamism and began by saying that it was important to know that only a small minority of Muslims in Germany can be considered adherents of Islamist groups, one of the teacher blurted out, "Then we don't care about Islamism. It's Islam that we don't want in our classrooms!" Other teachers nodded. Another teacher noted with a stern face, "You know, brothers telling sisters what to do, wearing headscarves, that kind of stuff. That's what we don't want. Tell us how we can do that." When the trainer reminded them that there is such a thing as religious freedom in Germany, and that they were prohibited from stating in their classrooms that they don't want Islam in their schools, the teachers became tense and told the trainer that they were not getting what they had come for. During a later conversation, the trainer told me that it was common for teachers to come to antisemitism prevention training courses offered by KIgA with very clear opinions as to how ill suited their Turkish and Arab students were to the values of German society. Teachers were quite unwilling to question their own suppositions and prejudices.

The second session of the antisemitism prevention workshop devoted to discrimination against Turkish Jews treats three anti-Jewish events: the 1934 pogrom in Eastern Thrace, the 1942 sinking of the Jewish refugee ship *Struma* by a Soviet submarine off the Black Sea coast of Turkey after the Turkish government had refused to allow the passengers to land, and the 1942–44 forced labor camps for Christians and Jews who could not pay the exorbitant taxes the Turkish government levied against them. "These events are not well-known in Turkey, but it is useful to know the historical developments" because "these events do not fit the picture that portrays Jews as having always had a happy life in Turkey. Everyone assumes that since the arrival of the Sephardic Jews in the Ottoman era five hundred years ago that Jews always experienced tolerance. But the material shown to participants [in the workshop] reveals different experiences—those of exclusion" (59).

The workshop's third session deals with antisemitism in contemporary Turkish society, covering themes that relate to theories about crypto-Jews (Dönme) ruling Turkey, Holocaust denial in Turkey, and comparing Israel to National Socialism. This session of the workshop has also been given to Turkish-background teenagers without success. It quickly became clear that the workshop materials—texts taken from Turkish-language newspapers—would have to be translated into German; the Turkish German teenagers could not read them. Even once the clippings were translated, the teenagers, who had grown up in Germany, not Turkey, found it difficult to follow the conspiracy theories.

The trainers later explained to me that Turkish German youth are not literate enough to understand newspaper articles and for that reason they had stopped attending the workshop. On the contrary, the articles used in the workshop were uniformly written in plain language and geared toward poorly educated readers in Turkey. What the young Turkish Germans did lack, however, was familiarity with the convoluted logics of Turkish conspiratorial thinking, to which they are not exposed while growing up in democratic Germany.

Antisemitism is indeed alive and well in the Turkey of today, as it has been in the past. A recent Anti-Defamation League survey suggests that 69 percent of Turks hold antisemitic views, ahead of Iran's 56 percent (Anti-Defamation League 2022). Following the foundation of the Turkish Republic in 1923, the Turkish government embraced a race-based ideology of nationalism. Like other non-Turk minorities, Turkish Jews and the descendants of Jewish converts to Islam have been subjected to severe forms of discrimination (Baer 2013; Bali 1999; Brink-Danan 2012; Guttstadt 2013). So, too, has a myth of Turkish and Ottoman tolerance of Jews been heavily promoted by the Turkish government, especially since the 1990s, as a counter to increasingly international accusations regarding the Armenian Genocide (Baer 2013a). Yet contrary to what the KIgA training program materials suggest, even these facts do not add up to any essential "Turkish antisemitism" that can be imported wholesale from Turkey to Germany. Inflected through a concatenation of local circumstances and forces that shift over time, ideologies are changeable things, particularly when they travel across distances, generations, and experiences. Holding training sessions designed to sensitize Turkish German youth to antisemitism in Germany by rehearsing the history and public discourse of Turkey at best is ignorant of the lived experiences of Turkish German youth, at worst traffics in racist tropes about a putative Turkish antisemitic essence, and most importantly misses the opportunity to address the conditions of contemporary antisemitism in Germany.

I interviewed participants in a Turkish-background-only Holocaust education program presented by the Wannsee Conference House. A group of fifteen twelfth-grade high school students spent the year studying the intertwined history of Germany and Turkey. The program culminated in a trip to Turkey. The first site visited was the Neve Shalom Synagogue in Istanbul, one of the two synagogues bombed in 2003 by Turkish Islamic terrorists with connections to al-Qaida, leaving fifty-seven dead and seven hundred wounded. Students told me that they were surprised to learn that Jews live in Turkey today, or had ever lived there. Unaware of the five-hundred-year Jewish presence in Turkey, they were also ignorant of the myth of Ottoman tolerance of Jews that KIgA blames for "Turkish antisemitism." A trainer who had worked with the Wannsee Conference House program for about a year told me that she had not once encountered antisemitic tendencies in the students. Most Turkish Germans are no better informed on the realities and myths surrounding Turkish Jews than were these fifteen bright students at an academic-track German high school. Were it not for organizations such as Wannsee Conference House providing Turkish German youth with translations of the antisemitic writings so common to Turkish-language media in Turkey today, these Turkish German youth might never encounter the distinct "Turkish brand of antisemitism." They would, on the other hand, be familiar with varieties of antisemitism that ebb and flow through time and circulate across different groups in Germany.

Over the course of the late 2010s and into the 2020s, the tone of the antisemitism programs directed at Muslims has changed. It is now common for program staff especially at KIgA to recognize the rising prevalence of xenophobia and anti-Muslim prejudice in Germany while discussing antisemitism among Muslim populations. Yet the assumption within these programs that immigrant-background populations are direct extensions of their ancestral lands has yet to be tempered by a less essentialist, more evidence-based approach. This is likely a reflection of top-down policyframing of the issue by these educational NGOs' major funding agency—the German government itself.

Persuading Young Palestinians That They Are Not Victims

If the myth of "tolerance" is the target of antisemitism prevention programs for Turks, the myth these programs aim to shatter for Arabs and especially Palestinians is that of "self-victimization." German reports explaining Arab antisemitism frequently mention how this population wrongly perceives themselves to be victims of Israel and the Western world. Deemed pathological, this misperception is assessed as more dangerous than the Turkish version because, experts warn, other Arabs and Muslims are likely to be swayed by this allegedly mistaken sense of victimhood. Attributed to all Arabs, victimhood was discussed in detail at a five-day conference in Berlin in 2006. The Strategies and Effective Practices for Fighting Anti-Semitism among People with a Muslim/Arab Background in Europe conference was organized by an independent research center called the International Institute for Education and Research on Antisemitism, and was promoted by the most important groups working against antisemitism in Germany today, many of which receive German government funding: Foundation Remembrance, Responsibility, and Future; American Jewish Committee Berlin; Friedrich Ebert Foundation; Anne Frank House (Amsterdam); Community Security Trust; and OSCE Office for Democratic Institutions and Human Rights.

In his panel paper for the conference, Jochen Müller (2007), the independent researcher who would later author the Amira report on Turkish antisemitism (Amira 2009), theorized without any supporting evidence that it is primarily Palestinians who see themselves as a "community of victims" (36) in relation to the policies of Israel. According to Müller, together with a hatred of Israel, a "desire for pride and power" (36), and antisemitism, this unfounded idea of victimhood is shared by the two main political ideologies of the Middle East: Arab nationalism and Islamism. This "self-victimization," Müller posits, is accompanied by the idea that the Western world, in the form of the United States and Israel, is conspiring against the Arab and/or Muslim world (36). Such ideologies are used by Arab nationalists and Islamists to spread their anti-Zionist propaganda as an expression of their antisemitism (35). According to Müller, this "self-victimization" and "desire for pride and power" is not an effect of living in Europe as a marginalized subject but rather "was and is imported to Europe by many [Arab] migrants from the region" (36). Furthermore, "self-victimization" is a crucial part of an ideology of collective identity, "the 'Gemeinschaft' of Arabs/Muslims" (35) that is "passed on from generation to generation" (36). This approach not only attributes pathological aspirations and ideas to all Arabs worldwide; it also views ethnic groups and their desires and ideologies as unconnected with the social and political context in which they live. In this framework, the fact that Palestinian refugees in Germany have been forced to leave their homes, live in precarious conditions, and are subjected to discrimination is irrelevant to the aspirations and ideas attributed to them. Such experts suggest that, devoid of any real cause for their claims to victimhood, Palestinians in particular and Arabs in general apparently "self-victimize" for no good reason. Worse, they are said to carry their pathological desires and ideas along with them wherever they travel and then pass them on to other Muslims.

Palestinians in Germany are the targets of the lion's share of programs in the fight against the new antisemitism. Especially in Berlin, they are a particular group, one with characteristics that differ significantly from Arab- and Turkish-background groups in Germany. Owing to their complicated legal status as stateless refugees, the actual number of Palestinians living in Germany is unknown.[20] Nikola Tietze (2006) reports that estimates vary wildly between eight thousand and thirty-five thousand. Most came to Germany in the 1970s, 1980s, and 1990s fleeing the violence they experienced in the Palestinian refugee camps during the Lebanese Civil War and the ongoing conflict with Israel. Because East Germany at the time did not require Palestinians to obtain travel visas, a considerable number of them arrived first in East Berlin, moving later to West Berlin. This makes many of them refugees three or four times over. Since 1985, Palestinian refugees in East, West, and reunified Germany have been registered as people with "unclear state belonging." This complication in their registration not only makes them difficult to count; it has also hindered their ability to access many of those basic civic rights enjoyed by other residents of the city. Most depend on social aid from the state, have very low levels of education, and live in precarious socioeconomic conditions. Many who experienced violence suffer from post-traumatic stress disorder. As a result, Palestinians in Berlin are a unique group who, as refugees to Germany originating in Middle East refugee camps that date back to 1948, have directly suffered from the Israel-Palestinian conflict and now live in a distinctly insecure and marginal position.

In the last few years the special place that Palestinians hold in the Muslim antisemitism discourse has become more prominent. According to Anna-Esther Younes, "the figure of the anti-Semitic Muslim carved out a special place for the figure of the Palestinian anti-Semite as one of the prime instigators or sources for this predicament, with the Israeli-Palestinian conflict as the prime site upon which anti-Semitism today is lived out" (2020, 252). After the German parliament passed a resolution that condemned the Boycott-Divestment-Sanctions campaign against Israel as antisemitic in 2019, pressure on Palestinian activists mounted, of which the following are but a few examples. Younus, a German-Palestinian scholar, was disinvited from speaking at a conference in 2019; she later successfully sued the Society for a Democratic Culture in Berlin for keeping a secret file against her and sharing it with other organizations (Akkad 2022). In 2021 the celebration of Nakba Day was banned, and Palestinian journalist Nemi al-Hassan was fired from her job at television station WDR when a right-wing website published a photo of her joining an al-Quds Day protest when she was seventeen in 2014 (Elger and Grossekathöfer 2021). In the summer of 2022 the work of Palestinian artists included in the Documenta 15 exhibition in Kassel was vandalized (Artforum 2022).

Over the past two decades, KIgA has developed educational methods to talk about antisemitism and the Israeli-Palestinian conflict with Middle Eastern/Muslim-background youth. For example, one module that discusses the establishment of Israel is "Jewish Dream—Arab Trauma: How Israel Came into Being." Another is *"Beyond Black and White: A Timeline of History and Historical Images of the Middle East Conflict until 1949."* The latter program's brochure (KIgA 2013) states that its aim is to "discuss" the history that preceded the establishment of the State of Israel in 1948. KIgA claims that such discussion is important because they want to "fight against problematic interpretations and views" (71) that leverage historical images in order to make territorial claims. The common interpretation they argue against is the idea that "Jews stole the land of Palestine from Arabs" (71). The interpretation of the region's history the program seeks to present to participants instead emphasizes that "over the centuries the various territories of the region were settled by Jews, Muslims, and other groups, and that a Palestinian state that might serve as the reference point for territorial claims has never existed" (71).

According to the brochure, the exercise aims "to sensitize teenagers to change in society and to question historical narratives that are used to legitimize territorial claims" (71). To achieve this goal, the program focuses on the flux and impermanence of history in the region: that it was ruled by different groups at different times; that its population changed frequently according to migrations and conquests; that the many peoples, cultures, and religions—especially Jews and Muslims—lived together for millennia without any single group having a state of its own. "In other words, by showing the diversity of rulers and populations in the region and by emphasizing that there was never an historical Palestinian state, the training aims to deliver the message that the idea that Israelis took land that belonged to Palestinians is not legitimate" (71). Following the presentation of this historical narrative is a timeline exercise that establishes that there are two sides to all historical events. The students are given a list of events that led to the establishment of Israel in 1948 and are asked to first place them in chronological order and then mark whether the event was good from an Israeli perspective or from a Palestinian perspective. The goal of this exercise, the brochure explains, is to show that there are both Israeli and Palestinian perspectives on any given event, thereby raising participants' awareness of the conflict's complexity. Palestinian students, it is foreseen, will see that there is no need to perceive themselves as victims or feel hostile toward Israel.

To complement the education of Muslim-background youth on the Middle East conflict, several organizations, among them the Wannsee Conference House, KIgA, and Amira, have organized study trips for Muslim-background youth to Israel/Palestine. These and similar trips build on the half-century-long tradition of taking young Germans to Israel with the aim of reconciliation and promotion of the "new Germany" in the world (Ayalon and Schnell 2014). ConAct (2010), the organization that administers government funding of the German-Israeli youth exchanges, reported that between 1961 and 2010, some 500,000 German and Israeli youth had benefited from the exchange. Until only recently, German participants of the German-Israeli youth exchanges were limited to ethnic Germans. An ethnographic account of a German-Israeli exchange (Bergerson 1997) documents how these exchanges are often positive experiences that focus on reconciliation and go beyond a simple victim-perpetrator dichotomy. Importantly, Bergerson's account demonstrates that tensions between German and Israeli youth were the result not of the shared past of World War II but prompted by discussion of the Israeli-Palestinian conflict. A more recent study of German study trips to Israel by two Israeli scholars (Ayalon and Schnell 2019) argues that such tours did bring Israeli and German youth "closer to each other, improved German's attitudes toward Israel, promoted understanding to Israel's security vulnerability and helped them live in peace with their German identity. . . . However, if the goal [was] getting to know Palestinian society and the conflict, it was achieved from a one-sided Israeli narrative that left only minimal room for empathy to the Palestinian cause and minimum tools to critically evaluate the occupation" (127).

In 2010, KIgA led a study trip for Muslim-background youth to Israel/Palestine titled "*What Does Palestine Have to Do with Me?*" The implicit goal was that the youth return from their trip devoid of any close emotional identification with Palestine. Although the trip built on the long tradition of German-Israeli youth exchange and even benefited from the same structures and resources, there were differences between the ethnic German and Muslim-background German trips to Israel. The founder and head of KIgA made clear in the video documenting the trip (Reichert 2011) that he interpreted these differences as having to do with something he called "image": "Most [German] youngsters who travel to Israel/Palestine from Germany already have a very positive image of Israel. But for this group, this was not the case at all." Perhaps the real difference was not something so insubstantial, malleable, or ideological as a positive or negative image of Israel and Palestine, but rather very different investments and personal connections to the area they were visiting, especially among Palestinian-background youth whose families had been forced to flee the country.

The Eberhard Klein Oberschule in Kreuzberg is a non-academic-oriented school serving mostly immigrant-background pupils. Funded through the Diversity Does Good program of the Ministry of Education, the school offered KIgA's "*What Does Palestine Have to Do with Me?*" study trip to sixteen teenagers of Turkish and mostly Palestinian background as part of a three-year-long educational program, called Pedagogical Concepts against Anti-Semitism among Youth with Islamic Influence. To carry it off, KIgA cooperated with several major organizations active in antisemitism and Holocaust education and German-Israeli relations: American Jewish Committee Berlin; Foundation Remembrance, Responsibility, and Future; the German-Israeli student exchange program ConAct specializing in intercultural contact; and Yad Vashem, Israel's memorial to the victims and resistors of the Holocaust.

As is the case with most antisemitism prevention and Holocaust education trips for Muslim-background youth, the KIgA trip represented the first time the youth had ever joined an organized youth trip, and in some cases, the first time they had ever traveled outside Germany. Of the sixteen, ten had German passports, four had Turkish passports, one carried a travel document for foreigners and one a travel document for refugees. Despite the involvement of the German and Israeli organizations listed above, it had been particularly difficult to obtain Israeli visas for the non-German passport holders. One of the students was able to join the group in Israel only four days later due to a visa delay. Also, many of them found it very difficult to contribute 100 euros for the trip (Demirel and Kassar 2011, 46–55).

The KIgA's "*What Does Palestine Have to Do with Me?*" program included participation in a series of workshops in Kreuzberg where the youth first talked about their own identity and background and their history of migration, then reviewed Jewish and Muslim life in Berlin more generally and the history of the Holocaust and the Middle East. While it is common for the German-background youth who take part in such study trips to Israel to attend educational workshops, the workshops for ethnic Germans educate them about Israel, without the topics discussed by the Muslim youth. "*What Does Palestine Have to Do with Me?*" assumes that Muslim youth are in need of rather different information: namely, a new angle on the Middle East conflict that gives them a glimpse into the Israeli perspective, the multiplicity of everyday life in Israel/Palestine, and the peaceful coexistence of Jews, Muslims, Christians, and other groups there. These topics were revisited during the trip.

The sleek brochure (KIgA e.V. 2011) documents the study trip in detail and provides candid statements from youth and organizers. When asked, youth talked about how not all of their family members were excited about the trip. Some had to endure comments from friends asking if they were trying to convert to Judaism. International reactions to the tightening of the Israeli-Egyptian blockade of the Gaza Strip posed a major obstacle to the trip. On May 31, 2010, the Israeli army raided the *Gaza Freedom Flotilla*, which included a cargo ship bearing a Turkish flag, that was attempting to deliver humanitarian supplies to Gaza by breaking the Israeli naval blockade. Nine Turkish activists were killed. This event radically changed the mood among the youth, and some of them came to the next meeting with T-shirts sporting Arafat and Hamas. They also accused the educators of being one-sided and of being Israel supporters. The educators described the effect the events had on the program: "Everything we had done previously with the youth was now being fundamentally questioned. Resentments that had begun slowly as questions posed bit by bit were now breaking out unfiltered" (25).

Two incidents occurred during the trip that brought the reality of the Israeli-Palestinian conflict home to the student participants. The first was their experience while entering and exiting a Palestinian enclave in the West Bank. At that point their German Jewish tour guide was not allowed to enter the Palestinian area because of the risk of him being kidnapped. Something more upsetting happened as the group was coming back from what had turned out to be a rewarding visit to the Palestinian area. According to the project booklet and interviews in the video, five of the youth took a wrong exit, which returned them to the Palestinian side instead of bringing them back to the Israeli side. At that point the five were threatened by Israeli soldiers at gunpoint. The tour leaders related that this made the youth furious because "they thought they had taken such a big step and made such a big sacrifice by participating the project and the trip, and now their reservations about Israelis had been borne out in reality" (36).

The second incident occurred when relatives of a Palestinian-background student, Mahmoud, drove hours to meet him. Mahmoud's family, who lived originally in the West Bank, had been unable to see their extended family since the Six-Day War of 1967 when they had fled, seeking refuge first in Lebanon and later in Germany. Mahmood had never met his extended family and was nervous before the very emotional reunion. This encounter revealed the living connections some of the Palestinian participants have to this land, and provided a powerful answer to the question "What does Palestine have to do with me?"

Despite these few tense moments that brought the Israeli-Palestinian conflict home to the Palestinian- and Turkish-background participants, the study trip did transform how students saw Israel and the conflict. The brochure includes a number of quotations from the students that demonstrate just how their perspectives were changed by the visit.

Bilal: I am most surprised that Jews, Muslims, and Christians can live together and are not enemies, as people always say they are. What I find bad is that people in the Palestinian territories cannot move freely. (41)

Ozan: My opinions about Israel/Palestine became more positive with respect to some things. I saw that there are Arabs and Jews who get along and help each other, and that there are not so many problems as one is told. (41)

Jenny: My opinions have already changed a bit. For example, I never thought that Palestinians and Jews could get along, or that Arabs could speak Hebrew well. I never thought I could sit down at a table with an Israeli and have a normal conversation. . . . There were some discussions with which I could not agree. But no one would say, "You're a Jew. I don't want to have anything to do with you," as it could have been were we in Berlin. (41)

Mahmoud: Thanks to them offering this trip, I have a complete picture of both sides. For the first time in my life, I had the chance to come into contact with people who experience it every day, who see it, who know what they're talking about, whether from the Israeli or the Palestinian side. Naturally,

> in the Middle East not everything is peaceful or happy, and there are still conflicts. But in the end, one has to be aware that a lot is happening that people don't really want to happen, but that politicians have been using as leverage for themselves. (43)

These quotations differ from the interviews I had with another group of Palestinian youth who had made a similar trip with another organization the previous year. At that time, the youth told me that the educational program they had been through and their trip to Israel had changed their perception of Jews in that they had learned to differentiate between Jews and Israelis. A few of them told me that their anger toward Israel for having taken their homeland remains.

Dislocating Antisemitism

In a country burdened by the guilt of a gruesome antisemitic history, public intellectuals and policy makers scrutinize the suitcases of immigrants in search of contemporary antisemitism's source. There is no question that immigrants arrive with their own memories, attitudes, and ideologies about the world in general (Rothberg and Yıldız 2011) and about Jews in particular. But there should also be no question that the German living quarters into which immigrants carry these beliefs and dispositions have never been fully cleansed of antisemitism. Muslim-background youth, who are the main suspects in the export-import theory of antisemitism, did not migrate to Germany but were born there. This means that the only antisemitism they might embrace is in fact part and parcel of life in the major European cities in which they were born and grew up. How, then, do we explain the popularity of the suitcase metaphor or the export-import theory as an explanation for contemporary antisemitism in Europe?

Above all, the recent discovery of what is termed "Muslim" or "new" antisemitism keeps the fight against antisemitism alive in Europe. Seventy years after the Holocaust annihilated two-thirds of the continent's Jews and the decades-long struggle to de-Nazify and democratize German society, right-wing antisemitism is alive and deadly in Germany. In a democratic Germany based on the negation of National Socialism, fighting antisemitism is central to national identity. This new campaign against "Muslim antisemitism" brings antisemitism back into the center of public concern and attention, renews an EU-wide consensus about the real malevolence of anti-Jewish hatred, and defines combating it as a European value. It displays to the world that Europe more generally, and Germany above all, is still highly sensitive to and intolerant of antisemitism.

At the same time, making Muslims the new focus of the European and German antisemitism prevention campaign shifts the blame to relative newcomers to European society, people who are still commonly called "foreigners" (*Ausländer*) in Germany. Accusing immigrants, or rather the grandchildren of immigrants, of having imported antisemitism to the continent successfully obscures non-immigrant European and German antisemitism. And despite the heightened attention paid to antisemitism and Holocaust memory in Germany, observers concur that increasing numbers of Germans report being weary of hearing about the Holocaust and no longer want to feel guilty (Margalit 2010; Markovits 2006). These findings suggest that shifting the blame for antisemitism onto Muslim Germans and depicting them as dishonorable and undeserving residents may work well to relieve mainstream Germans of guilt, in effect vindicating them as honorable opponents of antisemitism.

While the export-import theory of antisemitism accuses Muslims of being carriers of antisemitism, it attributes antisemitism's origin to Europeans, and especially to Germans. The theory blames Muslims for holding onto an antisemitism that European Christian missionaries and German Nazis taught them in the first place. Turkish and Arab cultures are depicted as quick to learn antisemitism, but unequipped with the moral character necessary to resist it. Antisemitism prevention program reports fault Turks for holding onto a myth of centuries-long Turkish tolerance toward Jews because it makes them feel wrongly superior to Europeans. The same reports criticize Arabs and especially Palestinians for clinging to a mistaken sense of victimhood and an ill-founded desire for power and pride. The antisemitism prevention programs designed for Muslims work to wear down these alleged self-perceptions. Turkish-background Germans are told that their forefathers were not really virtuous toward Jews, and Arab-background Germans, in particular Palestinians, are taught that their grandfathers collaborated with the Nazis and then sold their own land to Jewish settlers. The export-import theory attributes antisemitism's origins to Europeans, but stresses the inadequacies of Turkish and Arab cultures, posing them as obstacles to a proper, or properly European, repentance.

Perhaps the most pernicious outcome of understanding antisemitism as a malignant ideology exported from and then imported back into Europe by Muslims is that it makes perpetrators out of marginalized, racialized, and disadvantaged people. Once it is discursively established that Muslims are antisemitic—or worse, that they do not atone for their antisemitism—it becomes difficult to recognize their position as victims in relation to European racism. Critical race theorists of Europe have long ago pointed out that European variants of racism are built on an edifice of racial blindness and antiracist posturing that persistently ignores or refuses to recognize contemporary racial differences and, as a result, is oblivious to ongoing racism in Europe. They also agree that the memory of the extreme manifestation of racism that led to the Holocaust is partly responsible for this racial blindness/blindness to racism (Goldberg 2016; El-Tayeb 2008; Partridge 2010). In that respect, the discourse on "Muslim antisemitism" functions like its sister discourses on Muslim sexism (Ewing 2008) and Muslim homophobia (Puar 2008): by characterizing Muslims as immoral perpetrators and excluding them from the fold of the ethically normative European/German community. Complex processes that have recently moved the fight against antisemitism into the center of European identity have worked to distinguish this form of racism from all other forms, most especially from anti-Muslim racism. Depicting Muslims as past and present offenders against Jews, and doing so both officially at the national and supranational political level and as part of a consistent nationwide educational policy, serves to conceal the subtle and not so subtle ways in which Muslims are indeed victims of racism in today's Europe. It also depicts antisemitism as a problem that no longer belongs to Germany but now only exists there due to immigration. The next chapter provides a detailed account of how the group of youth from Duisburg we met in chapter 1 navigate this narrative of Muslim antisemitism in their everyday lives. How do they make a place for themselves in this foundational German narrative? At what cost? In what ways are they able to transform it?

CHAPTER 3

Wrong Emotions / Wrong Empathy for the Holocaust

Juliana has worked as a guide at a number of former concentration camps in Germany for many years now. I asked about her impressions of Muslim-minority Germans visiting the camps. "Many [Turkish and Arab German] immigrants have visited," she told me. "And I have a feeling that they were different from other visitors." After pausing briefly, she added, "Now I don't know if they really *were* different. But I could tell that the other guides were as irritated as I was by them. There was a sense that they didn't belong here, and that they should not be engaging with the German past. Somehow their presence at the camp didn't fit." When I pushed her further to explain what she meant, Juliana inferred from their behaviors what she intuited to be immigrants' emotions: "For example, when they go to the camps, immigrants start to feel like they will be sent there next. They come out of the camp anxious and afraid. I don't like it at all when they do that, and I don't even want to take them there."

Mehmet, a German history teacher of Turkish background, worked in a Holocaust education program for immigrants. He told me that some students didn't want to talk about the Jews' suffering "because according to them, it is always about the Jews, and no one cares about them." Arab students in particular, he said, "raise the topic of the Israeli-Palestinian conflict when we bring up the Holocaust. They compare Israelis to Nazis and say that Palestinians are the victims of the new Holocaust carried out by the Israelis."[1]

That Muslim-minority Germans, specifically Turkish and Arab Germans, do not engage with the Holocaust in the "right" way became a concern for Holocaust educators in the 1990s (Fava 2015). Victoria Bishop Kendzia ascribes this mismatching behavior to a lack of familiarity with the "performative guilt trope" (2018, 134), which has become a matter of public political discussion. In June 2015, Kurt Steiner, an MP from the Christian Social Union in Bavaria, declared that students who come from Muslim, refugee, and asylum-seeking families do not need to visit concentration camps as part of their education. Steiner explained, "Muslims and refugees do not have any connection to the history of German National Socialism. And this should remain so" (Smale 2015). He further explained, "One should be careful with such students because they face cognitive and emotional challenges." Left-wing politicians responded swiftly to his statement. Georg Rosenthal of the Social Democratic Party responded that visiting the scenes of Nazi crimes is "especially important for young immigrants so that they can understand why they need to assume responsibility for German history."

Although there is no consensus about what exactly is "wrong" about the way Muslim-minority Germans and Europeans engage with the Holocaust, recently there has been widely shared public discomfort with it (Allouche-Benayoun and Jikeli 2013). Newspapers run stories about how Muslim students refuse to attend concentration camp tours and do not engage with the material on National Socialism in history classes (Kouparanis 2008). It seems the core of the perceived problem is an emotional or even "cognitive" challenge seen as specific to the Muslim minority that prevents them from empathizing with Jewish victims of the Holocaust. Educators often complain to me about the inappropriate emotions Muslim-minority members express in relation to the Holocaust. The most common complaints involve the immigrants' fear that something like the Holocaust may happen to them as well, the envy of the status of Jewish victimhood, and the pride in their own national background. The Middle Eastern/Muslim minority is poignantly aware that despite all the work to ensure that they empathize with the Jewish victims, they themselves are not allowed to demand any empathy.

Holocaust educators' assumptions about immigrant-background Germans' engagements with the history of National Socialism are at odds with the more differentiated findings of one of the first studies ever conducted on this subject. In her book *Entliehene Erinnerung: Geschichtsbilder Junger Migranten in Deutschland* (Borrowed Memory: Historical Impressions of Young Migrants in Germany, 2003), Viola Georgi conducted interviews with thirty-two young people who did not consider themselves to be German. She identified four types of engagement with Holocaust memory. The first type focused on and identified with the victims of National Socialism. Immigrants who engaged in this way associated Germans with perpetrators, enablers, or bystanders and felt distanced from and cynical toward German society. The second type concentrated on the bystanders, enablers, and perpetrators and attempted to understand why Germans could have supported the National Socialist regime. Among immigrants who engaged in this way, Georgi observed an "active and empathic" perspective toward history. She argues that immigrants who engaged with Holocaust memory discourse in this way were primarily motivated by belonging to German society. "In being willing to accept the 'negative historical heritage' of Germans, the goal is to qualify as a 'full-fledged' German. . . . The perceived task and challenge are to rehabilitate the damaged image of Germany" (302). Even though this is the type of emotional engagement designated as most desirable by Holocaust educators, Georgi's description points up an emergent structure of feeling that exceeds the conventional history told within German memory culture and has a specific aim of fitting its immigrant subject into contemporary German society. In the third type, immigrants concentrated on their own ethnic community. Some members of this group go so far as to instrumentalize the history of the Holocaust in order to attract more attention to their community (304). The fourth type focused on the universal experience of the victims, trying to work out which conditions and which structures lead people to become victims, perpetrators, followers, or bystanders (304). Despite the rich variety of engagements and identifications among ethnic minority groups in Germany detected by Georgi, the complaints of Holocaust educators and public discussions on this topic typically infer immigrant engagement in terms of Georgi's first type. They assume that immigrants focus exclusively on the victims of National Socialism and identify with them. Educators' confirmation bias toward the first type has resulted in the development of education programs exclusively targeting this type of engagement.

In her long-term study of several coteries of Turkish- and Palestinian-background youth attending Wannsee Conference House educational programs, *Anerkennung und Erinnerung: Zugänge arabisch-palästinensischer und türkischer Berliner Jugendlicher zum Holocaust* (Recognition and Remembrance: Access by Arab-Palestinian and Turkish Berlin Youths to the Holocaust), Elke Gryglewski (2013) builds on Georgi's typology, expanding it to six attitudinal categories: open-empathic, processual learner, friendly interested, friendly uninterested, provocateur, and dogmatic thinker (145–217). The most desirable type of engagement, the open-empathic type, "is characterized by a great willingness to deal with National Socialism and the Shoah. It is not that the person is always looking for these topics, but if they are on the agenda, he is interested in them and shows great empathy for the fate of the persecuted and murdered Jews during the Nazi era, as well as in other victim groups" (145). Yet despite displaying the most desirable of dispositions toward Holocaust memory, in Gryglewski's estimation, even members of this group have a problem, for they are unable to take upon themselves the (potential) perpetrator position.

> The focus of interest is always on the fate and suffering of the victims and not on questions about the motivation of the perpetrators, the complexity of the crimes, or chronological or structural connections that might suggest lessons from history for current contexts. That is particularly troublesome insofar as this approach of focusing exclusively on the group perceived as the victim applies equally to current events. Also, with regard to current conflicts and human rights violations, the focus is on people's suffering and not on the question of what triggered such suffering or how [the precipitating events] could have been prevented. (145)

Gryglewski suggests that this is a combination of the first and fourth types in Georgi's categorization, which focus respectively on the victims of National Socialism and all of humanity. The example she uses to exemplify this type is Samira, a sixteen-year-old Palestinian-background girl. Throughout her education program, Samira showed complete open-heartedness toward the experiences of Jewish victims, but when they later discussed the Middle East conflict, she likened the experiences of Palestinians to Jews, something Gryglewski found problematic. Gryglewski takes particular issue with the way that Samira and two other Palestinian-background youths imagined the fate of Jewish victims through the experience of Palestinians: "The empathy the three youngsters show toward people in current conflict situations gets mixed up with a personal, family-related concern regarding the Middle East conflict, and lack of knowledge about historical, political, and social connections can lead . . . to historical flattening" (151).

It is obvious from her book, and especially from my observations of her during the Wannsee Conference House education sessions in which I participated, that Elke Gryglewski has great sympathy toward and rapport with the Berlin youth she works with. Yet these kinds of assessments also make it clear that the ideal type of engagement Gryglewski expects from this group is to achieve a very particular kind of interpersonal emotional connection in relation to historical actors: empathy with the victims and identification with the perpetrators. Her project steers Palestinian-background youth toward mimicking the publicly acceptable emotional formula for white Germans. To put it more bluntly, projects like hers aim to make Germans out of Muslims, at least in emotional terms and in relation to the memory of the Holocaust. Ironically, while embracing this emotional model gains political goodwill for the Muslim minority, it does not make them Germans because of the way the remedial Holocaust education programs set Middle Eastern/Muslim-background youth apart from white Germans.

From *Einfühlung* to Empathy and Back

In light of such judgments as to the inappropriateness of immigrants' interpersonal connections with German actors in the Holocaust, a foray back into twentieth-century discussions around the concept of empathy, especially as developed by German philosopher Edmund Husserl, reveals empathy to be a much more complex and nuanced experience of intersubjective connection. Introduced and developed first in the German language and the field of philosophy and then traveling to other languages and disciplines, empathy has not always been seen as a desirable quality necessary for the development of moral, social, and political life.[2] Only after World War II did empathy come to be understood as a measurable attribute in an individual or group (Dymond 1949; Norman and Leidling 1956), one that came to be seen as starkly lacking among many non-Jewish Germans during and shortly after the Third Reich (Parkinson 2015).

Before the arrival of the word "empathy" in the English language, "sympathy" was used to describe more or less the same phenomenon of understanding how others feel. But "sympathy" has a different genealogy in the English intellectual scene, one that begins in the mid-eighteenth century with discussions among philosophers and good friends David Hume and Adam Smith. Hume used the word in the sense of the capacity to read into the minds of others and promoted the idea that sentiment formed the basis of moral action (Kelly 2012). Smith shared the idea that sympathy is the basis of a moral community and of judgment in that society (Sayre-McCord 2013). But over the last several decades, scholars and lay intellectuals in politics, psychology, and neuroscience tend to deliberately employ the word "empathy" and avoid the use of "sympathy." Sympathy is now more often associated with feelings of sorrow or pity for someone who is sad or suffering. Despite the change in nomenclature, empathy as it is used today seems to be synonymous with what Hume and Smith meant by sympathy. An emotion akin to compassion, empathy is the ethical basis for individual action, the moral virtue necessary for proper political action, and the glue that binds communities together.[3]

Over the last decade, anthropologists have critically explored the role of the positive emotions of sympathy and compassion in humanitarian politics (Fassin 2005), noting that a politics based on the triggering of good emotions often ends in a disregard for universal rights.[4] Strong evidence demonstrates how this process works in the realms of political asylum (Kelly 2012; Ticktin 2011), charity (Elisha 2008), and foreign aid (Paragi 2017). Importantly, scholars have noted that compassion assumes a position of privilege (Berlant 2004). A tool of neoliberal modes of governance (Muehlebach 2011), its roots lie in colonialism (Balkenhol 2016). Echoing Hannah Arendt, Andrea Muehlebach (2011) argues that managing politics with emotions such as sympathy and compassion "unites citizens through the particularities of suffering and dutiful response, rather than the universality of rights; through the passions ignited by inequality rather than presumptions of equality; and through emotions, rather than politics" (62). But while the political and social ramifications of sympathy and compassion have been amply explored, a corresponding discussion of the political context of empathy has been lacking.[5]

Recent psychological anthropologists who have turned to earlier discussions of empathy in the German language, especially those of Edmund Husserl, promote a more complex understanding of how empathy works (Hollan and Throop 2011; Throop 2012; Duranti 2010). Empathy's complexity lies in the fact that although humans can imagine the possibility of swapping places and can therefore infer what others might be experiencing from their different standpoints, full access to their experiences is never possible.[6] How individuals fill in the gap between the experiences of others and their understanding of these experiences is as complex as the original intersubjective connection. Husserl's concept of *Paarung*, translated as coupling and pairing, can give us insights into how this process of filling in the gap works (Throop 2008, 403–4).

For Husserl, empathizers' previous bodily experiences shape their current experiences of empathy toward others through pairing, the embodied process through which we pair our bodies with the bodies of others. To bring the process of pairing closer to our physical home in our body, Husserl then describes the experience of his own two hands touching each other. "When my left hand touches my right, I am experiencing myself in a manner that anticipates both the way in which an Other would experience me and the way in which I would experience another" (Zahavi 2003, 104). While we can anticipate how it would feel for someone else to touch our hands based on the sense of our own hands touching, we can never really know how it feels for them on their side of the pair. The embodied intersubjectivity that arises from the process of pairing is central to Husserl's understanding of intersubjective empathy. But Husserl's concept of *Paarung* as the basis of intersubjective empathy can be extended from acknowledging the limits to intersubjective empathy imposed by one's "place" in one's own body to acknowledging the limits to intersubjective empathy imposed by one's "social place" in structures such as history, politics, and economics. Conceived of in this way, social positioning becomes a place that can be "paired" with that of another.

Husserl himself had already acknowledged the role of personal history in the intersubjective state of empathy. He especially pointed out personal histories influencing future experiences: "What I have learnt in the past does not leave me untouched. It shapes my understanding and interpretation of new objects by reminding me of what I have experienced before" (in Zahavi 2014, 132). It is thus precisely the diversity of our past experiences, brought about either by chance or structurally, that influences our stance or position on any given experience. Attending to these divergent pasts can help us account for how two different individuals may come to two very different experiences of a thing, even when they engage their capacity for intersubjective empathy and "swap places." Or how they can momentarily imagine themselves as swapping places in the present with an Other in the past, as is the case for minority and majority Muslims who empathize with the Jewish victims of the Holocaust to the point where they see themselves as walking in their shoes today. Intersubjective empathic experiences are situated not only in bodies but in histories and societies as well.

What is especially valuable in Husserl's approach to empathy is that it is clearly distinct from identification. He recognizes that person A empathizing with or feeling into person B can never exactly feel like person B, because she can never fully occupy person B's place. In the volume on the Holocaust and the Naqba with Bashir (Bashir and Goldberg 2018), as well as his individual essay on empathy, ethics, and the politics of Holocaust historiography, Amos Goldberg (2016) promotes Dominic LaCapra's concept of "empathic unsettlement" as most fitting to relate to trauma victims: "This concept recognizes the fundamental inherent otherness of the traumatized subject and the traumatic event. . . . It brings [the person] to identify precisely with the traumatic dimension of his existence, thereby recognizing radical separateness, deficiency, and otherness. . . . Empathic unsettlement compels us to react empathically to 'others' while being fully aware of their otherness, and at the same time helps us to recognize the component of closure" (61). While I agree that it is especially impossible to occupy the place of a traumatized person, an Husserlian approach suggests it is impossible for any two people to completely swap places and hence fully identify.

The situated nature of intersubjective experience is easier to understand if we explain Husserl's understanding of empathy with a simple analogy of swapping shoes. To put herself in another person's shoes, the empathizer does not take off just any pair of shoes; she takes off one specific pair. They may be her favorite pair, comfortable and well worn. Or they may be too tight and painful to wear. So, it is in the process of pairing that empathy is enabled, a process that is not, in fact, abstract or universal but concrete and specific. It pairs particular shoes worn at a particular time and place under particular circumstances by individuals of a particular social standing who operate under particular cultural influences. Anyone has the capacity to imagine themselves in someone else's shoes. But the emotional reactions that shoe-swapping triggers in each person will be shaped by individual past experiences and social positioning. By approaching the immediate experience of intersubjective empathy as always already influenced by history, society, and politics, we come to understand that there can never be one empathetic prescription for any given situation, not even one that prescribes how Muslim-minority Germans should empathize with Jewish victims of the Holocaust.

The Wrong Emotion of Fear

Nazmiye is a petite and well-spoken woman in her forties who was born in Turkey but has lived in Germany since she was seven years old. I met her after I learned that she organized Holocaust education for immigrant women, Neighborhood Mothers (*Stadtteilmütter*) in Neukölln, a program where immigrant women teach effective parenting methods to other immigrant women.[7] When she started working as a trainer in 2006, there was considerable discussion about pogroms against Jews.

> Because I grew up in Germany since the age of seven, I knew about the pogroms. But women who had grown up in Turkey didn't know anything about them. Around that same time, my friend's nephew visited Austria. There, he bought a copy of Hitler's *Mein Kampf* and was talking about it. At the time, there were many attacks against foreigners in East Germany. We wanted to learn why there was such an explosion of hatred.

Action Reconciliation Service for Peace, the main Christian organization in Germany dedicated to atonement for the Holocaust, is one of Neighborhood Mothers' partners. In response to this grassroots quest for the roots of such hatred, the Christian organization organized a program for the Neukölln mothers about the Nazi period. Nazmiye told me that although they learned a lot, the training was a very disturbing experience for them: "We were all shocked. How could a society turn so fanatical? We began to ask ourselves if they could do such a thing to us as well. We spent a lot of time wondering whether we would find ourselves in the same position as the Jews." This was the same stance Juliana had noted as being so disturbing to German educators when teaching minorities about the Holocaust. Other Germans apparently found it even less tolerable and reacted harshly when Nazmiye and her friends voiced their fear.

> A month later we were at a church in Nikolassee as part of our training program. We told them about our project and then told them that we are afraid

> of becoming victims. The people at the church became really angry at us. They told us to go back to our countries if this is how we think. I was really surprised at their reaction. I could not understand why this is not a legitimate question. Germans can ask this question, too. The National Democratic Party [a neo-Nazi front] is represented in Neukölln's local parliament. They are very strong in East Germany. Why should I not be concerned about the Nazis?

During the heated conversation, Nazmiye repeated Holocaust survivor Primo Levi's statement that it happened once, so it can happen again. But this made the ladies in the church even more furious. Nazmiye and her friends were asked to leave the church. Nazmiye's face turned red when she told me this story. She was reliving the shock she experienced when she was confronted with extreme anger while expecting to be admired for her interest in the history of the country of her new citizenship.

Since finishing my research in 2019, deadly Islamophobic attacks have increased dramatically in Germany. In the first official report of anti-Muslim hate crimes in Germany (Jones 2018), the German Ministry of Internal Affairs stated that close to one thousand hate crimes were committed against Muslims and mosques in 2017, leaving thirty-three people injured. These attacks intensify feelings of fear among the Muslim minority. At the time of my interviews, I found that intense fear was more common among first-generation immigrants than among members of the second and third generations. When I asked whether they thought something like the Holocaust could ever happen again in Germany, almost all second- and third-generation Turkish and Arab Germans who grew up in Germany confidently told me that this would be impossible, even though racism is still alive in parts of German society. A more common reaction I observed in relation to Holocaust memory among second- and third-generation Muslim Germans was a sense of unfairness because discrimination toward Muslims in Germany and around the world goes unrecognized. As racialized subjects Middle Eastern/Muslim-background Germans compare themselves to Jews and demand some of the empathy they receive. This emotional reaction is one that Holocaust educators commonly dismiss as envy or "victim competition."

The Wrong Emotions of Social Comparison

I joined an interfaith youth group tour to Auschwitz called "Where was G.d at Auschwitz?" initiated by one of the western German chapters of Muslim Youth in Germany (*Muslimische Jugend in Deutschland*).[8] Muslim Youth members explained to me that this was the second such tour they had initiated. As a group striving to develop a German Muslim identity, I was told, it was essential to learn more about this part of history and come to terms with it. Sixteen-to-twenty-year-old youth members from each of Dortmund's Catholic, Protestant, and Muslim communities and two from the Jewish community were present, along with two adult representatives from each group.

The first stop on the trip was the Memorial to the Murdered Jews of Europe in Berlin. The tour guide assigned to us was half Latin American, half Israeli, and a recent immigrant to Berlin. Our group started off with a discussion of how one should feel in relation to the monument and what it stands for.[9] A member of the Protestant group with a troubled look answered with one word: "Guilty." The guide shrugged his shoulders and asked rhetorically what feeling guilty is good for. The first young man tried to defend his feelings: "My grandfather was an SS soldier. I can't help feeling guilty here. The feeling just comes to me." A member of the Muslim group, a fifteen-year-old young man of Moroccan background, joined the conversation. "To me guilt is a very negative feeling. I don't feel guilty." The guide ended the discussion by directing them to how he thinks they should feel: "It's true that guilt is a negative and pessimistic feeling. It doesn't help anything. We don't want this. Empathy is the right feeling. We need to think about how this history is part of today."

That the guide wanted the group to make what is learned from history part of how we think about today visibly excited the Muslim members of the group. A few of them surrounded the tour guide when he gave the group some free time. Alaa, a young woman of Turkish descent, told the guide, "Look, I also feel like a victim in society. I am marginalized everywhere in German society. I want to show that I'm here too, but I can't get any support. The government didn't give us any support for this trip because we're a Muslim organization. And now that I'm here, I feel more frightened. What do you recommend I do?" The guide looked at the young woman sympathetically and recommended that she move to Berlin when she's old enough, reassuring her that in Berlin she will not feel like she is always being judged.

Not satisfied by the guide's dismissive response, Alaa and other Muslim participants kept trying to explain to anyone with an empathetic ear that visiting memorial sites makes them feel fearful of being discriminated against and frustrated that their fear is not taken seriously. At an earlier public event I had heard one member of the group, Esma, give a presentation on the similarities between antisemitism and Islamophobia, with images taken from the covers of respectable German weekly magazines of Muslims around the world. She mentioned there how a German politician had argued in 2012 that employers should inform the state about their Muslim employees, especially about whether or not they prayed.

This time our conversation took place in Oświęcim, Poland, the site of Auschwitz, and Esma brought religion up again:

Once you're here, do you realize how scary such things are? When you see the yellow stars Jews were wearing . . . Or when you stand in front of the Muselmann sculpture at the camp . . . Non-Muslims in this society do not understand why we feel afraid when we come here. They get angry at us and say mean things, like we try to belittle the Holocaust and we're antisemitic. Or they roll their eyes and say we try to play the victim role to attract attention.

Esma was referring to a representative statue in the Auschwitz exhibit. The name of the statue––Muselmann––was a slang word used in the extermination camps to refer to inmates who had become resigned to their fate and apathetic to their environment as a result of starvation, exhaustion, and hopelessness.[10] There is no consensus as to why the word *Muselmann* became the term for people in this desperate condition. The Italian philosopher Giorgio Agamben (2002) argues that "the most likely explanation of the term can be found in the literal meaning of the Arabic word *Muslim*: the one who submits unconditionally to the will of God" (45). According to Yad Vashem's Shoah Research Center, inmates likened the weak state of these individuals to images of Muslims prostrating in prayer.[11] Most likely the term builds on the well-worn Orientalist cliché of Muslims as fatalistic and abdicating all responsibility for one's fate and placing oneself in the hands of God, and in that sense it is an anti-Muslim slur. In reality, while Muslim captives were brought to the camp because they were Muslims, the idea that inmates in the worst condition were likened to Muslims or that "they became

Muslims" (De Koning 2015) visibly unsettled Muslim members of the group and intensified their feelings of fear.

Later that day, Esma shared her impression that the whole emphasis on guilt was an excuse for not doing anything about discrimination and racism today. "All these Protestant and Catholic people in our group who say they feel guilty and cry their eyes out are just swimming in history and in their own emotions. Most of their emotions have nothing to do with the Holocaust!"[12] Esma was referring to the group discussion after our tour of the first camp at Auschwitz, which had been very emotional for all of us. After a while, I noticed that a good number of the Christian Germans started bringing up the interpersonal trauma in their own lives. One girl talked about a friend who had committed suicide; another could not stop crying about her parent's divorce. Group discussion quickly moved from the Holocaust to the central question of "Where was G.d in Auschwitz?" or why God did not intervene when terrible things were taking place. Protestant youth in the group expressed particular anger at God for not having been there for their friends or for them, just as God had not been there to prevent the Holocaust.

As the group discussion became increasingly emotional and personal, Muslim members repeatedly tried to steer the topic toward current affairs. As a few participants sobbed, Alaa picked up the teddy bear that participants took turns holding to show that it was her turn to talk. "Today we experienced intense emotions. We all cried. But let's now think about what we bring to today. Let's talk about what's happening in Germany and in the world. Let's make sure that our tears are not in vain." Later Alaa told me that she wanted to bring up the topic of the suffering of Palestinians. Instead, because a few members of the group seemed to be overwhelmed by emotion, the social workers decided to end the group discussion. The next day, several Protestant social workers told me that they were extremely happy that the Muslims were there. They thought that making links between the Holocaust and today's events are good, but that care was needed to make sure that no tragedy or case of discrimination was compared to the Holocaust.

Banu, a nineteen-year-old Moroccan law student at the University of Maastricht in the Netherlands—the daughter of a nanny and an engineer—was convinced that the Holocaust and Jewish suffering are taught in schools at the expense of other forms of agony. During our conversation about her Holocaust education experiences, she told me about how she had gotten into trouble once in school for comparing French colonialism in Algeria to the Holocaust. On another occasion, she was scolded for trying to give a presentation on the wall erected between Israel and the Palestinian territories. In both instances, she was reprimanded by her teachers and told that she was spreading propaganda. Putting me in mind of many other statements from Turkish and Arab Germans I have heard over the years, Banu launched into her complaint:

> I know a lot of Muslims who have studied intensely and learned about what happened to the Jews. I think the Holocaust is very important. But I also think we should pay attention to what is happening now. There is too much focus on the Holocaust and the 9/11 attacks. It is prejudicial to say that Muslims don't condemn the Holocaust or don't sympathize with the Jews. I know a lot of people who do. But Muslims feel resentful (*verbittert*) about this [Israeli-Palestinian] conflict because it is not acknowledged. You know, Jews are not the only victims in the world!

Holocaust education experts and social workers in Germany commonly call these kinds of demands for empathy "victim competition." One important aspect of these feelings is that the emphasis on Jewish victimhood makes it difficult to talk about Palestinian victimhood in relation to the Israeli state. Here, comparison and demanding empathy is only one of the complex emotions that this trip to Auschwitz triggered among members of Muslim Youth. Yet during the trip, their frustration over the discrimination they have experienced as Muslims in Germany was not taken seriously, even when Muslim-background participants presented examples of contemporary racism and hate crimes. Members of Muslim Youth themselves reflected on what is to be learned from the history of the Holocaust and compared their experiences as Muslims to that of Jews in the Holocaust. That Friday, the Muslim group members first had a communal prayer, and one of them who took upon the role of imam held a brief sermon that focused on their Islamic duty to fight racism and antisemitism.

Wrong Identification with the Socialist Memory

In July 2010, I heard from a friend of a friend that the Berlin branch of the Socialist Turkish Workers' Union was organizing a trip to the Buchenwald concentration camp. I was told that I could participate as long as I shared the cost of the hired bus. Alper, the organizer of the trip, told me that they regularly organized events and trips that focus on German history. Recent events included a visit to the Bundestag, Sachsenhausen concentration camp, and the Soviet War Memorial at Treptower Park in Berlin. To prepare for this trip, I joined union members at one of their meetings, where the group of friendly, middle-aged, Turkish-speaking workers sit down to glasses of black tea and homemade snacks. The main purpose of this meeting was to watch *Naked among Wolves*, a 1963 East German film that takes place at the Buchenwald camp. Based on a true story, the film tells of communist prisoners who took great risks to hide and save a child and how they were instrumental in organizing resistance that partially liberated the camp just as American troops were approaching. In its depiction of communists and not Jews as the main victims of the Holocaust, as well as the people's united and heroic resistance to fascism, the film reflects the East German interpretation of the Holocaust. Members also talked about Ernst Thälmann, the leader of the German Communist Party who was executed in Buchenwald in 1944 after eleven years in solitary confinement.

On the bus, different members took turns on the microphone talking about the Holocaust, Buchenwald, the communist resistance, and Ernst Thälmann. One of the members reminded us that there are people in Turkey who don't recognize the Holocaust, "the biggest crime of humanity." He named Alev Alatlı, a Turkish novelist who had praised Hitler on Turkish TV a few days earlier. At one point during the journey a member told all of us something he had recently learned. When his nephew started working for Volkswagen, he was asked if he would like to join a group that helped to maintain the buildings at Auschwitz for a month. The Volkswagen administrator told the nephew that workers who go on this trip come back as more responsible and disciplined workers. Everyone in the bus appeared to be taken aback by this story. One person said, "So capitalists do this not out of guilt, but to discipline their workers!" Another man visiting from Turkey piped in, "This is a Jewish technique!" The man who told the story, still holding the microphone in his hand, became upset. "Hey, my friend! Watch out! You should not call this a Jewish technique. Especially not during a trip to a concentration camp!" The man looked puzzled. "Hmmm, I see. What shall I say then? [Pause.] A capitalist technique?" The man at the front of the bus looked relieved and smiled approvingly. "Yes, you can say that. Volkswagen sends its workers to do upkeep at Auschwitz to make it look like it's taking responsibility for its past crimes, but they use it [instead] to discipline their workers. This is how capitalism works."

At the door to Ernst Thälmann's prison cell, the visiting workers' group left a bouquet of red carnations, raised their left fists, and repeatedly shouted "Down with fascism!" in Turkish. Before leaving, they took pictures in front of the prison cell with earnest expressions. On the way back, the mood was very serious and contemplative. When one woman asked, "How can you ever trust Germans after all they did?", the others nodded in silence. Another commented on how the location of the camp was not clearly marked and that we had almost missed the entrance. Someone stressed how there were not enough explanatory exhibit labels at the camp. Mehmet, one of the organizers, took the microphone and said somberly, "I think it's important for us to think about how we can connect this history to today. In Germany, we're often told that we should not forget National Socialism. But sometimes such emphasis serves to blame socialism. There are people out there who say National Socialism and socialism were equally bad. If you noticed in this camp there was equal space given to victims of the USSR and victims of the Nazis. How can we forget that twenty million Soviets gave their lives to end German fascism? We should be careful not to fall into this trap."

Scholars concur that as West German memory culture became hegemonic after German reunification in 1990, the divergent public Holocaust memory discourses of East and West Germany also unified. I was therefore surprised to find elements of East German memory culture alive and well among members of this Turkish-German workers' union. This group was most invested in commemorating the socialist victims of the Third Reich and protecting the memory of the socialist rescuers that defeated the Nazis. They find mainstream memory culture in Germany inadequate in depicting the struggle between fascism and socialism because it reduces people to their national identities and ignores their class background and ideological commitments. It is true that some members of the group, especially those who arrived more recently from Turkey, one of the few countries where there is no Holocaust education in the school curriculum, were not sensitive enough to how eradicating Jewish existence was central to the Nazi regime. Yet, their approach recognizes the economic and political dimensions of National Socialism and emphasizes how socialist internationalism had been key to defeating it. In this framework, members of the Turkish-German workers' union do not carry any sense of the distance other Middle Eastern/Muslim-background Germans feel in relation to the history of National Socialism. This group of immigrant workers define their existence, as internationalist socialists, through the history of struggle against Nazism and any other type of fascism in the past and present. For them, the way to overcome fascism is through internationalist political consciousness, not identity-based intersubjective empathy.

Good Emotional Intensity

While many of the emotional engagements with the public Holocaust memory discourse displayed by immigrant-background Germans rubbed ethnic German Holocaust educators the wrong way, some did appreciate the intensity of those emotions. Over the years, I have heard Holocaust educators working with Middle Eastern/Muslim-background Germans comment on the unexpectedly strong emotions they encountered, with some responses triggering signs of trauma. Erhard, a white male Christian-background educator, recounted about such reactions occurring during their trip to Regensburg concentration camp, where they had stayed at a youth hostel located in houses used originally by the SS and later by Russian troops.

> The houses were originally used by the SS soldiers who ran the concentration camp. If you pay attention, even after lots of renovation, you can still see the camp insignia. The woman we went together with were shocked that we were going to be sleeping in what used to be part of the camp. I have taken many groups to these camps, and not a single [ethnic] German group reacted to staying in these houses, whereas the immigrant women had a very difficult time sleeping in the building.

The next day of the tour, they learned that the SS had used human ashes from the crematorium to pave the roads of the camp.

> The last time this happened was in 1943. The roads have been paved many more times [since then], so we were not walking on [the road] the SS had paved. But of course, we knew that the entire camp is a mass graveyard. There were many rushed burials for people who died of a disease, and they could have been buried anywhere. This information, and especially the fact that the roads had been paved with the ashes of the victims, was too much for the immigrant women. It was so strong that they refused to walk on the paved road and walked instead on the side of it.

At the end of the tour, Erhard said, they decided to stop taking immigrant-background women to visit concentration camps. They talked over the events with their colleagues and decided that learning was not possible when such strong emotions were involved. He said that he personally considered this level of traumatization to be an impediment to learning, calling to mind instances right after the war when American troops forced Germans to come face-to-face with their crimes. Once again, how Germans learned about the Holocaust immediately following the war is somehow seen as relevant to the question of how best to teach immigrant-background Germans some seventy-five years later.

> We have descriptions of how Germans were forced to confront the horrors the Nazis had committed after the war. One theory is that at the time, Germans could not come to terms with their crimes because it was too big [a crime] to confront. And I think that's what I have in mind. If people are in deep shock, how can they learn?

At that point, Erhard paused, leaving his judgment on this issue open ended. He, too, had been traumatized by what he had learned, he said, but he also wondered if being deeply unsettled would be better than simply remaining ignorant. In this conversation, it was clear that the way Germans learned about the Holocaust immediately following the war was a significant referent for ethnic German educators when approaching the education of immigrant-background Germans on the Holocaust today. But Erhard's uncertainty about what exactly had helped Germans confront their past crimes and what it was that had hindered them left him undecided about the best approach to teaching immigrants.

Overall, Erhard said, his impression of Middle Eastern people's reactions to the history of the Holocaust is very positive. But rather than relating their reactions to traumas they may have had in a recent past or their marginalization in German society, he provided a cultural explanation for it. "To me, it's similar to what we Germans think about Mediterranean people. They always have stronger emotions. They dance better, they sing better. And in relating to the Holocaust, again, they show their emotions better."

Other German Holocaust educators appreciated it when recent immigrants and refugees related their experiences with war to the Holocaust. One Holocaust educator at the Memorial to the Murdered Jews of Europe in Berlin recalled several Lebanese women from Beirut being deeply moved as they walked through the memorial and began crying while looking at the exhibition about the victims downstairs. One of them talked about how the memorial reminded her of Beirut during the civil war when they had to hide under the buildings and were fearful of going to the toilet at night. This woman had lost her mother when she walked out of the hiding place to gather water one night and never came back. The educator told me that the ethnic Germans don't engage with the memorial in this way. "Maybe," she said, "[the fact that] the immigrants were not fed the history of the Holocaust through their mother's milk means that it's new to them. They can really engage with it freely, much more than we are able to."

Immigrant-background and refugee responses to the Holocaust are appreciated when they connect the history to their own experiences of war and suffering elsewhere—unless, that is, their experiences of war took place in Israel/Palestine. What is not appreciated are responses to the Holocaust that speak from their marginalized standpoint as minorities in Germany today.

Modeling the Right Emotional Identification

Emotional engagements by immigrants with the Holocaust are deemed misguided when they do not correspond to the German model of the repentant perpetrator, the time-honored and officially approved way of approaching the darkest moment in German history. Ubiquitous across German social rituals from political speeches to Holocaust memorials, this model of the repentant German perpetrator is so prevalent that Holocaust education programs for Muslims often feature white Germans with Nazi perpetrators in their families performing pedagogical scenes that model the emotions ethnic Germans as collective perpetrators are expected to have toward the Holocaust.

I observed just such a modeling of emotions at a Holocaust education program designed for Muslim-background youth. The scene was part of a three-month-long training that prepared ten Turkish-, Kurdish-, and Arab-background youth to visit Auschwitz. The program was within the framework of Muslims in Auschwitz (discussed in chapters 4 and 5) and recruited youth from the youth club in Duisburg (mentioned in chapter 1). Fatih and Mehmet whom I introduced in the first chapter, were among the participants. Mehmet was also helping me—sometimes I could not keep up when many of the participants spoke at once. The training I discuss here took place during an intensive weekend retreat (two days and two nights) where the youth talked about antisemitism, the history of National Socialism, and what being German with a migration background means to them, all part of the preparation for visiting Auschwitz.

On the second afternoon of the weekend, we were sitting in a half-circle in the training room—the youth, the two trainers, and me; all of us nonwhite and from Muslim backgrounds. We knew that Sandra, the social worker in charge of the youth club where the program was hosted, and Rickie, an educationist at a local museum, had prepared something for us to watch, but we didn't know what to expect. Then the mood changed.

Sandra walked "on stage" in front of us and explained that both she and Rickie are the grandchildren of Nazis and that today they would dramatize the belief systems of their grandparents for us. She then placed on the wall a photograph from 1968 of herself as a little girl posing with her grandmother. "I will take on the role of my grandmother, Marie. Marie was born in 1921." She placed a black-and-white photo of a little girl on the board and said, "This photo of Marie is from 1929." Next to this, she placed another photo of Marie from 1942, when she was twenty-one. Sandra stepped away from the photos and took on the role of her grandmother. Her voice and her expression gave us strong cues that this was something serious and important for her. Even though it had been a long weekend with educational activities scheduled back-to-back, the audience of mostly teenagers sat silent and attentive.

"Marie" told us about the difficulties and challenges she had growing up as the daughter of a working-class family in Dortmund. "Things changed in 1933 when I was twelve," she told us cheerfully. "Hitler came to power, and everything was in order." Marie shared with us that her once Social Democrat father also joined Hitler's party, and that it had been good for the family. She worked at the

German Labor Front, the National Socialist state labor organization established by Hitler, which had replaced the banned independent trade unions. At that point Marie showed us her authentic identity booklet. Now they could go for vacations even when they did not have any money. When she was nineteen, Marie fell in love and married a young man who was a member of the National Socialist Motor Corps, a paramilitary organization affiliated with the Nazi Party. "I was so proud of him. He worked directly for the *Führer*. Look, here is a picture of him in his uniform. Isn't he handsome?"

At that point, Rickie walked "on stage" dressed in a nice white shirt and pressed trousers, barking orders at the audience in a loud voice to move out of the way. He introduced himself as Anton, an employee of the Reich Ministry of Public Enlightenment and Propaganda. In a booming voice, Anton said, "Today I am here to tell you what *Volksgemeinschaft* (national community) means. I will let you know who belongs to it and who does not. For example, German families belong to it, but asocial elements (*Asozialen*)[13] do not." In conversation with Maria, Anton explained to us that they were taking measures to ensure that everyone was healthy and would produce healthy babies. He explained how in Marxloh they had opened a clinic in the fight against "hereditary diseases so that drunks, the disabled, and criminals would not pass on their traits to future generations." He talked about other elements in society that needed to be controlled: intellectuals, communists, homosexuals, Jews. "Germans who have sex with other races are an embarrassment to our race. Social Democrats are traitors. Gypsies also do not belong to our nation. The ones who do not belong should get out! Jews, Gypsies, traitors, communists, asocial elements, drug users, all out!"

As they took their bows, Sandra and Rickie received a big round of applause from us. We were all moved by their performances. Sandra had projected the happiness and optimistic mindset of a young German woman who fit nicely into the nationalist narrative, while Rickie embodied the unquestioning passion and zeal of a dedicated propaganda worker. Both Sandra and Rickie looked emotionally exhausted. The youth had lots of questions. Everyone in the audience took turns complimenting them on the believability of their performances and how convincingly they presented the ideology. Kurdish-background Amed spoke up. "I was transported completely by your act. You really looked like you believed what you were saying. It made me wonder whether I would do as you did and believe in this ideology, too, had I lived in those times." Sandra answered Amed sympathetically. "This really is *my* biography, this is *my* grandmother. She was born in 1921 and was twelve years old in 1933. You could say that she was born into this ideology. I wouldn't say that she was a zealous Nazi, but she did believe in what she was told. Later in life, she would not admit that she had been a Nazi, but she continued to say that Hitler had brought order to chaos."

After a fifteen-minute discussion about the most convincing parts of the Nazi ideology for ordinary Germans and how difficult it would be to argue against them, the youth asked Sandra and Rickie what it was like to have acted out these roles. "It was very, very heavy for me," Sandra replied. "I really struggled. I ran through two rehearsals for it. But I think it's easy to influence people. The words I had my *Oma* (grandmother) say were very simple." She then added that there were some details she had not included. Her Oma's first lover had been a Jewish man. Her grandmother's parents had originally been Social Democrats. Her grandmother's father had to go into hiding for saying in public that Hitler should be killed. But her grandmother's mother had eventually decided to become a member of the Nazi Party. As it turns out, Sandra's dramatization of her family story for this audience had been carefully crafted so as to exclude any elements other than a straightforward and full-hearted commitment to Nazi ideology. She had depicted herself as the granddaughter of two committed Nazis, whereas the actual picture was much more nuanced.

Rickie confirmed Sandra's experience, telling us that playing a Nazi had been draining for him, too, and he had been especially worried that he might be too convincing. "If I had continued, I think it would have become like the experiment in *The Wave* (*Die Welle*). You would have started worshiping me." Rickie's reference to the popular 2008 German film and the German translation of the American young adult novel *The Wave* (Rhue 1981) explains the source of some of his ideas about the viral nature of the Nazi ideology. The novel and film both dramatize the five-day social experiment in fascism conducted in 1969 by Ron Jones, a California high school history teacher who sought to reproduce for his history class students how Germans could have come to accept Nazism. In the real-life experiment, the high school students accepted the movement's disciplinary and insider-only precepts with little hesitation, a trope driven home in the young adult novel, the German film, and the ninth- and tenth-grade high school lesson plan materials prepared for all sixteen German federal state school systems. Indeed, Rickie was fully convinced of the persuasive powers of the few sentences he had uttered based on Nazi logic, a conviction that echoed Sandra's belief that it was surprisingly easy to influence people. I wondered if Rickie and Sandra worried that their words might make an especially deep impression on a group of Muslim-background youth assumed not to have undergone the proper German stages of confronting the Nazi past and consequently not fully immunized against Nazi ideology.

The Holocaust education program had in fact been designed to help these youth trace the same steps Germans had taken. Taking on the role of dramatizing for the youth their forebears' Nazi past, Rickie and Sandra were genuinely worried that their target group might actually be convinced by Nazism after exposure to a fifteen-minute role-play. Underpinning the entire Muslims in Auschwitz program, such assumptions imagine Muslim-background Germans as being outsiders to the postwar anti-Nazi German ethos and overlook that, just like Rickie and Sandra, every one of these young people have been socialized into postwar German ideology. Moreover, they knew that Nazis would not be speaking to people like them, but rather excluding them from the *Volksgemenischaft*. Their reactions amply demonstrated their familiarity with and highly critical stance toward Nazi ideology.

To test the persuasive powers of the Nazi ideology on the youth group, Sandra asked us how we had felt when Rickie entered the room and started immediately issuing orders. Amed said that he would have obeyed out of respect, but for Rickie, not a Nazi propagandist. Another participant who was also an amateur actor asked Rickie whether he had given these orders to see if we would be convinced by them. Rickie looked troubled. "I don't know. I felt like doing it when I entered the room. I hadn't planned on it." He seemed unable to sort out why he had done it and whether it had been a good idea. Looking at Rickie's face, I thought perhaps the danger troubling him was not that he might convince the youth of the virtues of National Socialism, but that he felt he had gotten too carried away in his role as a party member. One of the immigrant-background group leaders said that he had indeed gone too far in barking out such orders, even if it was role-playing, especially when the audience doesn't know what they are about to witness. If he did this role-play again, he told Rickie, he should tone it down. Looking a bit embarrassed, Rickie agreed.

The rationale for including this role-play in the weekend training was to encourage group discussion about how the ideology of National Socialism could have taken hold. But with only two German-background individuals in the room playing the roles of the gullible German citizen turned Nazi, sandwiched between candid but carefully selected talk about their grandparents' Nazi pasts, the performance suggests that they were also displaying something else: how modern-day Germans have learned to despise National Socialism even though the ideology itself was so cunningly attractive to their grandparents. Sandra and Rickie were posing as role models for the right way to handle Nazism: accept your own family's responsibility in the regime unapologetically and by doing so repent for it.

As we were applauding the role-players, I couldn't help wondering what the lesson for the youth in the room had been; they had no family connection to National Socialism, as their parents or grandparents had not arrived in Germany until after the Nazis had been defeated. What could they take home from this stirring performance? An admiration for Sandra and Rickie's ability to denounce the Nazism their own grandparents had taken part in it? Or was there something I was missing?

Benefiting from a moment of silence following the applause, I asked the whole group: Do Sandra and Rickie have more responsibility than you do to remember National Socialism and the Holocaust, simply because their grandparents were Nazis? As soon as I asked this question, all hands in the room went up, and a long discussion ensued. No one in the group felt like Sandra or Rickie had a deeper responsibility or bore more guilt for the crimes of National Socialism. But they also confessed that it was difficult to put themselves in Sandra's or Rickie's shoes and to understand what it means exactly to be the grandchild of perpetrators. It was clear that the role-play led them to reflect more on Sandra and Rickie's positionality to their own ancestors than on the Nazi ideology itself.

Fuat: I don't think so. We're in the year 2017. We all want to change this society. Our grandparents are not innocent either. God knows what they did in Ottoman times. No one can say my past is cleaner than Sandra's.

Amed: It is difficult for me to put myself in Sandra's place. But I think there's a big struggle inside her. And whether she has more responsibility or not, this is something only she can decide. Maybe the difference between me and her is the sensibility, an entry point into these feelings of inner struggle. I can see that. I can never know exactly how Sandra feels. My grandparents came from Turkey. They were oppressed there as Kurds. So, I can't relate to Sandra's experience here.

Erol: Sandra is the granddaughter of a perpetrator. What she does here is a confirmation. By enacting this role-play here, she's separating herself from her Nazi forefathers. That's an act of resistance. She's putting distance between herself and her past, and she actively says, "I am not a Nazi, despite my family."

Baran: We all belong to the same race. We can all learn not to repeat the same mistakes, no matter who did it. What the Nazis did is not Sandra's responsibility. And I am not responsible for what happens in Turkey. Most of us here didn't show much interest in this topic until now. But we can all learn from it.

Fuat turned to Sandra and asked her what she thought about what they were saying. After a long pause, Sandra shared that she felt a tension between teaching Holocaust memory to those without a German background, as she was doing that weekend at Heroes, and advocating responsibility for the Holocaust by claiming it as her own because of her own family background.

Sandra: On the one hand, you're right that we're all responsible for shouldering the burden of the past. On the other hand, I personally feel very sensitive about this issue. In my youth, my friends and I hated hearing our parents complain about how Germany was bombed by the Allies. And still today I go crazy when I sense that Germans are being nationalist or saying or doing something racist.

Amed: Your sixth sense toward racism is very strong. You sense it immediately.

Sandra, smiling gratefully at Amed, replied: "It's because of my family. It took them a long time to accept that Nazism was wrong."

Sandra's political consciousness led her to become a social worker and to focus on creating a better, more tolerant, more inclusive, more gender-equal German society. It also led her to teach immigrants how to embrace the values she had learned by negating those of her grandparents. Her job is to teach young Muslim men and women how to make their own decisions even when they conflict with the values of their parents, how to claim ownership of their own bodies, and how to not only tolerate but actively support racial and gender equality. One important way in which she preached this doctrine to youth was by setting herself up as a role model: Her close relationships with and her unfaltering support of these immigrant youth was in itself her way of rebelling against a nationalism that has never fully disappeared and is now increasingly on the rise in Germany.

One of the expectations of Muslim youth in the Holocaust education programs, in addition to empathizing with Jews as the Holocaust's primary victims, is to first acknowledge and then empathize/sympathize with Germans for the hard work they have done on the long and difficult road they have traveled since their World War II defeat.

Socially Situated Empathy

Edmund Husserl contends that establishing an intersubjective connection based on our own bodily experience is the starting point for gaining perspective on what other persons might be experiencing in their own bodies. According to Husserl, we grasp the other's body as something similar to our own (Luo 2017, 45). The unanticipated and unprescribed emotional connections some minority Germans who have experienced discrimination establish with Jewish Holocaust victims demonstrate that our own socially situated experiences shape our understandings of others' experiences. When we encounter a racialized, classed, or gendered Other, especially one who experiences discrimination, we have insight into how they might feel simply by force of the fact that we each have standing in a society that ranks people in terms of such categories. This empathic ability to stand in the shoes of another is why, when confronted with reminders of the Holocaust, some Turkish- and Arab-background Germans fear they, too, might become victims should something similar happen again. Other minority Germans establish a likeness between their own current racialization and that experienced by Jews and demand that a small part of empathy given to Jews be given to Muslims.

The unexpected feelings expressed by Muslim-background Germans throughout my fieldwork run counter to the expectations of Holocaust education programs aimed at triggering feelings of remorse and responsibility. Muslims expressing feelings outside of that narrow framework were judged to be morally lacking, even at times lacking the capacity to be good citizens. Yet, a Husserlian understanding of empathy demonstrates that the emotions triggered by standing in someone else's shoes begin and end in the shoes one already has on. Beginning and ending their journey in very different shoes, an ethnic majority German and a racialized minority German will feel quite differently when putting themselves in the shoes of the victims. Of one thing there can be no doubt: whenever they do swap shoes, these minoritized immigrant-background Germans experience strong empathic connections with the Jewish victims of the Holocaust.

CHAPTER 4

Subcontracting Guilt, Policing Victimhood

I am sitting in the front row at an educational theater production in a majority-immigrant school just outside Duisburg. All eight actors are young men from Turkish and Arab backgrounds between the ages of sixteen and twenty. Most of them are involved with the Heroes program and take part in an extracurricular project with the attention-grabbing title, Muslims in Auschwitz. The rather sparse audience consists of local German politicians, German social scientists working on integration, and students from the school. This is the eighth time the piece has been performed, and I was told that the previous shows had larger audiences, with journalists, mayors, and pop stars in attendance. While the performance is not professionally polished, the actors are clearly giving it their all.

In one of the early scenes, set during World War II in the British Mandate for Palestine,[1] a Palestinian father teaches his son to hate Jews and gives him a gun. The father is wearing a long black leather jacket, which the actor will keep on for his role as a German Nazi in a later scene. A different German Nazi soon enters the stage. We learn that this German Nazi is also a convert to Islam.

German Muslim convert Nazi (*GMN*): I've heard a lot about you. I'm your friend.

Palestinian father (*PF*): What do you have to offer me?

GMN: Friendship, food, and oil. Is that enough?

PF: What shall we do in return?

GMN: Fight with us against our enemies: the British, the communists, and, most importantly, the Jews. I offer you a liberated Arabia.

PF: A liberated Arabia.

They shake hands.

GMN: First we find every single Jew and destroy their houses and synagogues.

PF: Where do we start?

GMN: Anywhere we find them. This will be our secret. We will eradicate every single Jew.

Why would a youth club that aims to improve the well-being and democratic development of lower-class immigrant-background young men stage a theater project that conflates German Nazis and Palestinian Arabs, merging them into the fantastical characters of German Muslim convert Nazis and Palestinian Nazis-in-the-making? More precisely, why would such a program turn Palestinian Arabs into the perpetrators of both the Jewish Holocaust and the Israeli-Palestinian conflict, an intercommunal conflict between British Mandatory Palestine Arabs and Jews after World War I that intensified after World War II, leading to Jewish independence in the new state of Israel and the mass exodus and continued statelessness of Palestinians? What do such characters and stories tell us about the grammar of being accepted into German society as respectable political actors and the state of Holocaust memory in a multicultural Germany?

Muslims in Auschwitz: A Problem of Memory or of Culture?

The idea for Muslims in Auschwitz arose after a pro-Palestinian Al-Quds Day[2] demonstration in Duisburg in 2011 during which a small group of demonstrators vandalized the youth club Zitrone and wrote anti-Jewish and anti-Israeli slogans on the walls. This occurred during a time in which significant government funds were being allocated for Holocaust education and antisemitism prevention programs directed at Muslims. Social workers quickly agreed that they should organize something to counter the vandalism. For the young white Christian-background social worker working at Zitrone at the time, the key goal was to wipe out all traces of antisemitism in the country that had perpetrated the Holocaust. For the Turkish/Kurdish-background educator, Burak, working at Zitrone at the time, the central focus of action was to fight the "honor culture" in which Muslim fathers pass their hatred and violence on to their sons. In other words, for the former, a problem of "memory"; for the latter, a problem of "culture." Despite these differences, the two Duisburg-native social workers shared a clear vision of what needed to be repaired: young Muslim men and their attitudes toward Jews.

When I met him at the Starbucks in the main Duisburg train station, whiffs of *döner kebab* and French fries from adjacent shops mingling with the acrid-sweet aroma of coffee, Mathe had already moved on to another job but still felt passionate about Muslims in Auschwitz. He told me that he had wanted for a long time to do something with immigrant youth about antisemitism. He was especially sensitive to this issue. He had performed his civil service residence at Auschwitz and had written his undergraduate thesis on Holocaust memory in Germany, Poland, and Israel. He proposed a trip to Auschwitz in the wake of the Al-Quds Day protests. He explained to the other social workers that his experience there had changed his life, and that he imagined a visit to Auschwitz might have a similar effect on the Muslim youth. The other social workers liked the idea and decided to name their project Muslims in Auschwitz.

Later in the conversation, Mathe told me that because his grandfather had been a Nazi, one of his missions in life was to rebuild what his grandfather had destroyed. Having the opportunity to fight against blatant expressions of antisemitism, as when immigrant-background youth called each other "you Jew," seemed like a golden opportunity, Mathe explained.

> It's my duty to fight against antisemitism. . . . When we're sitting here in a Starbucks, no one will openly say anything against Jews. For [white] Germans, antisemitism is well-hidden, more behind the scenes. Among [white] Germans you won't come upon many situations where you can interfere and say, "Hey, stop this!" With Muslims, though, it's common to encounter people discriminating against Jews. That was my motivation. . . . To take on this fight myself. To fix something that my grandfather had destroyed.

After a brief pause, Mathe shifted the story to his change of job. He was proud of what they had accomplished but eventually quit when he realized that it was too stressful for him.

> But then I realized that this kind of motivation was not really good for the work. It was too much for me. Whenever there were glitches in the project, I would be devastated. When they came back from Auschwitz and were still using antisemitic expressions, it was a big personal failure for me.

When I talked to Burak, co-founder of the Muslims in Auschwitz project, about what he thought went wrong with Mathe, he told me that Mathe was like their German teachers: they always expect a specific set of emotions—sadness, for example—and a certain way of being touched by history. Mathe had been very disappointed when the youth did not react in line with his expectations. When the youth became tired on their tour through Auschwitz, for instance, and crouched against a wall, Mathe interpreted this as disrespect, scolding them for forgetting where they were and making them stand up. Burak said that this approach simply didn't work for the Muslim youth. As Mathe became increasingly nervous and weighed down by the responsibility of correcting what his grandfather had done wrong, Burak told me, the youth started to withdraw from him. Burak thought that instead of focusing intently on their outward behavior, it was important to allow the youth to relax occasionally rather than continually keeping them on edge.

What Burak shared with Mathe was the perspective that Muslims in Auschwitz had something to do with grandparents. But unlike Mathe, for Burak it was an opportunity to change what is passed on not from German but from Turkish and Arab grandparents. For him, the project was closely connected to the fight they were already waging in Heroes against patriarchal "honor cultures." Burak had started working for the youth club when they had become an affiliate of Heroes. He and Mathe had launched Muslims in Auschwitz shortly thereafter. The target group for both projects was the same group of Turkish-, Kurdish-, and Arab-descent young men who are believed to come from patriarchal families or "honor cultures." Essentially, if Mathe was grappling with Nazi grandfathers, Burak was contending with patriarchal grandfathers who teach their children to defend the family's honor at all costs, even that of individual freedom, especially women's freedom. The Muslims in Auschwitz project showcased in a particularly poignant way how these two seemingly disparate sets of interests intersect.

In a blog entry on his personal website, Burak begins his discussion of the Muslims in Auschwitz project with the theater piece scene seen earlier in which a Palestinian father teaches his son how to hate Jews. For Burak, the biggest problem to be tackled to overcome antisemitism and violence in this community is the patriarchal family culture:

> The scene depicted above is part of our stage play *Coexist*, and it illustrates a basic educational pattern that can also be found in patriarchal families in parts of the Muslim community to varying degrees. The child receives the promise of power and land connected to a collective commitment against a common enemy. Hatred is necessary in order to preserve one's identity. The father isolates his son from what he perceives as alien and as the ultimate evil. He creates a bogeyman in order to unleash his son's aggression and subtly imposes a fatal way of thinking on him: "If you love me, you will follow my message of hatred!" (Yılmaz 2018)

Although in the project itself they talk often about racism and discrimination toward Muslims, the primary project idea behind Muslims in Auschwitz is how the many and varied form of discrimination toward Jews—everyday slurs, violence toward Jews, vandalism of Jewish symbols, antisemitic propaganda used by Hamas—can potentially turn into something like fascism and eventually lead to something like the Holocaust. Rather than connecting the dots between racism and fascism, the project connects the dots between antisemitism and genocide. During my conversations with Burak, I often noted my difficulty in understanding why the project downplayed the ongoing discrimination against Muslims in contemporary Germany. Burak would then patiently explain to me that one of the central points of the project was to move Muslims out of the victim role and have them confront their perpetrator position. He repeatedly told me that Muslims in Germany have the potential to turn into key perpetrators in relation to Jews, precisely *because* they see themselves as victims. In our private conversations and in public forums he repeated the refrain, "We want to free ourselves of the victim role."

Victims and Perpetrators

In a 2016 documentary film about Muslims in Auschwitz made for the national public television channel ZDF, Burak explained the problem that they aim to fix: "Young people's interest in [the Holocaust] comes from the Israeli-Palestinian conflict. They see Israel and Jews as perpetrators and Palestinians as victims" (Wolf-Graaf and Presnick 2015). In his lone blog entry, he elaborates on the other side of the same coin in Muslim populations: "Jews are not perceived as victims during and before the Holocaust, but as perpetrators and occupiers in the Middle East conflict" (Yılmaz 2018). If one wants to change this perception, writes Burak, informing Arab- and Turkish-background youth about the Holocaust and giving them a different narrative about the Israeli-Palestinian conflict will not necessarily help because the root of the problem lies in deep-seated cultural features and patriarchal family structures: "Viewing 'the Jew' and Israel as the bogeymen is a distinct feature of these Muslim families with patriarchal family structures." What needs to be tackled, he says, is the narrative passed from generation to generation: "We the Arabs are the victims, they the Jews are the perpetrators." According to Burak, the problem is not limited to Arabs. Turks are just as culturally ill equipped to see themselves as perpetrators. In Turkish nationalism, "Atatürk's War of Independence, the conquest of Constantinople, and the wars of independence in North Africa are highlighted. Heroic memories [fail to] expose their own people as perpetrators of any kind. Neither the Ottoman system of slavery nor the Armenian Genocide are mentioned because they are subjects for which there is either collective silence or laws interdicting public discussion." In aiming to transform Arab- and Turkish-background youths' moral position and identity from that of victims to past and present perpetrators, Muslims in Auschwitz offers them a chance to repent, and by repenting become legible within the grammar of the German political narrative.

By connecting Holocaust history and the Israeli-Palestinian conflict in innovative ways, Muslims in Auschwitz and dozens of other Holocaust education and antisemitism prevention projects designed for Muslims seek to guide Muslim-minority Germans beyond seeing themselves as victims of racism in Germany and the Israeli occupation in Palestinian territory. These connections are laid down in a fivefold manner. First, the programs, operating on the assumption that Muslim minorities do not perceive Jews as having been victims in the Holocaust, are designed to reverse that perception among the youth. Second, they teach the youth that Arabs, defined as a generic collective, collaborated with the Nazis and were on the side of the perpetrators. Third, they conflate contemporary anti-Zionism with Nazi antisemitism. Fourth, they provide as positive role models the handful of "righteous" Arabs and Turks who used their positions of power to help Jews. Fifth, they move quickly and seamlessly from treatment of the Holocaust to a history of the establishment of Israel and the roots of the Israeli-Palestinian conflict, emphasizing the view that Palestinians are not victims but are rather equal partners in a two-sided conflict where Jews have also been victimized.

Burak defines the ultimate aim of the Muslims in Auschwitz project: to persuade Muslims to empathize with Jews and their victimhood, with empathy as both the goal and the solution to their problems. He explained to me and in his blog that the visit to Auschwitz works as a "brain crash" in the following way: "Each time the word Jew or Israel occurs, a box blinks in their minds that is filled with strong feelings of hatred and aversion. There is no other box related to this topic. In the concentration camp, a second box appears out of the blue, although there is no space for additional emotion. The second box is filled with unsettling emotions such as empathy and compassion. All of a sudden, the youngsters develop empathy for their enemy" (Yılmaz 2016).

I spoke with participants at length to try to determine if and how they have been transformed by Muslims in Auschwitz. For twenty-eight-year-old Turkish-descent Mehmet, whom we met at chapter 1 and used to be closely identified with the Palestinian cause, taking part in Muslims in Auschwitz four years prior had been a very intense experience, one he credited with having changed him profoundly. He recounted his emotional transformation with a great deal of passion and insight when I first met him at a Duisburg café.

> This project gave me the chance to see Jews as victims for the first time in my life. I used to believe that Jews oppress us, that we are their victims. It's thanks to this project that I came to empathize with Jews as they were being victimized. For the first time in my life, I could see them as victims and not as perpetrators. I cried for Jews for the first time in my life. Before I could cry only for the Muslim community. This was a golden opportunity for me. I learned how to establish empathy at such a high level: I empathized with my enemy.

Building on their work teaching participants to see Jews as victims, the programs usually encourage youth to move beyond their perception of Israel as a perpetrator country. As I discussed in chapter 2, all Holocaust education programs designed for immigrant-background Muslim youth in Germany include a major section on the Israeli-Palestinian conflict in which they make the connection between the Holocaust and the establishment of Israel. Most often, the main take-home point is that the conflict is complex and the position of Palestinians as victims is not as clear-cut as they might think. The kind of empathy Mehmet, and earlier Burak, brought up—"love your enemy"—is already different from the kind of empathy white Germans are encouraged to have in relation to Jews, who had little chance to engage in resistance during the Holocaust. The "Jews" that Mehmet is learning to love and empathize with are not only the Holocaust victims but also the Israeli Jews who are in active conflict with Palestinians. It is possible that these two groups of Jews have become fused in this project, with Mehmet's empathy for the Holocaust victims allowing him to accept the Israeli Jews who he sees, or used to see, as his enemy.

In a private video recording of the second trip of the Muslims in Auschwitz in 2012, Ahmad Mansour, who aided the project by leading the discussion on the Middle East, saw his role as showing the youth the nationalist Israeli perspective in relation to the Israeli-Palestinian conflict: "The Israel issue is not a black-and-white conflict. The youth are unaware that there was once a possibility to establish a Palestinian state, that Israel offered to divide it. Nor do they know that there were one million Jews who became refugees because of the establishment of Israel."[3] He added, "The youth gained a new perspective, a differentiated, complicated approach to the whole issue. Now they see that Jews are also victims." To be liberated from their patriarchal culture, violent tendencies, and antisemitism, Arab- and Turkish-background youth must, it seems, learn that they are not victims, but perpetrators.

The most powerful strategy used by these programs for distancing Muslims from their alleged "self-victimization" syndrome is to teach them about the controversial figure of the Grand Mufti of Jerusalem, Muhammad Amin al-Husseini, as in the Muslim-only antisemitism prevention programs I discussed in chapter 2. On his blog, Burak describes how teaching Palestinians about the mufti works in the Muslims in Auschwitz project: "Jamal is a proud Palestinian and gets excited when he learns that a Palestinian imam, Amin al-Husseini, worked for and was on the payroll of the Nazis. There is even a video recording of the imam greeting Hitler with the Nazi salute" (Yılmaz 2018). When I asked Burak why he emphasizes al-Husseini during the program, he told me that this allows the youth to learn that the Holocaust is also their history. More importantly, they learn that their ancestors were also perpetrators, not powerless victims.

Participants in the Muslims in Auschwitz project learn that Turks also had close relations with the Nazis. On his blog, Burak explains the connection:

> It is important to note that before seizing power, the Nazis saw Kemal Atatürk as a model [leader] who had the nationalist awareness to liberate the nation and dispense with "parasites." At the end of the 1920s and in the early 1930s, German newspapers called for a "German Atatürk," and Hitler used the phrase "student of Atatürk" many times to describe himself. (Yılmaz 2018)[4]

Adnan, a soft-spoken twenty-three-year-old Palestinian medical technology student, was one of the first participants in the Muslims in Auschwitz project, and project leaders told me he underwent the greatest transformation. I asked him about how he had felt upon learning about the Mufti of Jerusalem for the first time.

> I heard about the mufti for the first time in school. It stayed with me. We learned about him again in the project. When we visited Auschwitz, I felt that it was not only the Germans but also the Arabs who were responsible for Jewish suffering. I told myself, "If I try to run away from my connection to Germany, which I can do in my community, where could I run to? We [the Arabs] also share the burden of responsibility somehow. So there really is no escape."

Adnan recounted this story while we were sitting together in the Duisburg train station Starbucks café with an Egyptian-background German female researcher who had traveled to Duisburg with me. When he had finished, I noticed that my researcher friend's eyes were wide open as if in disbelief. After a few moments of staring at his coffee mug under her incredulous gaze, Adnan took his scarf from around his neck and said, "But I have to honestly tell you that I don't really feel this responsibility to be equal on both sides, the Germans and the Arabs. And even if I try, it's not really possible for me to do so."

Despite this, Adnan told us, the greatest gift from his participation in Muslims in Auschwitz was being liberated from feelings of rage and hate. With a contented smile, he said, "Now I don't have to walk around with this heavy feeling of victimhood on my shoulders anymore. I don't obsessively follow and analyze what is happening in Palestine and how Jews are treating my people." Adnan told us that he was proud of himself for having been able to establish a friendship with a few Israelis through an exchange program, something his parents would not be happy about. He told us this transformation allowed him to concentrate on his life in Germany and generally feel happier from day to day. Adnan also said that he had told his parents that he was no longer interested in the documentation they had brought with them from Palestine testifying to the property they owned and its appropriation by the state of Israel. Adnan told them that he is free now: he's in Germany and doesn't care about it. Unlike Mehmet, he did not tell me that he loves his enemy, but he said he feels lighter by disconnecting himself from the conflict and his family's material and emotional loss in Palestine.

The amalgamated characters of the Nazi and the Arab collaborator—here Hitler and the Palestinian Mufti of Jerusalem—are used with the aim of moving Adnan away from his sense of victimhood and toward an affiliation with perpetratorship, one that is placed alongside the history of German perpetrators of the Holocaust. Adnan first learns about and then internalizes a feeling of guilt and a sense that he and/or his forebears share responsibility in the Holocaust. Adnan also recognizes, however, that learning about Palestinian collaboration in the Holocaust does not bring him any closer to German identity. He acknowledges that the Muslims in Auschwitz education program was extremely challenging for him. I was told of dramatic scenes from Adnan's group's visit to Auschwitz, including a particularly difficult moment when the group ran into an Israeli youth group wearing Israeli flags and acting provocatively. Heavy tears of intense emotions were shed at this first encounter with Israeli citizens in the middle of the camp, and walls were punched as a way to relieve the tension of conflicted feelings between loyalty to family who had lost their homeland to Israel and the suffering witnessed in the death camp.

Having fully internalized during his trip to Auschwitz the expected emotional orientation to the Holocaust and the Israeli-Palestinian conflict demanded of him in order to be accepted into the moral makeup of German citizenship, Adnan now needed to navigate how his new perspective affected his relationship with family and friends. Upon his return from Auschwitz, there was community fallout waiting for him: some of his relatives accused him of being a traitor, and his Palestinian circles excluded him. By the end of a challenging educational program designed specifically for Muslims who identify with the Palestinian cause, Adnan, a young man born and raised in Germany, had opened his heart to the suffering that Jews experienced during the Holocaust. Because the Mufti of Jerusalem had collaborated with Hitler, Adnan now feels that as an

Arab, and even more so as a Palestinian, he bears a certain co-responsibility for the suffering of Jews. Adnan's status as a model participant in the project is thus fully dependent upon his giving up his emotional commitment to Palestine and his family's property rights in Israel. Paradoxically, in order to be accepted into the moral makeup of German citizenship, Adnan's responsibility for the Holocaust must be accomplished as a Palestinian, not as a German. Yet unlike the ethnic German grandchildren of Nazis whose assumed "direct genealogical descent from Nazism" can be traced back only a few generations within their own family, Adnan's family has no direct connection with Nazism. None of Adnan's grandparents or family members were Nazis. This poses a problem for Adnan in terms of his fit in public German Holocaust memory discourse, itself based on a self-identity as perpetrator. To compensate for this genealogical mismatch between ethnic Germans who are the descendants of perpetrators and immigrant-background Germans who are not, the Muslims in Auschwitz project works to expand Palestinian-, Arab-, and Turkish-background family genealogies to a field of culpability as large as the nation. Because Adnan has no Nazis in his family, he must be made to bear not a personal familiar responsibility but an ethnonational responsibility that he "inherits" from a Palestinian religiopolitical leader—the Mufti of Jerusalem—about whom he has only recently learned in the context of Holocaust education. Importantly, to achieve the emotional goal of identifying himself as a perpetrator rather than a victim, Adnan's non-German, ethnonationalist Palestinian background must be highlighted. Rather than turning immigrant-background German citizens into invisible members of German society, the project instead highlights their ethnic difference.

The Coexist model of the theater play demonstrates the specific type of genealogical connection with the Nazis that immigrant youth must display in order to gain legitimacy and visibility. In this model, by connecting themselves ethnogenealogically to the Mufti of Jerusalem, Palestinian-background youth assume a responsibility for Nazism not on behalf of their families but of their nations, and in this way they are allowed to form the necessary conditions for taking part in the German social contract. But there are other young men in the group who are not Palestinians and find it harder to establish a connection with a Nazi collaborator like the Mufti of Jerusalem.

The German Nazi Who Converted to Islam and the Search for a Perpetrator in the Family

Selim, a young Turkish-background man at the time studying law with a focus on human rights in an eastern German town, played the role of the German Nazi who converted to Islam. Social workers told me that it was a big deal for him to move so far away from his family to an eastern German town. I got the impression that the decision had been a combination of his desire to live on his own and the fact that, given the popularity of law as a career choice, it had been easier for him to gain entry to that university with his graduation scores. I could see that the social workers who knew Selim were proud of what he had accomplished.

When I asked him what it had been like to play the converted Nazi, Selim told me that he was glad to take on that role. He said that his visit to Auschwitz had left him confused. He could not understand why anyone one would take part in such horrific crimes. He had taken on the role of the Nazi to better understand Auschwitz. He also told me that at Auschwitz, he had felt like he was in "double trouble" in relation to Jews, both as a German connected to the Holocaust and as a Muslim connected to a new wave of antisemitism. When he told me that they had created the roles themselves, I asked him why the German Nazi character in the play was a convert to Islam. Selim explained to me that most people don't know that the Arabs collaborated with the Nazis, or that they at least tried to collaborate with them. They created the character of the Nazi convert to show the cooperation between Arabs and Nazis. He confessed that he did not know if there were any German Nazis who had converted to Islam, but that the character brings together what he saw in himself as being "double trouble" for Jews.

Later in our conversation, I asked Selim whether engaging in this project made him more German in the sense that he had shouldered responsibility for the German past. Selim explained that for him, it works the other way around.

> I actually already feel pretty German, even without the Muslims in Auschwitz project. But the project makes people think that I *am* German. Every time I say I'm from Duisburg, people ask where I'm *actually* from. They don't see me as German. But if they knew that I'm involved in such projects, that I fight for human rights, maybe they would be convinced that I *am* German.

Selim also told me that after his return from Auschwitz, he began thinking about his own family history and his grandfather. He had begun asking what his grandfather had been doing when the Armenians were being killed. I had heard him make a similar statement in one of the post-performance conversations with the public. His mother, too, denied that the Armenian Genocide had taken place. He said that he had begun to compare his grandfather's role to that of the Nazis. "When I meet old Nazis today, they are perfectly nice people. My grandfather is also a nice guy. So maybe he was a Turkish Nazi. Maybe. But I don't know."

Rather than focus on the feeling or the motivation behind this comparison, I was carried away by the temporal unlikelihood of his grandfather having been a "Turkish Nazi," a Turkish/Ottoman soldier who had carried out the Armenian Genocide of 1915.

Esra: Did you ever ask your grandfather about this?
Selim: No. That's something we don't talk about.
Esra: He might be a bit young to have been alive during the Armenian Genocide. How old is he?
Selim: Very old. He's ninety-two.
Esra: Even then, he was born after the Armenian Genocide. He could not have been involved. Your grandfather is safe.

Selim laughs.

Esra: Did you really never ask him?
Selim: I asked my mother. She denies that the Armenian Genocide ever happened. When I bring it up, she wants to talk about Israel.

While it is temporally impossible for Selim's grandfather to have played a role in the Armenian Genocide, there is a possibility that his great-grandfather could have played a role in it. Perhaps Selim does have a stain somewhere in his bloodline. Researching such a connection—for a crime that is officially denied—is no easy task. He would have to travel to Turkey and be granted permission to access archives that are heavily guarded, open to few researchers, partially uncatalogued, and whose integrity has been open to question. He would need to be able to read Ottoman, a language he does not know. That would be an extraordinary and near-impossible undertaking for Selim. How, then, can we understand the motivations of a Turkish-background law student who is actively involved in understanding German history who overlooks the fact that his grandfather was born two decades after the Armenian Genocide took place? Selim did have a sense of the temporal nature of history. In our conversation, he noted that the Holocaust happened before Israel came into existence. Was his desire to have a perpetrator grandfather like the perpetrator grandfathers of his German friends so great that he could ignore this most basic of temporal calculations?

Of all the young men I met in Muslims in Auschwitz, Selim was the most eager to take on difficult challenges. He claimed to have a Turkish Nazi grandfather. He made this claim in conversation with researchers and in public after theater performances. He wore a bracelet with an Israeli flag that an Israeli woman had given him during one of the youth exchanges programs. He created and took on the role of a German Nazi who had converted to Islam to make it easier to collaborate with Arabs. He decided to move away from his family to another town for his university studies. He confided in me that he was so different from his sisters and brothers that he would never discuss his opinions openly with them. He had felt like a traitor to them by joining Muslims in Auschwitz. But he was glad to have taken on this challenge, saying with a contented smile: "It's been really good for me." Of his own accord, Selim moved as far away as he could from anything that might identify him as a victim, identifying instead with the roles of the German Nazi who converted to Islam and the "Turkish Nazi," and with Israel, whose flag he wears on his wrist. What he hopes is that his choices will be enough to persuade others that he really is a German.

The Theater Project: *Coexist / You Must Hate, My Son!*

In her analysis of postmigrant theater in Germany, Lizzie Stewart (2017) argues that although "theater, as an art form, is seldom considered a major social or theoretical mover today" (56), a new theater movement in Kreuzberg, Berlin, has been instrumental in bringing the new concept and story of postmigration into the public realm. According to Stewart and Shermin Langhoff, the director who began postmigrant theater in Kreuzberg, the concept is especially powerful because it allows postmigrants—people with a migration background—to rewrite the stories circulating about them, generating a postmigrant literature. "For us," Langhoff noted, "postmigrant means that we critically question the production and reception of stories about migration and about migrants which have been available up to now and that we view and produce these stories anew, inviting a new reception" (quoted in Stewart 2017, 57). According to theater researcher Azadeh Sharifi (2013), postmigrant theater is a way of "telling stories from the margins and still knowing the center" (quoted in Stewart 2017, 57).

While youth theater projects in the underprivileged margins of German cities rarely act as "social or theoretical movers," the *Coexist* theater project was nevertheless an attempt by marginalized immigrant-background youth to redefine the stories circulating about them. As a way of opening up space for themselves within the German temporality, the play demonstrates the youths' deep knowledge of the stories Germans tell about them and their motivations in changing these stories.

Coexist is the second theatrical production developed by the Muslims in Auschwitz team to showcase for a select public the work the youth were doing. Some of the scenes from the first production, *The Others* (*Die Anderen*), made their way into *Coexist*, while others were dropped. *Coexist* was later renamed *You Must Hate, My Son!* In 2018, a third version of the play, *Benjamin and Muhammad*, was presented. While each production and each scene has its own theme and pedagogical message, the overall intent of these three theater productions is to relate Muslims, especially Arabs, both to the Holocaust and to the hatred of Jews from the position of a potential perpetrator, without reciprocal recognition of the historical and contemporary suffering of Palestinians in the Middle East or of discrimination against Muslims in Germany today.

The play begins in contemporary Germany. A young man is wandering around a train station. He walks up to people, one after the other, each of them busy on their phone or in a rush, and tells them that he wants to know the truth (*Wahrheit*). Some people ignore him. Others stop and ask what he means, "Which truth? The good one or the bad one?" Overwhelmed, the young man decides to rest and falls asleep on the floor. The rest of the play is his dream. The dream he has blends scenes from the past and the present, from Nazi Germany and the Middle East, leaving the audience wondering at times when and where a particular scene is located.

His dream opens to the sound of Arabic music. A man wearing a long black leather trench coat down to his calf and black boots walks onto the stage. He is pushing a service cart on wheels. On it sits another male actor, eyes blindfolded, playfully dangling his feet as a cue to the audience that he is a child sitting in a buggy. In an innocent tone, he asks, "Where are we going, Daddy?" His father answers seriously and determinedly. "You'll see!" After a few rounds on the stage, the father stops, unties his son's blindfold, and shows his son around with a proud expression. "Do you see the apple trees, the olive trees? They're yours. Yours and mine." Then he turns around and looks closely at his son, "But there are horrible creatures out there. They want to come and take our land." The father takes out a gun and gives it to his son. The boy is excited. "Thank you, daddy! A toy gun!" "No, son," the father answers. "This is not a toy. It is for you to shoot Jews with." The father helps his son point the gun. The boy is curious. "The Jews?" The father nods affirmatively. "Yes, the Jews. They have big noses." The boy asks, "Like your nose, Daddy?" Father looks aghast. "Like my nose? No! They are like beasts and they smell. You should kill all of them. Kill them! Hate them, my son!" The son repeats after his father, "Kill. Hate. Kill." He then turns to the audience and says, "I hate you all!" and points his gun at the audience.

This was one of the first scenes the project's youth and educators all agreed on. Mariana, the theater director, told me that it was clear to the youth that their fathers had passed the hatred of the Jews on to them. They thought that as young Arabs and Turks they were innocent, and that it was their fathers—wearing Nazi-like long black coats and boots—who were responsible for the antisemitism. If they could rebel against their fathers and not take up this hate, antisemitism among Muslim communities could be resolved. The scene reflects well the psychological work the same young men do at Heroes. As they try to free themselves of what they see as the honor culture they grew up in, the young men struggle with their own families, reflecting on the violence they were subjected to at home and which they sometimes passed on to their younger siblings.

The scene depicts the subjects of the Muslims in Auschwitz project as innocent boys, blindfolded and pushed in a buggy, possibly kidnapped, by their Nazi-like father who forces them to learn that Palestine belongs to them and that they should hate Jews. The journey with the blindfold indicates how far away the idea of Palestine is to the Arab boy: he needs to be taken in a buggy to a place that clearly is distant and foreign to him. Without his father, he would not know how to get there, not know that he is the owner of olive and apple trees, not know that there are Jews he needs to hate. It is important that the antisemitic stereotypes the Arab/Palestinian/Muslim father is passing on to his son—the big-nosed and smelly Jew—are German antisemitic stereotypes, not Palestinian ones. This image strengthens the export-import theory of antisemitism discussed earlier, where Arabs and Muslims are accused of having imbibed German antisemitism exported to them and now regurgitate it in the present.

The next scene involves an Arab terrorist in the making. A Palestinian man called Hassan walks onstage smiling, wearing a *thawb*, the traditional ankle-length cotton-white attire for men. Another man walks over to him, offers him a gun, and asks him to kill someone for him. Hassan refuses. "I came to Germany to work and not to kill." The man places the gun to his head. "You must kill or be killed." Hassan takes the gun, looks at it, and in a distressed voice says, "I have children. Why should I kill someone?" Hassan, a Palestinian-background German father, then runs offstage in a panic.

The following scene opens on the Palestinian father who taught his son to hate Jews now talking to a German Nazi officer who has converted to Islam, the scene we saw earlier. Blending together what happened in the Middle East and in Europe in a fictional montage, the now Muslim German Nazi officer offers the father a Palestine that is free of Jews. In return he asks the Palestinian to hunt down every single Jew, destroy their houses and synagogues. Later, the Palestinian and the German Nazi shakes hands cheerfully, the Nazi pronouncing, "This will be our secret. We will eradicate every single Jew."

Next, Hassan from the previous scene walks onstage with a baby in his arms. The baby cries. The converted Nazi from the previous scene asks him whether the baby is Jewish. Hassan asks, "How do I know? It's a baby." The Nazi asks him which language he cries in. Taking the baby, he smells it and says that it smells like a Jew. "He must go." Next, we see Hassan crying, gesturing as if he is praying and at the same time trying desperately to wash his hands. Another man walks in and looks to Hassan. "You must help me." "I cannot help you," Hasan replies. "I just killed a baby." The man responds in a hushed voice, "I hid a Jewish family. Don't tell anyone."

In these two scenes, time and place are blended unintelligibly. Nothing is clear: when or where Muslims are killing Jewish babies and destroying synagogues at the instruction of Nazis; when or where they are saving Jewish families from the Nazis. In his first scene, Hassan said that he had come to Germany to work, not to kill, suggesting that the time frame is post–World War II. But the man who puts a gun to his head and orders him to kill the Jewish baby is a German Nazi who has converted to Islam and was just seen in Palestine. The scene mixes the disparate elements of the German Nazi experience during the Third Reich, Palestinian experience both then and now, and Muslim immigrant experiences in Germany in the postwar and contemporary period. Indeed, the scene seems to span all of these elements. This scene and another that follows it counterbalances the Arab Nazi collaborators with Arab saviors. Suggesting that while some Arabs collaborated with the Nazi's Final Solution plans, others saved the Jews, offering this as an alternative for all times and places, perhaps even now. Arabs and Muslims can choose even today, the play seems to suggest, to save Jews instead of killing them. But where this can be done is not clear.

Although it is unclear whether Hassan is killing a Jewish baby in the 1930s, the 1940s, the 1950s, or even today, or whether he is killing the baby in Germany, in British Mandatory Palestine, or in Israel, the ZDF documentary about the Muslims in Auschwitz project (Wolf-Graaf and Presnick 2016) discusses this scene as "the scene with the Arab terrorist." According to the theater educator, this scene provides an important opportunity to have the youth explore ways to act when in a position of power. In the documentary we see how the rehearsals were used as role-play opportunities for internalizing the perpetrator position and opening up possibilities for alternative action. We see one of the participants aiming his gun at another. Mariana tells the one holding the gun, "Now you are in position of power. You can shoot him. Will you shoot him? Will you shoot him?" After hesitating, the young man puts the gun down. It's clear that Mariana is not directing her question to the character in the play; she is asking the young man himself to make a choice. Although in the play Hasan kills the Jewish baby, here in the documentary footage of the rehearsals-cum-project-role-plays, the youth manages to put down his gun when given the opportunity to kill a Jewish person. Paradoxically, the theater project also teaches the youth that they are in a position of power in relation to Jews: in that sense, the gun is in their hands and they have the power to chose whether or not to use it. What is not clear is whether this powerful position may be negotiated in Germany, in British Mandatory Palestine, or in Israel/Palestine, or whether Jews are in danger at the hands of Muslims everywhere. In changing the dominant story being told about them, Arab- and Turkish-background youth are encouraged to change the way they think about themselves. No longer victims, they are now potential perpetrators who are nevertheless able to show empathy toward their potential victims and, by doing so, learn to control themselves.

While I interpreted this scene as having replaced the German perpetrators of the Holocaust with Arab ones, some of the young participants in the project interpreted the scene where Hassan kills the Jewish baby as reflecting a distinctly Arab/Muslim predisposition toward violence. In the documentary, one of the participants says, "This play reflects our society. In our communities there is readiness for violence. This stereotype reflects reality. This scene occupied me for a while. I was raised with this [readiness for violence], but I was not happy with it. The scene is an example of how these biases came about. It reflects the Arab world." Many of the youth buy into the stereotypes they perform in the theater, eagerly demonstrating their willingness to change themselves.

The next scene takes place in a Nazi office. A German officer kills a Nazi soldier after learning that he is in love with a Jewish woman and wants to marry her. The Nazi officer wears the same long black leather coat the Arab father was wearing in the earlier scene. This scene is reminiscent of the role-plays the youth enact as part of their work in the Heroes project, where falling in love with a German woman has grave consequences. In the role-plays, their fathers do not kill them, but they do disown them, leading to social death in their minority social circles. Enacting the dilemma of people who fall in love with someone beyond their sociopolitical ingroup, the scene highlights the circumstances that can limit one's capacity to love or to act on that love, or, alternatively, to enable a person to go beyond hate and prejudice.

In a later scene in the same office, a Jewish man wearing a striped prison uniform cleans the floors on his knees with a piece of rag and is constantly humiliated by a Nazi officer who holds him at gunpoint. When the Nazi officer steps outside, the Jewish man runs away and looks for a place to hide. He enters a room where the Palestinian son from earlier, now grown up, is talking to himself while reading a newspaper. "Damned Jews . . . I got the land from my father." When the Palestinian son sees the Jewish man, still in prison uniform, he demands to know who he is. The Jewish man stutters, "Jew . . . Jew . . . Jew." The Palestinian son says, "I will hide you. Stay here." His father walks in with a gun in his hand, wearing the same long black leather jacket shared with the Nazi, saying that he is going to kill every single Jew. He asks his son if he has seen a Jew lurking about. The son points to the newspaper. "Papa, did you see that? They want my land." When his father walks out, the Palestinian son asks the Jewish man if he has seen the news. The Jewish man, who was just a minute ago cleaning the floor in a Nazi office, stands up and declares, "Palestine is mine! I inherited it from my father!" The Palestinian and the Jew keep arguing back and forth, making reference to their fathers like two little children: "It's mine!" "No, my papa said it belongs to me!" After a few rounds the Jewish man says, "I don't want this anymore. Why all this killing? Can't we just share?" The Palestinian son says, "Sharing is good, but how are going to do that?" The Jewish man explains, "Look, this part will be for you and this part will be for me. We can divide the trees, the houses." The Palestinian son asks, "You mean, like East and West?" The Jew says, "Exactly." At that point they are both smiling and looking content. The scene goes dark. Then we hear the father's voice yelling from offstage, "You traitor!" We hear two loud shots, indicating that the father has just killed both the Palestinian son and the Jewish man as they were about to reach an agreement. The Jewish man who had earlier been imprisoned and converted to slave labor by the Nazis is killed not by a German Nazi but by a Palestinian. But along with the Jew, the Palestinian father has killed his own Palestinian son. The Jewish prisoner, the Palestinian son, the Nazi soldier, and the Jewish baby are all killed at the hands of Palestinian fathers or Nazi officers. Palestinian fathers and Nazi officers have now been made equal in their perpetratorship, while Palestinian sons and Jews are now both positioned as their victims. But there is a big difference between the Palestinian sons and Jews in that the Palestinian son killed a Jewish baby, and so while he is a victim, he is also a perpetrator.

In the very last scene, the young man from the opening scene who had fallen asleep in the train station while looking for the truth wakes up. He recounts a bad dream in which Arabs and Jews are all mixed up in it. He wanders around the train station, asking people if they want a war. As with his questions about truth, most seem too busy to answer him. But some do say, "No, we don't want war." Someone asks him whether he has had a dream or a nightmare. When the man answers that he has had a nightmare, the stranger tells him not to let the media get to him and to always be critical. Another stranger answers by saying that war is a crime.

The people onstage then turn toward the audience and say in unison, "Hey people, do you hear? We don't want war. We want to talk." In ending the play in this way, they are playing a double game: they repeat the commitment to peace made by Germany after its loss in the second of two world wars and after the revelations of the atrocities they committed in the Holocaust, and they also seem to be saying that they do not want war elsewhere, in Israel/Palestine, the other space occupied by the play. By not stipulating which war they do not want, by rejecting war in general but not in the specific, they draw a clear connection between the two time-spaces of the play: World War II and the Israeli-Palestinian conflict.

Before and After the Theater: Framing the Play for the Audience

After the applause dies down, the actors sit on the stage and invite the audience to stay for discussion. This part of the performance is as important—arguably even more important—than the play itself. It is during this discussion session that the youth convey their redemptive narrative and confess that they themselves used to hold antisemitic prejudices but, thanks to the project, have now changed their point of view. They share repeatedly the message that this transformation had not been easy for them, that their families and communities had made things difficult for them, but that nothing could stop them. As a result, they now feel liberated from their sense of victimhood and from the hate they claim was instilled in them by their families, in particular by their fathers. Having shed these commitments to their ethnic communities even at the cost of being disowned by their fathers, they are now free to take part in a democratic, tolerant, empathetic, and redemptive German society.

Because it is interactive, this last part of the play takes different forms depending on the audience. Yet a closer look at the interactions with two very different audiences—one at a school in a small western German town where most of the students were of minority background and the second at a leftist organization in an eastern German town—sheds light on the fact that there appears to be space in German society to allow movement from talking about the Holocaust memory to talking about contemporary racism in the country.

The audience at the school performance in western Germany is somewhat sparse: students, teachers, a few parents who were mostly of immigrant background, several local politicians, adults who were involved with the project. At the end of the play, after announcing to the audience, "We don't want war. We want to talk," the youth take turns explaining how their strong feelings against Jews have been transformed by the project.

Mahdi: Throughout the project there was a struggle raging between my heart and my mind. I learned certain stereotypes about Jews from my family. You know how we all come from certain environments here. My parents have an Arab Muslim background. I grew up with a lot of antisemitism. Religion and politics are mixed in that respect, and it really is difficult to question this set of assumptions. Heroes allowed me to get to know myself in general. But Muslims in Auschwitz was a totally different experience.

Mehmet: After I came back from Auschwitz, I was in emotional chaos, and the theater [project] helped me to organize my feelings.

Mustafa: I'm a Palestinian, and I, too, grew up with antisemitism at home. Going to Auschwitz gave me a different perspective.

Yassin: I don't have an Arab background. I'm Turkish, but I also grew up with these attitudes.

After the youth confess to having been antisemitic and describe their difficult road to recovery, guests of honor—significant social and political actors or individuals who work closely with the project, almost all of whom are white Germans—stand up to vocally acknowledge and celebrate the youths' transformation. As at other performances, the local white politicians praise the youth enthusiastically, speaking in superlatives about how wonderfully they have displayed their emotions. The handful of white participants in the audience, which include researchers from the local university, ask the youth how their families have reacted to their focus on the Holocaust. Mustafa answers that the project created conflict within his family. In the beginning, they accused him of being a traitor and of betraying his family. But as he continued on with the project, his parents saw how much public acknowledgment he received because of it, and they now support him. Mustafa reiterates his commitment to the project's goals by saying that he is extremely motivated to continue with it. The theater educator appears onstage and tells the audience how proud she is of the youth, how far they have come as actors. After a round of applause, the youth take a bow.

In *Scripting Addiction*, anthropologist Summerson Carr (2011) demonstrates that homeless drug users enrolled in a government drug addiction program they must attend to gain access to shelter, food, and custody of their children use a strategic practice they call "flipping the script" in which they perform the narrative they believe therapists want to hear from them. By convincing the therapists that they are on the path to recovery, drug users are able to gain access to rights and services and avoid unwanted treatments and consequences, thus improving their lives, which for most people is the necessary precondition to stop using drugs. Carr also notes that in contemporary Black American culture, "script flipping" refers to the ability to change one's social trajectory and become upwardly mobile. According to Carr, script flippers are able to give successful performances because they have "schooled themselves in . . . 'contextualization cues,' the communicative indexes that let people know what is going on in any given situation and how they are expected to proceed" (193). Alternatively, Carr suggests, drug users may have a high level of metalinguistic awareness, "the practical ability to read the range of authorized, acceptable discursive possibilities within an institutionalized set of discursive linguistic practices" where "the focus remains on the contextual dynamics of the linguistic practice [in the program] rather than the innate verbal talents of particular people" (194). I suggest an additional explanation: the marginalized youth "script flippers" who participate in the Muslims in Auschwitz program are also highly skilled "anthropologists" who are able to crack the cultural and linguistic codes of public German Holocaust memory discourse, find the right script, and flip it so that they can enter into it, be seen and heard, applauded and honored as equals in the German social contract.

Let me be clear here: the youth of the Muslims in Auschwitz project are not in any way misleading the program social workers, educators, political actors, journalists, and other concerned members of the majority society. They are not dissembling. Rather, by mobilizing a high level of metalinguistic awareness of the contextual cues within the Muslims in Auschwitz program and German society at large, the youth successfully perform a script that enables them to insert themselves into public German Holocaust memory discourse as authorized and acceptable members. To do so, they create a literal script, a theater play, and act it out in front of audiences across Germany. Part of the text of this Holocaust memory discourse script is more scripted: the play is written out beforehand and then acted out verbatim. Part of the text is less scripted: when the youth sit down on the stage at the end and interact with the audience in a give-and-take manner, the stories they tell about their self-transformation have been tweaked beforehand; before each performance they talk about who is in the audience that night and which strategy will be most effective in their storytelling. Their aim is to simultaneously please, surprise, and challenge their audience.

Most importantly, their successfully framed narratives give the youth a chance to present social performances of their commitment to German history. In Jeffrey Alexander's words, such performances or rituals are "episodes of repeated and simplified cultural communication in which the direct partners to a social interaction, and those observing it, share a mutual belief in the descriptive and prescriptive validity of the communication's symbolic contents and accept the authenticity of one another's intentions" (2004, 527). The success of such performances, Alexander argues, lies in the actors' ability to ensure viewers believe that what they see and hear is an authentic expression. To do so, they engage in what Alexander calls "cultural pragmatics" (2004) and draw upon the various elements of social performance, not so different from theater productions generally. It is this process of authentic performance, as in the "flipping the script" discussed above, that leads to success for the Duisburg youth, meaning access to a new social trajectory. From being unrecognized, stigmatized, and even despised members of German society, they are able through authentic presentation to become prized German citizens who receive multiple public awards, appear frequently in the media, are invited to meet with local and national politicians, and are interviewed by the press and foreign academic researchers traveling from afar. The most dramatic example of flipping the script is the case of Burak Yılmaz, who, because of his contributions as project leader in the Muslims in Auschwitz project, was awarded the Order of Merit, Germany's highest civilian honor, by German president Frank-Walter Steinmeier. Burak was also awarded a book contract to write about his experiences in the project (Yılmaz 2021). His high level of metalinguistic awareness and ability to perform the meaning of German history and his commitment to it authentically allowed him to change from being perceived as an undeserving, sexist, and violent antisemite to being recognized as someone who is leading the fight to further German values.

The *Coexist* performance in Leipzig played to a very different kind of audience, who did not buy into the attempts of "flipping the script." The actors could not make the viewers believe that they were committed to the lessons of German history. When a left-wing, antifascist cultural organization in Leipzig invited

Muslims in Auschwitz to perform, I joined the group. The play was to be hosted by an German-Israeli society and displayed at left-wing cultural center Pöge-Haus Leipzig, home to the antideutsche branch of the German left. In the 1990s the German radical left split on the question of Zionism/Palestine into opposing camps. What is called the traditional left in Germany have an anti-imperialist focus and affiliate themselves with the Palestinian cause. The so-called "antideutsche," on the other hand, see the primary aim of left-wing activism as the fight against antisemitism. They define themselves as antideutsche because they see antisemitism as the deep-seated essence of German culture and psyche. Hence the antideutsche movement is fiercely Zionist and see the pro-Palestinian movement and Muslims as their primary enemy (Moghadam and Wyss 2018). Leipzig is a particular bastion of the antideutsche student left, where students come from across Germany.[5]

Hosted by an all-white audience in a city where there are few Muslim immigrants, Burak introduced the theater project participants by asking them questions that revealed their different situations and capacities and how far each of them had come by participating in the program. Burak began with Mustafa, telling the audience that in Auschwitz Mustafa had asked how it was that we could still have racism in Germany despite what we witnessed there at the concentration camp. Mustafa then recounted how every time he drives, he has trouble with the police. He also said that the extreme right party AfD had received 13 percent of the vote where he lives in Duisburg and that he often attends demonstrations against racism. This had been his main motivation for participating in the Muslims in Auschwitz project—to fight against racism.

Burak followed up by asking Mustafa what kinds of reactions he receives when he talks about the project with his family and friends. Mustafa said that a lot of people tell him that he has nothing to do with National Socialism and that he should not bother with it. "My family comes from Palestine. I'm German, but I am not accepted as a German." Mehmet chimed in that the project had taught him to separate Jews from Israel and antisemitism from the critique of Israel.

Burak then introduced Huseyin, a young Yazidi man originally from Syria, reminding the audience that Yazidis are persecuted by ISIS and that Huseyin had played the role of a Jew in the theater.

Burak: Huseyin, during the project you frequently compared the past with the present. . . . You had a chance to reflect on the victim role a lot. What can you tell us?

Huseyin: The Jewish perspective was very important for me. Throughout the project, I had one eye concentrated on the Holocaust and the other concentrated on the Yazidi genocide. People tried to exterminate my race. While performing this play in a synagogue, an old lady came up and said, "I used to think all Arabs are aggressive and now I see that it is not the case." I was very happy to hear that.

Burak then turned to Selim, who focused on the perpetrator perspective and the fact that he studies law. Selim explained to the audience that there had been no emotional dimension to their Holocaust education at school, that he had only learned to engage with it during this project, and that he hated what had happened in Auschwitz. Burak told the audience that Selim was so troubled by what had happened in the Holocaust that he had decided to study human rights law. Selim said that he had learned a lot from acting the role of a Nazi who had converted to Islam because then he could see what it means to have the power to choose in one's own hands.

Burak was doing a lot of mediating, trying hard to frame both the Muslims in Auschwitz story and each participant's individual story of transformation for the audience. The audience, however, was not willing to make the connections Burak and other participants were establishing from racism in the past to racism in the present. When Burak opened the floor to questions, the first audience member to raise his hand accused the group of being antisemitic for having separated antisemitism from the critique of Israel. Mehmet tried to respond to the accusation by bringing in his own perspective. He said that when he was eleven years old, he had visited Lebanon for six days during the 2006 Lebanon War, a two-month-long military conflict between the Israel Defense Forces and Hezbollah paramilitary forces. "I didn't know what was happening. I woke up one morning to explosions everywhere, and it was Israel who was doing it." It was there, he told the audience, that he first learned to hate Israel and Jews. "Four years later, I came to this project. I was very critical. I kept telling them that they are only showing one side, that they never show the Palestinian perspective. But then I wanted to learn more. And now I have Israeli and Jewish friends."

The second question was directed at Huseyin. The audience member accused him of being opportunistic. "Don't you think it's unethical to use the memory of Auschwitz to establish empathy and solidarity with the Yazidi issue? This is not true empathy. You're using [German-Jewish] reconciliation to help your own cause." Another audience member voiced a different critique: "In this project you're equating racism with antisemitism. You should know that racism is directed toward people one views as inferior to oneself. Antisemitism is directed toward people one views as higher [more powerful] than oneself; it's an attempt to explain what one cannot control. The Holocaust is an absolutely unique experience, and you should not compare antisemitism to racism. The attempt to annihilate the entire Jewish population is a break with civilization. It was a machine of extermination that had never before existed." The statement received enthusiastic and long-lasting applause from audience members. Looking troubled by the accusations, Burak said, "You're right. Maybe what we said came out in a way we did not intend. Huseyin should not have used the word racism." Mehmet once more resorted to personal experiences and emotions: "This play is about *our* emotions. We did it to understand and process *our* feelings. Our aim isn't to compare the Holocaust and antisemitism with anything else. We're trying to understand and represent the antisemitic structures we live in."

The audience members then began pressing the Duisburgers with questions designed to reveal their true colors. "How did you feel during the Gaza conflict in the summer of 2014? Some Arabs said Jews should be sent to gas chambers. Did you also want that?" Burak answered simply by saying, "I hope such a thing never happens again." When another audience member challenged them again by asking them which role in the project they thought of themselves as playing, a perpetrator or a victim, Mehmet's answer, "I am the Nazi in the theater," was meant to show that he wholeheartedly embraced the perpetrator role and does not shy away from the responsibilities that attach to being one.

Despite the project members' earnest efforts to carefully frame the project, to read the contextual cues in this unfamiliar all-white antideutsche room, and to take upon themselves the role of the repentant perpetrator, these immigrant- and Muslim-background Duisburgers would find no acceptance into redemptive German identity. This all-white radical left audience accused the youth of a laundry list of trespasses: of not doing enough to shoulder the role of Germans as perpetrators; of being antisemitic for criticizing Israel when they have personally suffered under Israeli military aggression; for trivializing antisemitism by comparing it to racism; for comparing the Holocaust to the Yezidi genocide. One audience member after another questioned their sincerity, their motivations, and their "correct" understanding of the importance and meaning of German history. Once again, they were marked as Muslim-background immigrants who, regardless of what they insisted, could not relinquish their antisemitism.

Exclusionary Incorporation into the German Social Contract

New Holocaust education programs designed especially for and often by Muslims open up space for immigrants to enter into Holocaust memory discourse through affiliation with the German perpetrator. Participants learn about and enact the stories of the Mufti of Jerusalem who collaborated with the Nazis and righteous Arab and Turkish Schindlers who saved Jews. Through this engagement, some Muslim-minority Germans attempt to enter the realm of moral German citizenship. At the same time, this same model prevents them from claiming the victim position as Palestinians and Lebanese in relation to Israel, as Yazidis in relation to ISIS, and as Muslims and immigrants in relation to white Germans. The Holocaust memory script adopted, perfected, and performed by members of the Middle Eastern/Muslim minority compels them to engage with the Holocaust in relation to their own forebears but not in relation to ethnicity-based German nationalism. Hence, while incorporating them into this foundational narrative of the nation, initiatives that aim to educate Muslims on the Holocaust already exclude them (Partridge 2008).

All of this emotional and intellectual hard work of taking the guilt and responsibility of the Holocaust on their shoulders gives participants of Muslims in Auschwitz partial and exclusionary entry into what I call the postwar German social contract. They receive funding for their projects—even if not steady or predictable. They appear in newspapers and documentaries, they get invited to different parts of the country or the world to present their projects. They receive many awards and attention from researchers like me. As a result of the social support they have, most of the participants finished their schooling, entered universities, and expanded their social networks. However, none of this makes them full and equal members of German society. After a big applause in an award ceremony or at the end of a theater play, they will be stopped in traffic by the police, they will not be let into clubs, they will have a harder time getting jobs and renting apartments. Worse, they also still will be routinely accused of being antisemitic and sexist. This is why I contend that taking on or subcontracting the perpetrator role gives them only partial and conditional entry into the German social contract.

CHAPTER 5

Visiting Auschwitz as Pilgrimage and as Shock Therapy

Holocaust education projects aimed solely at Muslims often utilize a visit to Auschwitz as a form of shock therapy, a tool designed to shake them out of their antisemitism and instill in them the "right" kinds of feelings toward Jewish victims of the Holocaust. Muslims who participate in these Holocaust education projects aim to transform themselves, and at the same time become anxious about whether they will be able to achieve such a transformation. Equally important, these projects also seek to grab the attention of the mainstream German population through such an unexpected engagement with the Holocaust by Muslim- and immigrant-background Germans at Auschwitz, a place that has attained semi-sacred status in postwar German national identity. Muslim participants in projects that engage with the Holocaust aim to demonstrate to mainstream white German society both that they are willing to shoulder the burden of the German Nazi past themselves and that they empathize with the Jewish victims of the Holocaust. By doing so, they demonstrate their belonging in German society.

Yet, there is no one model for Middle Eastern/Muslim-background Germans to follow as they visit Auschwitz. For example, Muslims in Auschwitz seeks to bring about an inner transformation in its participants by having them embrace the emotional position of being a potential/repentant perpetrator and therefore affiliating themselves with white Germans in whose name the Holocaust was committed. Another concentration camp visit project yearly organized by the Muslim/immigrant organization Muslim Youth in Germany (*Muslimische*

Jugend in Deutschland), takes a different approach in that it aims to establish connections with Jewish and Muslim experiences and uses Holocaust memory to develop a deeper understanding and appreciation of multiple racialized groups, including racialized selves and others. However, despite these variations, the visits to Auschwitz serve the common purposes of pilgrimage and also as a kind of shock therapy with a dual aim: to transform the participants and to challenge the perception of white Christian-background German society that accuses them of not engaging in German history.

Auschwitz as Pilgrimage

One cannot overestimate the symbolic importance of Auschwitz in the memory and imagination of the Holocaust globally, but most particularly in Germany. As the biggest Nazi death camp, 1.4 million people were killed in the two main camps that constitute Auschwitz I in Oświęcim and Auschwitz II in Birkenau, 90 percent of them Jewish. In Germany especially, the name Auschwitz is synonymous with the Holocaust. It is a UNESCO Heritage Site and every year a new record is set for the numbers of visitors; according to its official website in 2019, 2,390,000 individuals visited the Auschwitz-Birkenau Memorial and Museum, three percent (73,000) of whom were from Germany.

Of all the groups who visit Auschwitz, the best studied are Israeli and North American Jewish groups. The first and most detailed is Jackie Feldman's (2008) study of the Israeli youth trips to Auschwitz organized by the Israeli Ministry of Education since 1988 for Israeli Jewish teenagers when they are about to finish high school and start their obligatory military service. Noncompulsory and requiring negligible monetary contribution from students, the trips attract half the Israeli graduating high school students each year. In terms of sheer numbers, scope, and the level of organization involved, German and Muslim German trips to Auschwitz or other death camps pale in comparison with Israeli trips. The Israeli and North American Jewish visits have the additional function of passing on the victim and survivor perspective from generation to generation, whereas the German Muslim visits aim to break down the victim perspective that Muslim-background youth in Germany may have and encourage them to take on the perspective of the repentant perpetrator turned empathetic citizen. Despite the differences, Feldman's analysis of Israeli youth trips to Auschwitz provides insights into how pilgrimage to Auschwitz works, even for Muslim-minority Germans.

In Feldman's view, the primary aim of the annual Israeli youth trips to Auschwitz is not to gather information about the Holocaust and the death camps, but rather to perform a ritual; more precisely, a pilgrimage. Feldman adopts Victor Turner's (1973) approach to religious pilgrimage as a process where the pilgrim leaves his or her home and endures an often difficult and dangerous journey in order to arrive at a sacred but peripheral place, which then becomes the center of sacred religious experience for the pilgrim for the duration of the pilgrimage, effecting in Turner's words an "inward transformation of spirit and personality" (214) that develops into "the source of miraculous healing and rejuvenation" (Feldman 2008, 3). Equally important is that the experience of pilgrimage creates a strongly connected group, a *communitas*, out of the disparate individuals who have shared the pilgrimage experience. Upon their return, society recognizes that pilgrims have undergone a transformation and are accordingly granted new social status (3–4). Feldman argues that the trip to Auschwitz provides Israeli youth with a model of Israeli citizenship rather than a mirror of it (7–9). Working from within the framework or ritual, he argues that the "ultimate purpose [of the voyage] is to root the sanctity of the State in the experience of the Shoah. The voyage is a civil religious pilgrimage, which *transforms* students into *victims, victorious survivors*, and, finally, *olim* (immigrants, ascenders) to the Land of Israel and witnesses of the witnesses" (3).

Likewise, in her ethnographic study of contemporary discoveries of the Jewish past in Poland, Erica Lehrer (2013) notes the ritualistic and quasi-religious aspects of voyages to places both where Jews were killed and where they lived. She notes that the word used in Jewish communal circles for visits to spaces inhabited by Holocaust victims just before and at the end of their lives is a "mission," and that these missions are "almost always advertised as an opportunity to enhance one's Jewishness" (57). Lehrer states that mission tours "offer a chance to make a difference, have a spiritual awakening, or undergo a life-changing experience. They attempt to transform communal ideology into embodied reality. They create group memory" (57). For Israeli and North American Jews, trips to Poland make and solidify group identity as Jews and as survivors.

Scholars who study organized Israeli and non-Israeli Jewish trips to Israel concur on the centrality of the Zionist narrative. In their independent analysis of the March of the Living trip, "an annual education program, bringing individuals from around the world to Poland and Israel to study the history of the Holocaust and to examine the roots of prejudice, intolerance, and hatred,"[1] Rona Sheramy (2007) stresses that Jewish groups who take part in the march establish contact with and relive the mythical collective past in Poland, reaffirm victimhood in Auschwitz, and relate to the Jewish future by ending their trip in Israel. In Ian Lustick's (2017) analysis, Israeli and Jewish American trips to Israel are based on a model in which the Holocaust becomes a "template for Jewish life" where "the catastrophe [reveals] an unbridgeable abyss separating Jews and gentiles—the slaughter of millions of Jews by the Germans and their allies in almost every occupied country; the unique aspects of the Holocaust as an industrialized, ideological, and fanatical effort to extirpate an entire people, the willingness of governments and peoples around the world to acquiesce in the implementation of the Final Solution; and the world's refusal of refuge to those seeking to escape" (154). Feldman (2008) also notes that Israeli youth trips to Poland right before they start their military duty aim to highlight the necessity of defending Israel in light of what happened to Jews when they did not have a nation-state.

If visits to Auschwitz serve to help North American and Israeli Jews feel united within a Jewish community that has been persecuted in the past and that is now protected by Israel, what kind of an emotional transformation happens and is expected to happen when Muslim-background Germans visit Auschwitz in organized tours? What kind of spiritual awakening are they expected to have? How will their lives transform? Which communal ideology will be introduced or reinforced for them? What kind of group memory will they create, and with which group?

Although differing in many aspects from the Israeli youth trips to Poland, the Muslims in Auschwitz program does have important parallels. As with Israeli and North American Jewish travelers, Muslim-minority Germans experience the trip to Auschwitz as a civil religious pilgrimage, but as one that finally invites immigrants into a post–World War II national German civil religion from which they have been excluded. Its aim is to transform Muslim-minority youth who are at best indifferent to, at worst hostile toward, Holocaust memory into reliable and unswerving witnesses of the need for democracy, empathizers of Jewish victimhood, and defenders of a strong Israel that protects Jews in a world so hostile to them. All of this turns Muslim-background immigrants into deserving German citizens.

Beyond serving as a civil religious pilgrimage, visiting Auschwitz also serves as a form of shock therapy for Muslim-background Germans, one that aims to replicate and fast-track the journey Germans have taken over the last seventy-five years. Their emotional engagements with the victims of the Holocaust, virtually impossible to avoid during a visit to Auschwitz, turn Muslim-minority Germans into proxy repenting perpetrators. Middle Eastern/Muslim-background Germans at the same time hope to shock white Germans by showing them that they are willing to visit Auschwitz and take the responsibility of the massive crime on their shoulders.

Auschwitz as Shock Therapy

An organized trip to Auschwitz assumes that visitors will be transformed by standing physically in the space of horrific crimes because once there, they cannot possibly avoid its reality. Trips to Auschwitz evoke strong emotions. Some visitors become depressed; others feel empowered. When the visitors are Jewish, organizers do not expect them to be shocked by encountering a reality different from what they already know to have happened. By witnessing the suffering of their ancestors, Jewish participants expect and often experience a strengthening of their commitment to the Jewish community, an outcome common to most pilgrimages. After witnessing places of extreme suffering, they are expected to testify in witness-like fashion to others about the Holocaust.

An organized Muslim-minority German trip to Auschwitz, on the other hand, assumes invariably that visitors will be radically transformed through the shock the space will trigger. This expectation is related to the perception of the extraordinary power Auschwitz has in transforming those who encounter it, independent of the will of the individual. It also assumes that in order to be aligned with their fellow German citizens, Muslim minorities are in need of a treatment strong enough to bypass their commonplace beliefs. The shock produced by the encounter with Auschwitz is expected to transform not only their relationship to the Holocaust but their standing as human beings overall.

According to the American Psychiatric Association, shock therapy as electroconvulsive therapy is a treatment that involves passing small electric currents through the brain, triggering a seizure.[2] The intention is to cause a change in the brain chemistry and reverse the onset of certain mental health conditions, such as severe depression or mania. The negative associations and subsequent fascination with the treatment derive from the fact that when it was first invented in 1930, it was applied without anesthesia and with a high dose of electric current, often leading to loss of memory and other severe side effects. The Canadian activist and author Naomi Klein (2007) recently popularized the usage of the term outside of its medical context. In *The Shock Doctrine: The Rise of Disaster Capitalism* she argued that man-made crises have been used to force countries to adopt neoliberal market policies because the shocks kept citizens emotionally and physically stressed and prevented them from resisting.

The idea that visiting Auschwitz has the power to shock and transform individuals who cannot be rehabilitated in standard ways has not only been applied to Muslims. In 2009, the Polish prison system utilized a system where the most difficult convicts would visit Auschwitz as part of their rehabilitation program. As a newspaper article reported:

> "It's going to be shock therapy for them," said Major Luiza Salapa from the prison service, explaining that by learning in graphic detail about the horrors of the camp the convicts might move away from the criminal behavior that brought them to prison. "They'll learn that a terrible system was created through the acceptance of violence and oppression." Materials given to prison guards extol the visits saying that they should help "shape the prisoners' moral outlook toward the community and stop them displaying contempt and intolerance." (Day 2009).

Similarly, in 2018 the Chelsea Football Club offered its fans who had been accused of being antisemitic the opportunity to visit Auschwitz instead of being banned from Premier League matches (Press Association 2018). Or, in a more extreme case, Laurent Louis, a former Belgian MP who was convicted of Holocaust denial in 2015, was asked to visit Auschwitz annually and write about the experience in the blog where he had originally denied the Holocaust (Pettitt 2019). According to this view, there is something in Auschwitz that would transform even the most difficult of Polish convicts, antisemitic football fans, and established Holocaust deniers. And, perhaps, Muslims in Germany who might otherwise not be open to rehabilitation via the usual methods. A trip to Auschwitz is seen as the last chance for otherwise lost cases to embrace a moral stance on tolerance toward Jews and others.

Of all the surprising visitors to Auschwitz, Muslims, and more specifically Muslim Arabs, attract the most attention, even when they regularly visit Auschwitz. In 2019, thirty-two hundred people from Arab-majority countries visited Auschwitz, demonstrating that Arab visits to the former death camp are not an anomaly. When Raed Saleh, chairman of the Social Democratic Party's group in Berlin's senate parliament, visited Auschwitz in 2013, it made national and international news.[3] Similarly, when a group of Muslim leaders visited Auschwitz in January 2020, it was touted internationally as "ground-breaking."[4] Virtually every time the Muslims in Auschwitz and Muslim Youth projects have planned a trip to Auschwitz, a journalist has followed them, creating news about that particular "rare" and "surprising" occasion.

While some of the projects that take Muslim-minority members to the space where Nazi criminality reached its height in the industrialized murder factories of Auschwitz are designed to include them into the German national narrative through shock therapy, Muslim-minority participants who take part in these pilgrimages aim also to shock the German public by showing them that they are, contrary to popular German expectations, willing to go to Auschwitz. It is in this way that participants in these programs hope to reverse the assumptions the German public holds about them.

I visited Auschwitz, other Nazi concentration and death camps, and Holocaust memorial spaces in Germany with several Muslim and Muslim-background groups on seven different occasions. Here, I recount my observations of the months-long preparation for the trip, which focused on the intersecting histories of National Socialism, antisemitism, and the Israeli-Palestinian conflict for the fifth trip the Muslims in Auschwitz group made to Poland. My aim was to document and analyze the multifaceted reverberations generated by a visit to Auschwitz among a relatively small group of Turkish-, Arab-, and Kurdish-background youth from Duisburg. The group had a very strong sense of awareness of being seen by mainstream German society as lacking the capacity to empathize with the Jews. As a group, they worried that they might fail to develop the proper feelings of empathy, and they were also anxious about actually experiencing feelings of empathy. As they learned more about the victims of the Holocaust and visited the places where Jews were executed en masse, the youth constantly scanned their own feelings that bubbled up in response. Their own observations of their interior lives proved to be more critical, demanding, and full of doubts than the scrutiny they are subjected to by mainstream white German society.

Joining Up and Preparing for the Visit

Muslim-background youth of Duisburg have various reasons for joining the Muslims in Auschwitz project. While some are already enthusiastic members of the Heroes project and understand the Muslims in Auschwitz trip as yet another intensive group activity that furthers the goals of Heroes, other youth join after hearing about the project at school, thinking simply that a free youth trip to Poland might be fun, not fully aware of the project process and aims. I asked Apo, a Turkish-background high school student, why he had joined the project.

> I came here thinking it would be like a vacation, I have to admit: I thought it would be fun to travel to Poland with friends for free. I didn't think about what we would be doing here. Had I known how much training we would have to go through, I may not have joined up. But once I was here, I learned a lot. I understand now that Jews had no chance. They would either be killed immediately or be worked to death. There was nothing they could do to get out of it.

Kurdish-background Erol had a different orientation to the project. He told me that he had always had strongly positive feeling toward Jews and had always wanted to learn more about the Holocaust. Long before he joined the project, he taught himself how to read the Hebrew letters and learned as much about Judaism as he could. When he was offered the possibility of visiting Auschwitz, he was thrilled.

Orhan, who was visiting Auschwitz for the second time, first as a participant and then as a group leader during the trip I observed, told me that he suspected that Heroes thought he needed to come here for a second time because, for reasons not clear to him, he used to have animosity toward Jews. "I had no encounters with Jews. I had no personal experience. But I guess because of my socialization, I used to have this animosity." When I asked him what exactly his antisemitic ideas were, he said, "I used to think that all Jews are wealthy, that they own banks, that they are strange people. This project helped me understand that they are normal people, and that our religions have many similarities."

Depending on the amount of funds they are able to secure from multiple sources, the Muslims in Auschwitz project involves up to four months of preparation for the trip to Auschwitz. During the preparatory meetings, participants discuss their own family histories and learn about Germany's Nazi past, the logic of antisemitic propaganda as utilized by the Nazis and by Hamas today, and the nature of the Israeli-Palestinian conflict as viewed from within the victim/perpetrator framework. In an activity unique to this project, participants learn about the history of their own neighborhood during National Socialism. In my conversations with the young participants, they referred back to this activity often.

Rickie, an educator from a local museum, asked for the participants' addresses and located former Jewish residents who had lived closest to their homes. Participants told me how surprised they were to learn that had they not been killed during the Holocaust, they would have had Jewish neighbors, Jewish school friends, and Jewish bakeries to shop from on the way to school. Fatih and Mehmet, whom I introduced in the first chapter, gave me a tour of Marxloh from the perspective they had gained in the workshop. As we walked, we looked at the *Stolpersteine* (stumbling stones),[5] brass-plated stones that have been placed in the pavement outside the last known homes of the many victims of National Socialism, inscribed with names and life dates. We calculated how old the victims were when they were taken away. Mehmet showed me a wedding garment store he worked at and told me that this store used to be owned by a Jewish family and that they also sold clothes. Fatih told me how surprised he was when he learned that there used to be a Jewish family right next to their old apartment in Marxloh.

> Through the project we couldn't help thinking about what our life now would be like if the Jews were not murdered. We would live in the same apartment buildings, go to the same schools. They would be in our close friendship circles. We would play soccer with them and just hang out and be friends. We were really taken by this idea, and we felt sad to be deprived of this possibility.

Out of this activity, the idea of a friendship between two young Jewish and Muslim men was born and later became a theater play called *Benjamin and Muhammad.*

Arriving in Oświęcim

On July 12, 2017, I meet the group at Kraków Airport. To save on funds, they took a red-eye flight from Düsseldorf. They look energized but tired. Upon our arrival at the youth hostel in Oświęcim, we are greeted by two young Germans who will help us for the duration of our visit. Both women, affiliated with the Action Reconciliation Service for Peace (*Aktion Sühnezeichen Friedensdienste*), work as volunteers at the hostel for a year. The hostel's accommodations are basic but comfortable, with a lot of open space and separate meeting rooms for the various groups staying there to reflect in the evenings on what they have seen on their tour of the camps.

The youth are excited about having finally arrived at the location for which they have been preparing themselves for so long. They are also excited about being in a foreign country and in a big hostel full of young people like themselves. It takes them a while to decide who is staying with whom, and whether all the rooms are the same or not. The biggest excitement is the realization that there are plenty of nice outdoor tables where they can smoke the shishas they have carried with them with great care all the way from Duisburg, along with the pineapple, apples, and oranges they brought to add to their shisha concoction. Shortly after we put our luggage in our rooms, we are scheduled to join a tour of the Oświęcim Synagogue, which no longer has a community and now forms part of the Auschwitz Jewish Center.

As we walk to the synagogue, the youths' excitement is visible. There are giggles and lots of hugging and pushing each other around, probably the result of being abroad with friends, finally having arrived in Poland after months of preparation, a giddiness following a sleepless night, and for some of them, the anxiousness about entering a synagogue for the first time in their lives. As we are about to enter the building, two of the boys who are not part of the Heroes group but are taking part in Muslims in Auschwitz run to hide and then jump out in front of one of the boys to scare him. The boy, caught by surprise, lets out a scream. The two pranksters laugh out loud. The group leaders gently tell them to quiet down, and they comply.

At the door of the synagogue sits a big basket full of kippahs, and the group leaders tell them that men are supposed to cover their heads when entering a synagogue. All the Heroes reach into the basket without hesitation and place kippahs on their heads. The two pranksters are still looking restless and do not want to put on the kippahs. The group leaders tell them that they don't need to put on the kippahs, but that their heads need to be covered. One of the group leaders explains that he will put his sweatshirt hood up. The two youth decide to hang their sweatshirts over their heads in a distinctive way that attracts attention. They point out the donation boxes at the entrance and ask if we have to give money to the Jews. As soon as we sit down on the benches inside and are waiting for the German-speaking volunteer to talk to us about the history of the synagogue, one of the boys puts his head on the desk in front of him and closes his eyes, pretending to be asleep, perhaps in a gesture of denial about being in the synagogue.

The tour guide is a white Christian Austrian volunteer, most likely doing his community service. He tells us briefly about the history of the synagogue and about the basics of the rituals and ceremonies performed in a synagogue. When he performatively asks us whether there is anyone in the group who knows any Hebrew, Erol, raises his hand. His friends pull his hand down, saying, "No, you don't know Hebrew. You're confusing it with Arabic." Erol says assertively, "No, I learned the Hebrew letters. Doesn't that count?" His friends give him a look of surprise. When the tour guide shows them the shofar, the ram's horn trumpet used in certain Jewish ceremonies, and asks if anyone would like to try blowing it, a few boys volunteer. They say they have tried it before in football games. One of them is able to blow it loudly and really enjoys himself. Some of them take selfies with kippahs on, holding the shofar and smiling broadly.

On our way out, I ask the group leaders what they think about the commotion while entering the synagogue and if they are worried that the two boys will be resisting each and every aspect of the visit. They knowingly tell me that it's too early to worry and that they expect things may change over the next two days, especially when we visit the camp. Only then will we know their dispositions. They speak confidently from a decade of experience working with adolescent boys and having taken five groups to Auschwitz. Mehmet shares his opinion that most likely the two boys who made a scene are struggling inside. "Look at it from their perspective. For years they heard antisemitic things from people around them. These two are devout Muslims, so they feel anxious about being in a synagogue. At the same time, they chose to come on this trip. They participated in many of the preparatory meetings and had a number of opportunities to change their minds and drop out." Burak makes a thoughtful suggestion: it's possible the boys want to show us what people around them at home might be thinking about this trip, that they may be trying to make these voices and opinions visible here without completely buying into them.

As is often the case, I am impressed by the familiarity the group leaders have with each of the young people they work with, and their deep concern for their well-being. I am also convinced that much of the group leaders' confidence that the youths' uncomfortable attitudes toward Jews will be transformed and that they will learn to respect the memory of the victims of the Holocaust is due to the fact that we are in Auschwitz. That the two young men kept showing up for the project trainings and had come to Poland of their own free will is surely a good indication that they are ready to face the physical remainders of the brutal reality of the Holocaust. After so much preparatory training, it is unlikely that anyone could imagine the trip to Auschwitz would be anything like an ordinary fun-filled outing. The group leaders assume that walking though the camp will do something that months of training activities could not do for these two youth, who now seem wholly uncomfortable in their encounters with anything Jewish.

Unlike these two young people, the rest of the group expressed enthusiasm for what they hoped would be an emotional experience unlike anything they had ever felt before. Each of them shared that they were hoping to be able to relate to the Jewish victims of the Holocaust in a new way and, as one of the participants put it, "prove to themselves that we are not antisemites."

A Strong Desire for Strong Emotions

That night, after a shared dinner at the hostel, we have our first group meeting. The atmosphere is relaxed but also serious. We are sitting in a circle on chairs in the empty room that has been provided for us. The room is made especially to facilitate such group meetings, with indoor and outdoor space, including an outdoor fire pit for all-night discussions. Burak and Orhan ask the youth to think about why they are here in the first place. Orhan tells the group in a stern but not overly dramatic voice that this entire town is a graveyard where the ashes of people burned in the gas chambers were indiscriminately scattered. He asks all of us to keep this knowledge uppermost in our mind. After letting the boys sit silently for a brief moment, Orhan asks us to share our hopes, expectations, and worries about our visit to Auschwitz tomorrow. The youth are enthusiastic to talk about their emotions and the mood in the room is now energetic. It turns out that their biggest worry is not that they may be overwhelmed, but that they may not be moved enough. Many say that this will be a successful visit only if they are able to experience strong feelings in relation to the suffering of Jewish victims. Any lack of such feelings will indicate a personal lack of moral depth, and, worse, an underlying, persistent antisemitism.

Anxiety around not having sufficiently strong feelings and failing to be deeply moved by Auschwitz is not limited to Muslim-minority visitors who are under suspicion of lacking empathy for Jewish victims. Jackie Feldman (2008) notes that Israeli teenagers who participate in voyages to Poland also experience anxiety about not being able to have strong emotions while visiting Auschwitz. Judging from the statements recorded by Feldman, the cost to Israeli youth of not having had strong emotions is a sense of personal inadequacy and frustration in missing out on an important part of the experience and facing social exclusion from the communitas that has been formed through the pilgrimage experience (2–7). Feldman makes note of how a number of American Holocaust educators working at Auschwitz feel like visitors have gotten the right message if they shed tears (220). Compared to Israeli and American visitors, the cost to Muslim Germans of not experiencing strong feelings is much greater, as it can be seen as proof of their assumed lack of empathy and, worse, their lack of differentiation from the Nazis. Each of these potential outcomes is cause for concern for both individuals and the group. The group discussion that took place the night before the visit to Auschwitz provides a window onto their anxieties about their own emotional performance.

Erol: I'm worried that I may not be moved as much as I want to be. I really want to have strong feelings. I hope I have a chance to have strong feelings tomorrow.

Altan: I'm afraid of feeling tired tomorrow. I'm afraid of not being sufficiently moved due to exhaustion and possibly not being able to sleep well tonight.

Amed: I want to have a strong sense of empathy. I don't want to feel pity for the people. I want to empathize with what they experienced.

Barış: I hope no one tries to horse around tomorrow. Even if it's boring or difficult, I hope we all hold out.

In response to this outpouring of anxiety, the group leaders try to calm the youth down. But then their own anxieties begin to surface.

Orhan: Calmness and respect are all we need. No one has to cry. Everyone processes emotions differently. We're on a mass grave. Millions of people died here. It does something different to everyone. Some people cry, some people stay quiet. Don't judge yourself based on that.

Burak: We'll spend five hours on the first camp tomorrow. We'll pay attention to what we see. Sometimes feelings about it come later. And everyone experiences different feelings. Don't compare yourselves to others, either.

Rickie: I'm here for the first time. I know that a lot of the places are reconstructions. This knowledge makes me worried that I may not have strong feelings. What touched you the most, Orhan?

Orhan: Seeing that there were children here. And also seeing the toilets.

Rickie: Five hundred people from Duisburg were brought here.

Erol: Does it look like the concentration camp in Berlin? I wasn't moved at all when I saw that camp. I hope I'm moved here.

Orhan: I think there are very different atmospheres in camps in the summer and in the winter. Now the weather is beautiful, we have trees, the flowers are blooming. That sets up a different kind of mood. So remember that before evaluating your own emotions.

Barış: I think you shouldn't expect too much from yourself. Then you'll be forcing yourself, and it won't work.

Rickie: It might be very crowded. There are so many groups.

Amed: What if we get bored?

Barış looks seriously worried now.

Barış: I think everyone should just reflect on their feelings by themselves, without comparing themselves to others.

As they sit together in the circle, the group looks very serious, in anticipation of an important test the next day, a test in which the kind of emotions they display will reveal the kind of a person they are, and one where external conditions might inhibit their ability to develop strong feelings. The leaders and a few of the youth try to mitigate the group's anxiety by reminding everyone, including themselves, that is not a test and that being stressed about it will not help. A bit later, Metin introduces a new issue: he is worried that he might not be able to feel, as distinct from strong emotions, the expected emotions during their tour of the camp the next day.

Metin: I'm afraid of not being able to empathize. I have no personal connection to a Jewish person. What if this lack of connection prevents me from empathizing? This is my worry.

Amed: I think empathy is a personality trait. Not everyone is equipped with it. So it depends on what kind of a person you are.

Metin does not seem especially relieved by Amed's intervention.

Metin: I am afraid of not feeling for people. Until now, I've seen them only on TV or on the internet. I have met one Jewish person in my life—the one who came to meet us in Essen last month. What if I can't empathize with the victims? I believe that you can empathize with a person just because they're human, too. But what if I can't? I'm really worried about that.

As he goes on, Metin looks increasingly stressed. The fact that Metin rarely speaks makes his words seem louder than they actually are. A short silence falls in the room. We are all feeling Metin's anxiety. To help him delve deeper into his feelings, Erol asks a thoughtful question. Metin's answer reveals why it is exactly that he is so anxious.

Erol: OK. What do you think will happen if you can't feel empathy for them?

Metin: I'm afraid that it will be proof that I'm an antisemite. I'll be like the Nazis. They couldn't feel for the Jews, they didn't see them as humans, and that's how they were able to do all these things to them. Then I'll be just like them.

Amed: Did you feel like that in the synagogue? Did it feel so foreign to you?

Metin: No. I actually found it beautiful.

After his reply, Metin looks relaxed and starts smiling.

Metin: The synagogue didn't feel foreign at all. I saw a synagogue for the first time in my life, but it felt very familiar as soon as I stepped in.

Metin's close friends Erol and Amed start smiling and nodding as if to say, "See. We knew you could handle this! There's nothing for you to worry about!" Metin returns to his original reasoning, but this time around, he seems to have found his way out of it.

Metin: I think some people become antisemitic because they can't empathize with Jews. But maybe you're right, Amed . . . Maybe those people aren't able to empathize with anyone.

I have never heard Metin speak this long or this much. But this evening, he has more to share.

Metin: I'm also upset at our group's behavior in the synagogue. That was totally disrespectful. OK, there are no longer any Jews there and the guy was not a rabbi. And no one told us that we were misbehaving. Maybe some of us felt distant because we're not familiar with the writing on the walls. Maybe if our friends who acted up there had acted differently, we would have had the time to ask what the writing on the walls was. It is like entering an empty mosque that's no longer in use. I think we would not behave like that in a mosque that is no longer in use. Some of us could not feel for the Jews who used to congregate in this synagogue, and they acted disrespectfully. Maybe the Jews who once used it would not want us to be there. We entered without having a chance to ask them. And on top of that, we acted so rudely. I was really bothered by that behavior. I feel like because of what happened, we won't be able to meet any Jews anymore. And because of this, we can't ask them any questions, we can't learn from them. And as a result, we can't feel for them. And some of us end up acting rudely and inconsiderately. And this is very unfortunate.

While saying the last few sentences, Metin is looking at the floor. He appears pensive, as though facing an unfair situation he is unable to change. It is obvious that Metin already has a deep empathy for the Jewish victims of the Holocaust. I am struck by his sensitivity and his ability to think through whether Polish Jews who used to congregate in this synagogue a century ago would be bothered to have seen our group in their synagogue or not. Such a perspective displays a respect for the memory of the Jewish victims, because it places the self in their afterlife shoes, imagining how the departed Polish Jews would feel today from their place in the afterlife about the afterlife of their synagogue as a museum.

Yet despite his deep empathetic connection with the Jewish victims of the Holocaust in their afterlife, Metin is still worried that his empathy might not be able go deep enough, simply because, until meeting the Ukrainian-background representative of the Jewish Community Center in Essen who sat with the group for an hour and a half, he has never had the chance to meet Jews. Metin's fear-based beliefs are strong. He believes that he has been deprived of the opportunity to meet Jews, which is bad enough in itself, but even worse, this lack of opportunity and familiarity might make it difficult for him to empathize with the Jewish victims of the Holocaust, or so he fears. Worse still, this possible lack of empathy for Jews may make him similar to Nazis; they, too did not empathize with the Jews, albeit not out of lack of contact.

Later, as I reflected on the meeting, I am touched to have observed Metin work so hard to peer deeply and critically into his own heart and wonder if he might find any obstacles to his empathic experience. Equally touching was that his good friends noticed his struggle and that he was being unfairly harsh with himself. Amed's intervention—asking Metin how he had felt in the synagogue—was productive and most likely relied on having observed Metin's sincere engagement with the space in the synagogue. Having realized that he was in fact able to empathize despite having never been in a synagogue before, Metin visibly relaxed and a big smile lit up his previously troubled face. He also expressed his disappointment with the group members who acted disrespectfully in the synagogue and accused them of stripping the entire group of being able to deepen their experience of getting closer to the disappeared Jewish lives by learning more about the synagogue. The two youth who had been disruptive in the synagogue had their heads down and looked pensive. Soon after that moment, the meeting had ended.

Thanks to weekly Heroes meetings where they are asked to look deeply into themselves and reflect on their thoughts and feelings, the youth in Muslims in Auschwitz are extraordinary in their ability to express their emotions. The importance they place on their emotions fits Auschwitz well. During another trip to Auschwitz in which I participated, initiated by the Dortmund chapter of Muslim

Youth for Protestant, Catholic, and Jewish youth groups, the tour guides prepared the young people in quite a different manner. During that visit, there was no pre-tour encouragement to explore or discuss their emotions. Instead, the Polish guide who accompanied the group told us through the bus microphone as we were approaching Oświęcim that we should approach this as an "extreme sport." She told us that we should push ourselves to the limit in terms of the way we experienced what we saw. At the same time, she told us that we should also recognize our limits and stop when we realized that we had reached them. "If you feel you have reached your limits, you can always come back to the bus or approach one of the adults in the group and let them know that you are feeling overwhelmed." As one of the adults in the group, I was told separately that it was very important that I keep an eye on the youth, and that if I thought that any of the young people were overwhelmed or saw anyone crying, I should approach them with a packet of tissues they handed me. The leaders of the Protestant group, who had previously brought in a number of youth groups to the death camp, told me that it was important to talk about feelings in the moment, because they had observed some of the participants becoming depressed after the trip.

Although I was one of the adults who had been trusted with an unopened packet of tissues to hand out to overwhelmed young people, I proved to be unfit for this extreme sport of emotional overload. I fell apart shortly after we started the tour, began sobbing unconsolably, and used up the entire packet of tissues myself. One of the adult supervisors approached me as they had advised me to approach the youth, put her around me gently, asked if I needed another tissue, and whether I would like to go to the bus and take a break. I calmed down after a few minutes and was soon enough able to concentrate on my surroundings.[6] I don't know if the tour organizers evaluated me more positively or trusted me more after seeing me cry, but in interviews with Muslim-minority participants, I heard stories where tears shed for Jewish victims of the Holocaust garnered them new appreciation from authority figures. A young Turkish-background German woman told me about how her teachers' perspective of her changed dramatically when they witnessed her cry uncontrollably while watching a film about Anne Frank at school.

Selma was born in the late 1980s as the daughter of a Turkish-immigrant worker in southern Germany. When I met her, she was an MA student at a university in London. When I asked her what it was like learning about German history as a non-German, she quickly told me that from a young age, she had learned not to open her mouth on this topic. Her first interaction with Holocaust history in the seventh grade at the age of thirteen marked her for the rest of her student life.

> We were learning about the Holocaust for the first time. The teacher told us that six million Jews were killed in the Holocaust. When I heard that, I thought the number must have been bigger. I raised my hand and asked, "Did only six million Jews die?" The teacher became very angry at me and said, "What do you mean by *only* six?" I swear to God that I had no intention of belittling the number of murdered Jews. I didn't know much about the Holocaust, and I had thought the number was higher. After that incident, my teacher was not nice to me at all.

Selma explained to me how her teacher's attitude changed later in a way that was again puzzling to her.

> At the end of that year, the same teacher wanted to show us a film about Anne Frank. She took us to a darkened room in the basement and set up a projector. It was the first time I watched this film. I was so touched by it that I couldn't keep from crying and sobbing throughout the film. Although I was lost deep in my emotions, I suddenly felt someone looking at me. When I raised my eyes, I saw that from the corner of the room my teacher was looking at me and grinning. After the film, she came over to me and put her hand on my shoulder. After that incident she was very nice to me.

Both reactions left Selma puzzled. "Since then, I always remain quiet when the topic of the Holocaust and National Socialism is discussed. I'm afraid I might say something wrong and leave the wrong impression." Barely a teenager, Selma had already learned that her reactions had consequences and that she would always be held under scrutiny as to whether she related to the Holocaust in the right way.

Reflection Round after Visits to Auschwitz I and II

Although the original plan was to dedicate separate days to Auschwitz I and Auschwitz II, due to an organizational mishap we had to complete the two visits in one day, making the tour physically and emotionally exhausting for all of us.

We walked a lot, learned a lot about unspeakable brutalities and details of camp life, saw marks left by the prisoners, and viewed exhibits that gave us a glimpse of Jewish life in Europe prior to the Holocaust. At the end of the day, I was ready to retreat to my room, but the group wanted to have another reflection round to process what they had seen.

Orhan started the round by asking simply "what did you feel?", leaving out other possible questions such as "what have you learned?" or "what did you think?" The result was another intense two-hour discussion about feelings. Needless to say, the youth had strong feelings. Most were overwhelmed by what they had seen and learned. But most were also disappointed that they had not experienced a specific set of emotions, such as being shocked or crying.

Orhan: What did you feel?

Altan: I had more intense feelings at Auschwitz I. I felt like I was living there during that time. Auschwitz II didn't give me such strong feelings. I was very tired by the time we got there. I saw the gas chambers, but I couldn't feel them. Of course, having seen them gave me a new perspective.

Faruk: I of course had feelings, and I was shocked by a lot of what I saw. But I can't say that I was about to cry.

Orhan: Everyone has different feelings. We don't need to compare our feelings.

Erol: I can say that my expectations were met. I had a lot of feelings, but I wasn't immobilized by a feeling of shock, and I didn't cry. Seeing the shoes and the hair, the quantity was the most shocking thing for me. It made me take it much more seriously. I exited Auschwitz knowing much more compared to when I came here. It was different from what I expected. For example, I learned that they killed Jews from all of Europe. And there were people from Duisburg. That was especially touching.

Fatih: I didn't feel like crying. But I kept wondering how this could have happened! All that hair! And the smell of it. I can't find the right words to describe how I felt. The marks of the nail scratches in the gas chambers. Children in the camps. People squeezed in tiny rooms. It was a very emotional experience for me.

Amed: I also thought the first part was much more emotional. Everything there was very interesting. The second part was a bit boring. I'm disappointed that we didn't enter the gas chambers.

Erol: The guide gave us a lot of information, but it wasn't emotional enough. The music in the exhibits carried me to another level. I feel like I needed to spend an hour in every room by myself. And I think personal stories touch one more. I think the trip was not what I had in mind. Maybe I should have prepared myself better about what to expect.

Orhan: This is my second visit, so I was not as shocked as I was during the first visit. But still I noticed many things I had not noticed the first time. I didn't know that seven hundred to a thousand people stayed in one barrack. How can you fit so many people in one room?

Apo: Their beds and their toilets were awful. We couldn't see where they worked.

Davut: I learned so much. But I can't say that I was deeply moved.

Fatih: What really bothered me was that they took people from their peaceful lives and they brought them all the way here to kill them.

Davut: And when they were coming here, they didn't know what to expect. They made this complicated organization just to bring them all the way here and kill them. That is really gross.

Throughout the reflection round, the young people went back and forth between recounting how they had been moved by what they had seen and confessing disappointment that they had not cried or were not so shocked by what they had seen as to become immobilized. They noted how much new information they had acquired throughout the day, but it seemed that the real test was whether the intensity of their feelings had matched their expectations.

For most visitors to Auschwitz, it is hard to imagine oneself living through the radically inhumane conditions people were forced to endure there. When faced with the material remains of the Holocaust's most brutal experience, it is extremely difficult to ground oneself in human connection and feel what it would have been like to have made a week-long journey in an overcrowded cattle train alongside dead bodies, to have slept in overcrowded bunkbeds with diarrhea dripping down from the upper bunk, to have endured two-square-meter punishment rooms where four people would spend days in a standing position, to have been forced on pain of death to help the Nazis in the crematorium. While there in the camp, the experience produces more of a shock than a feeling of empathy where one puts oneself in the victims' shoes and feels at one with them.

While the material remains of camp life were effective in inducing the visceral shock that educators so often talked about, it was the family photographs from victims' lives before the Holocaust that engendered empathy in the Muslims in Auschwitz and Muslim groups with whom I visited the camp. Viewing these family photographs from before their internment, these young men felt an intense connection with the victims, likely because they were better able to picture themselves in the shoes of people leading regular lives. Looking at these images, the youth not only related to them as fellow individuals but also likened the victims' lives to their own.

Amed: I was really touched by the family photos at the end. That was really hard. One of the girls in the pictures looked like my sister. She could be my sister. She had a very charismatic smile. That really touched me, and I felt like crying. All those beautiful girls, handsome boys. Why did they have to be killed like this?

Amed was upset, head down, staring at the floor. There was a pensive silence in the room.

Metin: I was in shock the entire time I was there. People were made to work until they died. They killed children. I feel like I learned too much and kept being shocked. But you can see that the people who were killed there were human beings—you can see that from the pictures. They weren't just masses of victims; each was an individual human being. But they weren't treated as such. Who did all those masses of eyeglasses belong to? Those shoes? When I saw the pictures depicting life before the Holocaust, I could relate to them as individuals. I think I wouldn't be able to have these feelings without visiting Auschwitz and being able to put myself in their place. But in the end I don't think I was able to process and understand everything. It was too much for me.

Fatih: People were treated like bugs.

Metin: Maybe if they told us who each pair of glasses belonged to, it would be more difficult for us? Is that why they put them there in a big pile?

Unsurprisingly, the youth who were most worried about not being able to empathize with the victims were the ones who had the most intense feelings. Metin, having fretted beforehand that he might not be able to empathize because he did not know any Jews personally, was immensely moved and able to verbalize his strong feelings about relating to the victims at an individual level. Looking at a mountain of eyeglasses, he considered how each pair had once belonged to an individual and was upset that these individuals were not treated as people. Metin accomplished precisely what he had wished for himself the day before—to be able to relate to the victims as fellow humans. As he put it, he was able to put himself "in their place." Emotionally overwhelmed, he had reached a feeling of excess that others had wished for themselves and that some reported as being unable to achieve.

During our conversations the next day, Metin told me that he felt deeply moved when visiting the Auschwitz I photograph exhibit room. These small black-and-white photographs brought by the victims to the camp displayed them in their most meaningful moments of family life: families together at weddings, bar mitzvahs, and on vacation; couples posing with their children; children proudly starting school. Metin told me that he had a strong feeling of connection with those families.

> The people in those pictures looked just like me and my family. They were all quite integrated into German society. For most of them, you can't tell whether they're Jews or Germans. But they still have their different religions, traditions, and they have their distinct communities. I felt like they were exactly like me.

Metin paused a moment.

> I thought that if I had had the chance to meet them, I would have a lot to talk about with them. I felt like they would have understood me, and I would have understood them. And if they had not been killed, maybe I would be able to have them as friends. That made me very sad.

In both Oświęcim and Duisburg, Metin shared with me that he has difficulty making friends and feeling like he belongs in Germany. "I live here, but I feel like I don't belong here. I don't like the German language. I prefer to use Turkish or English. I feel like I can express myself better in English. I feel like the German language has too many rules, just like the country itself." He also complained to me repeatedly that he has a hard time finding people who think like him. Over the years, I have observed Metin as an introverted and sensitive young man who mostly stayed quiet in group discussions and spoke out only when he had something meaningful to say. He would voice his words quietly, without imposing himself on others. I would often find myself more impressed with what he had said while reading my notes. At the university, where he is a second-year information technology student, he told me that there is a great divide between Germans, many of whom he experiences as right-wing, and international students. He was able to connect with a small group of Indonesian students, and, so far, he is able to relate only to them. As we were chatting in Oświęcim, an unpleasant fight was taking place in his university cohort's WhatsApp group. Earlier that day, a couple of Russian students wrote texts in Russian to the whole group. German students who are known to him as right-wingers wrote angry responses like "Foreigners need to be kicked out of the school" and—pertinent, given the theme of our trip to Auschwitz—"We need to throw them out or burn them. Germany belongs to Germans." Especially in relation to his hostile university social environment, Metin longed for a diverse Germany where he would be able to have friends who were similar to him. The visit to Auschwitz and the Muslims in Auschwitz program reminded him that had German Jews not been murdered, he could have lived in a more diverse Germany and Duisburg.

At the end of the reflection session, Burak came back to the topic of empathy. Despite that they clearly had intense feelings for victims, the group were still disappointed that they did not feel enough. Much of this disappointment centered on the sense that they had not always been able to achieve the right kind of bodily disposition for displaying their empathy for the victims.

Burak: Yesterday we talked about our wishes and fears, and a lot of you talked about your wish for empathy. What do you think today?

Altan: I think we had empathy, but there was no room to really experience it. The guide was telling the story without emotions. We didn't have the space or the time to get emotional.

Erol: I also think we had empathy. We took what we learned very seriously. I'm confident that everyone in the group was moved. I was very moved by the piles of hair. Yesterday I was afraid of not being emotional. Today that sounds strange. Why should we be afraid of that?

Rickie: I felt like we didn't show enough respect. If I told you my grandmother was killed here, then you would be acting differently. No other group was as loud as we were.

If simultaneously feeling sad and performing sadness are de rigueur in public Holocaust memory discourse, such concurrence takes on an extra weight for Muslim minorities who stand accused of not showing enough empathy for the Jewish victims. But this was not the first time that tension concerning the right kind of behavior displayed by Muslim youth at the death camps surfaced in the project. Mathe, the German-background social worker at the Zitrone youth club in Duisburg, had earlier expressed disappointment that the youth would take selfies or squat when they were tired. On this trip, Rickie, the German-background museum worker from Duisburg who was one of the project contributors, expressed his disappointment about what he observed to be a lack of respect from the group. Comparing our group to other groups, he concluded that ours was the loudest: at the beginning of the tour that day, the young people had been full of energy, holding onto each other, at times jumping on top of or hitting one another—the kinds of homosocial acts of intimacy I have observed them engaging in regularly, whether in Duisburg or in other places. I assumed that, after months-long preparation, entering a place that produces fear and anxiety in them created a need to connect with and comfort each other. Although they were louder and more active than other groups, they were not disruptive or a nuisance to other people. Our group did, however, stand out as the only all-male youth group whose members looked both Middle Eastern and working-class. The other German speakers who joined our tour were older middle-class white Germans who all stayed together and a little apart from our group, albeit staring curiously at us. At one point, Hamit quietly approached and then jumped on the back of his friend, who let out a scream, the same kind of behavior they had engaged in while entering the synagogue the day before. The tour guide turned around with a frown and told us that this was a cemetery and we needed to show respect. The way she said it gave me the impression that she was annoyed, but that it was not the first time she had had to discipline a group of rumbunctious young people visiting Auschwitz.

When reflecting on their behavior, Erol took responsibility for Rickie's criticism and said, "It's true that we sometimes lost our concentration." But Orhan felt the need to defend the youth. "In terms of respect, I would say that it was bad for about half an hour. But overall, you all did well." Burak agreed: "Yes, let's not forget about the six and a half hours where you did really well!" Some of them defended themselves by saying that they needed to talk to each other not out of disrespect but because they were trying to process things.

Mehmet: It's true that we were constantly speaking among ourselves, and the tour guide told us several times to be quiet. But I feel like we had a lot to say.

Metin: I personally was really curious to hear what others were thinking, how they were processing it.

Behaviors that looked on the surface to be outward signs of a lack of empathy, concentration, or care stemmed in fact from a desire to deepen their understanding and experience of Auschwitz. A group of young Muslim-background German men who are also good friends may at times express their interests and experiences differently than a group of older white Germans who do not know each other, or even than a younger group who is there with authority figures such as their teachers. In addition, behavior that might be ignored if performed by white, German-background youth is quickly noticed and commented on when performed by a group of Muslim-background youth who are always under close scrutiny during Holocaust education.

Toward the end of the reflection session, Orhan furthered the conversation by asking the youth to write some adjectives about their experiences on the blackboard and then to explain what they meant by them. Everyone took turns walking up to the board quietly and writing: "worth seeing," "interested," "informative," "fascinating," "influential," "impulsive," "disturbing," "real," "unreal," "unworthy," "sad," "engrossing," "multisided," "scarry." Erol said that he had written the word "impulsive" on the board and explained why.

Erol: I'm really struggling to convince myself that what I saw is true. I can't get emotional. I kept deceiving myself that this is not true. And this gets in the way of experiencing strong feelings.

Mehmet said that he had written the words "disturbing," "unworthy," and "interested," and explored the development of his feelings over the last five years of his active involvement with Holocaust memory. He seemed to be of two minds about where emotions can lead us in relation to the "right way" of engaging with the Holocaust.

Mehmet: I feel like I want to learn more and more. I want to understand this thing that is not understandable. I'm disturbed by the fact that I can't know, understand, or explain what happened during the Holocaust. Over the last five years I've played the role of a Nazi officer. I saw a photograph of a dead baby with her head dangling. I was here on my eighteenth birthday, and looking that day at that photograph, I cried. Today I know more. I'm not only a bundle of emotions the way I was that day. As heroes, we want to help people approach events with their emotions. Today, I felt like the emotional part was not sufficient. Everything was concentrated into one day. I will think more about what I saw today. Some of my thinking must be postponed for later.

Orhan: Do you think you're especially moved because you acted the part of the Nazi officer?

Mehmet: I will never forget about antisemitism and war. In our theater performances, I say out loud to the audience that I am against war and antisemitism. And for this I feel proud of myself. I'm able to look at antisemitism differently from people around me.

Most likely all visitors who come to Auschwitz with a strong intention to learn from it and a wish to be transformed leave the site feeling overwhelmed and confused. Particularly notable about this trip—organized by members of the Muslim minority, who see themselves as heroes who are ready to face things others will not and who also regularly perform on stage the kinds of transformations they believe themselves to be going through—is that the stakes are higher. While this group is unique in their commitment to embracing human rights and fighting against antisemitism, other Muslim-minority groups in Germany who engage with the Holocaust do it both to transform themselves and to demonstrate their self-transformation to mainstream German society in the hopes that they, too, can be accepted into the moral fold of postwar German identity.

Recognizing Themselves as Germans

During my interviews with earlier participants of the Muslims in Auschwitz trip, I heard again and again that one of their most transformative experiences was to recognize themselves as Germans in a way they had never done before. Indeed, recognizing themselves as Germans is not an unintended consequence, but is rather the project's starting point. Feeling themselves to be unapologetically German is an important part of the Heroes project, and although the Muslims in Auschwitz project is technically distinct from the regular Heroes programming, it is very much connected in terms of the way the project is imagined. Despite most of the group members having thought at length about the ways in which they are Germans, the moments in which they have felt or almost felt like white ethnic Germans have surprised them and at times left them confused.

For many participants of Muslims in Auschwitz, if we do not count their trips to their grandparents' or great-grandparents' countries of origin, their trip to Poland is the first time they have been outside of Germany. A number of participants told me that their main motivation for joining was the opportunity to take a free trip to Poland with friends. When their schools had organized school trips to other European cities, their families either had no means with which to send them or did not prioritize these trips in their budgets. This was a point Mehmet made, both in his interviews with me and to audiences who came to watch their theater project: there was usually no one who looked like him on any of the school trips, definitely not in school trips to Auschwitz. Whereas family trips to Turkey, Lebanon, or Iraq made them think about the complicated ties they have with these countries as part of the diaspora in Germany, the trip to Poland made them aware that for the first time in their lives they were being perceived not as Turks, Arabs, or Kurds but as Germans.

Part of this experience is the sensation of finding oneself suddenly a German as soon as one is outside of Germany. Staying at a youth hostel reminded Mehmet of the time he first felt himself to be a German: it was during a Europe-wide youth camp that had nothing to do with Holocaust education. Mehmet was eighteen years old at the time. Because he had come from Germany, he was given the nickname of Mercedes, after the prestigious German luxury car. Although this had happened four years before he told me the story, he giggled joyfully and repeated the name "Mercedes" a few times. He had loved being named after a Mercedes, but shortly after, he wondered whether because of this nickname he was "seen as being responsible for the Nazi crimes as well." He wondered whether the youth in the camp would ask him about World War II and was relieved when they did not. Having the feeling of being German in Poland, the first country to be invaded and occupied by Nazi Germany, and in Auschwitz, where being a German is not about being a Mercedes but is about the Third Reich and its crimes, adds multiple layers of complexity to their perception of themselves as Germans. During a Holocaust education journey, is it then any wonder that the youth reflected on their relationship as Germans with the Polish people?

Like Mehmet, Mehmet Can, a Turkish-background history teacher who also works as a Holocaust educator, told me that for him, being German was very much connected to the Holocaust. When I asked him how he had come to be interested in the history of National Socialism and why he had become a Holocaust educator, he said that it was mainly to impress a teacher he liked in school. He told me that he doesn't remember the Holocaust or even Jews being a topic of interest for him until he was in his last year of high school. At that time, he had a history teacher who was very interested in the Holocaust. Wanting to impress her, Mehmet Can looked for a way to demonstrate his knowledge on the topic. When she took a group of students to Auschwitz, he couldn't go because his family didn't have the money. He said that the group was all-white, made up of children from middle-class German families. He realized then that he stood apart from them. To show the teacher and the German students who had gone to Auschwitz that he was as German as they were, Mehmet Can set about studying the Holocaust and chose it as a topic for his final *Abitur* exams.

Turning into Germans becomes visually salient at the moment when visitors to Auschwitz are given color-coded stickers to mark the language in which their tour will be given. In a coincidence so ironic that it makes one wonder if the color was intentionally chosen by the Polish Auschwitz museum employees, yellow stickers, reminiscent of the yellow stars that Jews had to wear during the Third Reich, mark the German-speaking visitors. Although the youth did not reflect on the color of their stickers, being given stickers that marked them as Germans was a powerful experience for them, coming as it did at a moment when their emotions were already heightened by standing at the gates of the camp. During their reflection round that evening after the tour, they discussed their experiences of being marked as German speakers and thus treated as Germans by the Poles.

Mehmet: I don't know if you noticed, but we were all given yellow stickers at Auschwitz. It showed that we are Germans. British people had green stickers, Polish violet. We got yellow. I felt like others who were in the same group with us [all white Germans] were looking at our stickers and our faces. They didn't associate the stickers with us. We didn't look like Germans to them. I'm happy that we're here and can show that to Germans. We, too, have yellow stickers, and we deserve our stickers.

Here, Mehmet reveals that he was moved not only by the fact that the groups had been given German-language stickers and had thus been recognized as Germans, but, more importantly for him, by the fact that white Germans had witnessed it. The middle-aged, middle-class white Germans did stare at our group for a long time and seemed to comment among themselves while staring at us, but they didn't say anything directly to us. On the recommendation of our tour guide, we quickly put on our headphones and got busy figuring out which channel we needed to tune in to hear her. As it turned out, Mehmet would have other chances to make white Germans in Auschwitz face the fact that he was there and that he "deserved" his yellow sticker.

Unlike Mehmet, who reflected on his relationship to other white Germans as a fellow yellow-sticker wearer, Erol reflected on what the sticker did to him in relation to our Polish tour guide, whom he treated as the descendant of the Polish victims of Nazi Germans during World War II. In that interaction, Erol felt connected to the former German perpetrators who were facing their former victims. He found it moving that the Polish tour guide took the time to describe to them what "we" as Germans had done to them.

Erol: I thought about the Polish people who work here and who talk to us Germans about what happened here. Germans really oppressed them, but they still tell us what we did here.

Burak: They welcome us here, don't they?

Amed: Don't you think they treat everyone the same?

Erol: I feel like they're extra nice to us. They explain everything to us in German. Just think about it.

Burak: Do you think they treat us differently because we come from Germany?

The group: No.

Erol: I mean that they're being extra nice by treating us like everyone else.

Studies of organized Israeli and North American Jewish youth trips to Auschwitz note the minimal contact between the youth and the Polish locals (Feldman 2008). Feldman describes how the Israeli Ministry of Education tours do not allow the Polish guides to provide spoken guidance to their youth groups and asks them instead to stay silent. This is part of a larger calculated effort to prevent contact with contemporary Poland. The trip is treated as a journey in time where Poland has remained a land of death. Others note that this is the case for other non-youth North American Jewish tours as well. Lehrer (2013) notes that this treatment of Poland as a land frozen in time does not apply to "quest" visits where Polish-background Jews in diaspora come back individually to get in touch with their roots through contact with contemporary Polish society.

The Muslim youth trips to Auschwitz I observed are closer to "missions," in the sense that they are organized, educationally prefaced, and have the primary aim of witnessing the death camp. However, they differ from the Israeli and North American Jewish youth tours in one significant way: the Muslims visitors don't consider Poland to be a source of antisemitism. For them, Germany and Germanness is the unquestionable source of Nazi terror; the Polish role in the mass murder doesn't factor into that history hardly at all for them. Muslim-minority German visitors don't code Poland as a land of perpetrators and antisemites, but as a nation that was invaded, occupied, and victimized by the Germans, suffering enormous human and material loss.

This perception of Poles as the victims of Germans often became complicated by the fact that during these visits, Muslim youth, especially headscarf-wearing young Muslim women, are commonly harassed by local Poles. While the Muslims in Auschwitz group I took part in did not have any bad experiences with the locals, I heard that other groups had been harassed by the locals. In another trip to Auschwitz, organized by the Where Was G.d in Auschwitz group, I witnessed headscarf-wearing Muslim women walking to town from the youth hostel being harassed by a local man. Behaving as though he was either drunk or mentally ill, the older man called the women in headscarves, of all things, "Jews." Because this was not the first time they had experienced racist harassment, the women told me that they had avoided interaction with the man, lowered their gaze, and walked as quickly as possible back to the hostel. In an incident that made international news in 2017, a group of Muslim girls from Berlin were spat upon by local Poles and even threatened with a knife during a study trip organized by the Wannsee Conference House, a prominent Holocaust memorial and education organization. The students claimed that while reporting the incidents to the police, the officer only grinned and would not help them. Ironically, the youth were there to learn about the victimization of Poles by the Nazis.

If encountering Poles drove these Muslim youth to relate to their German identity in complex ways, their encounters with Israeli youth groups were more contentious and emotionally charged. On none of my research trips to Auschwitz did the Muslim groups encounter an Israeli group. But in my interviews with earlier Muslims in Auschwitz trip participants, I learned that such encounters left a big impression and stirred up unexpected emotions.

Feldman's (2008) ethnography of Israeli youth trips to Auschwitz demonstrates that while the primary aim of the trip to Poland was to catalyze the internal transformation of Israeli youth about to start their military service, the trip was also staged for an imaginary audience of Poles. The youth wear Israeli-flag T-shirts and carry Israeli flags both for their own purposes as a group and so that they will be visible to their local Polish audience. Feldman notes that many group leaders and organizers assume that the young Israelis will be perceived as "an extension of pre-War murdered Jews, and that the Pole on the street feels a sense of guilt and complicity in the murder of the six million Jews" (Feldman 2008, 75). Feldman notes that some of the Israeli teenagers hoped for the opportunity to pick a fight with the Polish youth, who they perceive as the antisemitic descendants of the Nazis' willing helpers.

The Muslim youth in my groups did not bear any visible markers of their multiple identities as Germans, Arabs, Turks, or Kurds. But they did look different from most of the white European-background visitors to the camp, with their darker, typically Middle Eastern phenotypes and their male-only group composition. Participants of earlier Muslims in Auschwitz trips related two encounters with Israelis there. In one instance, two of the youth walked up to the Israeli group and introduced themselves, telling the group leader that they were Turks and Arabs from Germany. While the narrative did not give me a clear indication of what the Israelis made of their presence there, letting the Israelis know that they were visiting Auschwitz as both Muslims and Germans was clearly important to the Duisburg group. In the presence of the Israelis, even their languages became suspect as sources of antisemitism. As one of the participants told me, "We didn't want to speak German with each other because we felt embarrassed. When I wanted to speak in Arabic to my friends, I noticed the Israeli groups, and I didn't want to do that either. I felt like I represented the two worst enemies of the Jewish people. I didn't know what to do. So I just kept quiet."

The next day, our group was scheduled to attend a witness narrative organized by the youth hostels. A central part of any organized Auschwitz tour is a meeting with a witness who experienced the horrors of the Third Reich firsthand. The audience consisted of more than a hundred visitors, mostly middle-aged, middle-class white Germans who had also come to Auschwitz in organized groups. The witness was a Polish physicist born in 1926 who had been part of the Polish resistance. He was arrested and sent to the camp in 1944 at the age of eighteen, shortly before the end of the war. Most likely his young age and the relatively short time he spent in the camp led to his survival. He recounted his experiences in the Polish resistance: how he had been caught, and how he had survived in the camp.

Before the meeting, Rickie, who the day before had been upset with the behavior of the youth in the camp, was worried that they might not be respectful enough. He had warned them how important it was for them to listen to the witness quietly. Contrary to Rickie's expectations, the youth sat patiently, even though it was not always easy to follow the long and winding narrative of this elderly Polish man speaking in German with a thick accent. Observing them there in the audience and during the reflection round afterward gave me the impression that coming face-to-face with a witness was not one of the more impressive things they experienced during the trip. They didn't mention the Polish witness in any of their discussions or my interactions with them. I imagine this has partly to do with the fact that the survivor was Polish and not Jewish. When the Jewish representative of the Duisburg Jewish community came to meet the group, the youngsters were visibly excited, and they returned to the experience of meeting a Jewish person over and over again, even though he had not discussed his own family relationship to the Holocaust. The youth were not very interested in listening to what the Polish witness had to say, in "witnessing the witness." They were, however, extremely excited about giving the German audience a chance to witness their witnessing in Auschwitz. When the question-and-answer time came, some of the youth were animated and wanted to speak for and represent the Muslim youth in their engagement with German history.

As soon as the witness's narrative came to a close, the first hand to jump in the air was Mehmet. He walked confidently onto the stage at a calculated pace, took hold of the microphone, waited for a few seconds for the audience to recognize that he was there, and told them that his name was Mehmet and he was part of a group from Duisburg, Germany. I immediately recognized Mehmet's actor self on stage. He told the audience that he was about to ask a question that was of particular importance to his group. His looks, his accent, the fact that he was from Duisburg, and, most noticeably, his name marked him as a member of the working-class Muslim minority in Germany. Even before he declared who he and our group were, the German participants in the room were staring in our direction. Looking both at the witness and at the audience, Mehmet asked, "What was the role of religion for you in your survival in the camp? Did you ever think about killing yourself?" His question highlighted the fact that he was not asking the question for himself, but for his group: he was underlining the fact that their difference there at Auschwitz and in the audience was marked by religion. The witness answered that he felt strongly about God, that his belief did not diminish in the camp, but that he had contemplated killing himself by refusing to eat. Even after he changed his mind, eating was difficult for him. The second question was posed by a white German woman, who asked what the man thinks now about Germans. I have heard various versions of this question asked in many such meetings where German audiences encounter Jewish or non-Jewish survivors of the Nazi atrocities. On other occasions, I have heard audience members ask whether the victim has forgiven the German people. The Polish witness on stage that day offered a half-answer to this question, saying that in Poland they had been subjected to the propaganda that only the West Germans were bad, and the East Germans were the good Germans. He had traveled to East Germany, he said, and Polish relations with West Germany had improved since Willy Brandt, the West German chancellor from 1969 to 1974, and his rapprochement with the Eastern Bloc.

After the witness had gone, a few white German women came up to our group and asked us who we were. Mehmet and Fatih proudly explained that they were with Heroes, a group that works for gender equality and against the oppression of women in the name of honor, and that they were now doing a project called Muslims in Auschwitz where they learn how to face history. With a truly impressed look on her face, one of the women said, "It's really amazing that you're here doing this work at a time when *our* young people are no longer interested in these issues. Keep going!" She walked away with a broad smile on her face.

After the session, I walked up to Mehmet and asked him whether he had wanted to know if religion had helped the Polish survivor, or if he had really wanted to show off the fact that we were there. Looking happy with himself, he said, "Of course what I wanted was to show people that we are here, that we are listening to [the testimony of] a witness, that we are engaging with him." Mehmet had managed to shift part of the spectacle away from the witness and toward them. He had made the German audience witness their witnessing of the Holocaust as Muslims in Auschwitz.

Scholars of trauma survivor testimony concur that witnessing can occur only once the survivors themselves bear witness. Primo Levi ([1947] 1991) maintained that Holocaust survivors speak on behalf of the real victims—those who did not survive. Shoshana Felman and Dori Laub (1992), on the other hand, argue that because the Holocaust was so unbearably and incomprehensibly traumatic, the only way it can be witnessed is for the survivor to give their testimony of their own trauma experience to another, an impossible but necessary act. No matter in whose name they speak, this presence of another, of an audience, is necessary to witnessing. Without a witness, there is no witnessing. "To testify: from *testis* (witness) and *fie* (make). The act of testifying, then, constitutes the making of the witness. Much as the witness produces testimony, testimony produces the witness" (Horowitz 1992, 51). Listening to a victim's testimony transforms listeners into secondary witnesses who have a different relationship to the traumatic event. Esther Jilovsky (2017) argues that it is this fundamental difference in the experience of secondary witnesses, their lack of presence at the originary event, that leads second- and third-generation Holocaust victims to journey to Holocaust memory sites.

The Muslims in Auschwitz participants' engagements with the Polish camp survivor demonstrate that the experiences of secondary witnesses are not homogenous. Although the Muslim youth were listening to the same survivor testimony, sitting in the same room as their white German counterparts, their transformation into secondary witnesses proceeded differently. To become legible as secondary witnesses, they themselves needed to testify to a white German audience. It is for this reason that Mehmet felt the need to walk onto the stage, say out loud that his name was Mehmet, which is one version of the Prophet Muhammad's name, and they were from Duisburg. He needed to show the white Germans in the audience that they were there. In so doing, he turned the white Germans in the audience into witnesses to his and his friends' witnessing of the Auschwitz survivor. Mehmet and other Heroes participants utilize every opportunity to display their efforts in shouldering the burden of German history and their work for gender equality. They talk to journalists and researchers, use social media aggressively by posting updates on their activities, and create online, print, and live content about fighting antisemitism and sexism within Muslim contexts. They hope to shock the German public with their engagements, change their mindset, and teach them to accept Muslim heroes into the moral compass of the German identity.

Muslims in Auschwitz in a Night Club

The Muslims in Auschwitz trip was planned for four days. After one day of observing Jewish life in Oświęcim and two days touring the camps at Auschwitz, the final day was reserved as a time for relaxing and reminiscing in Kraków before making their way home to Duisburg. At that point, I had the mistaken sense that their Holocaust education was over, but the good sense to realize that although the participants appeared to like me, having a middle-aged woman whom they deferentially referred to as "older sister" continue to observe them, notebook in hand, would limit their ability to relax in a foreign city with their friends. As the group was heading toward Kraków with a sense of accomplishment on their faces, I headed back to London.

The next day, I received a WhatsApp text from Burak. "Esra. You will not believe what happened! On our last night in Kraków, the two conservative Turkish guys were kissing Polish girls in the night club! I think this is a major success!" When I read this message, I was frankly taken aback. After all we had experienced and discussed together, I could do little more in the face of what seemed to be a quick sloughing off of our Auschwitz experience than struggle to stay in the present moment and feel joyful. The youth whom I thought to have felt emotions about our Auschwitz trip even stronger than my own had evidently spent their last night dancing and making out with girls they just met in a club.

The next time I saw Burak in Duisburg, I asked him how going to a night club in Kraków fit into the Holocaust education program. He told me that it is important for the youth to relax after the heavy emotional labor they perform there. And more importantly, he added, their hard emotional work was clearly paying off as the two youth who had not done the Heroes program and who had identified themselves as virgins during our conversations were finally breaking free of their religious conservatism. The Muslims in Auschwitz program understands religious conservatism as one of the primary sources of antisemitism. That they were drinking and making out with Christian Polish girls was a sign for Burak that they were finally taking their first steps into the German understanding of democracy, a democracy assumed to entail both religious and sexual liberation. I told Burak that my hunch is that these conservative youth will consider the night as an exciting adventure experienced outside the bounds of their regular moral universe and will most likely not transform that moral universe's approach to gender roles and sexuality. Burak agreed with me that the events at the night club might very well not have a long-lasting effect on their lives. He also reported that the two youths had never returned to the youth center, but that he had run into one of them on the street. Because the young man had complained to him that his parents were trying to convince him to marry a girl he was not interested in, Burak remained convinced that the shock this boy had experienced in Auschwitz may have at least partly liberated him from some of the antisemitic and gender-oppressive values held by his family and community.

Public Reactions to Muslims in Auschwitz

I was far from being the first outsider to have recorded the Muslims in Auschwitz trips to Poland. Each of the earlier trips was monitored and studied by someone: a journalist, a researcher, a documentary filmmaker. The organizers themselves even made their own films. In 2018, the sixth trip of Muslims in Auschwitz was covered in the highly regarded national weekly newspaper *Die Zeit*. The reporter focused the piece on one of the Turkish-background participants and called it "Berat Goes to Auschwitz" (Schrader 2018). The article was framed in terms of the shock therapy model and attempted to demonstrate how a simple-minded, working-class immigrant youth with less than honorable views on Jews was almost completely transformed by his trip to Auschwitz. At the end of his trip and the piece, Berat not only understood how much the Jews had suffered during the Holocaust but also how everything now was so much better because "Germany is a democratic country."

The article starts out by marking Berat as working-class and immigrant. Berat smells of aftershave, wears Adilette slides and the same pair of shorts two days in a row. He sports a silver chain, and on his arm a silver bracelet upon which his name and that of his ex-girlfriend are engraved. Berat smokes the shisha, talks a lot, is loud. His body, his language, the way he smells, his gear, and the way he expresses his emotions—all this sets him apart from the middle-class ethnic Germans for whom the democratic postwar national memory culture was established.

The piece documents what the journalist sees as Berat's transformation from an underclass immigrant to a German with democratic sensibilities in Auschwitz. At a key moment in the journalist's story arc, the youth pause outside the Auschwitz prisoner barracks, fresh from the shock of having viewing the exhibition of mountains of suitcases, cups, bowls, shoes, hairbrushes, eyeglasses inside. They are silently angry, an apparent invisible transformation happening inside them:

> Berat sits down on the steps of the bare brick building and says, eyes narrowed, "Brother, I was so angry when I saw that. I wanted to scream. I wanted to smash the glass." You can't see his anger. You don't see anything here. They sit and are silent. It's no longer about Zidane's dismissal as Real's coach, as before, when they sat eating pizza under the geraniums in the Oświęcim market square. Now no one raps out a line, the way they did the previous evening at the hostel. No one jostles or fools around.

Apparently, words fail them:

> Tim says, "This is so awful," and Berat answers, "Yes brother."

We hear from the journalist that, after a night's sleep, Berat suddenly has had his first complicated thought:

> "I had the feeling in the camp that my two identities intersected: on the one hand, I am German, and as a German I would have been the perpetrator, I would have shaved the head of the woman in the camp." But then he imagined that as a Turkish woman his mother might have been a prisoner; how she would have undressed and how he would have had to cut off her hair. "That made me angry." He raises his arms to sort out his thoughts. "In any case, I won't be making any more jokes about the Holocaust, although I suspect that from time to time I might say 'You Jew.' I won't say 'I'm going to burn you like the Jews in the gas chamber.' Because to have seen it was just awful." And if his friends say such things, he will scold them.

At the end of the narrative, the desired transformation is complete. After a brief visit to Auschwitz Berat is able to reflect on the way German history is depicted and how the past plays a role in making Germany even better than other nations today. According to the journalist, Berat has even begun to use the pronoun "we" when referring to German history for the first time.

> Berat says he sees a rift in German history: Germany is now a democracy. In Germany people are cool and fun. The old Germany is not today's Germany. But history will always belong to Germany, he says. "That's why Germany cannot say we are not taking in refugees; because we are the reason the Jews fled." He says it that way, as a matter of course. But for the first time, he uses a "we" for "Germany."

And so the journalist's narrative arc is complete: after touring the death camp and claiming German history as his own, Berat finally arrives in contemporary Germany and the "we" of German society.

I talked to Berat a few days after this feature article was published. He was proud to have been the center of the story in *Die Zeit*, a weekly he does not read. He repeated to me some of the things written in the piece. In our conversation about the trip to Auschwitz itself, what came out heavily was the fear he experienced there, something not covered in the *Die Zeit* piece. He told me that while at Auschwitz, he worried whether Turks had also died there and that he felt like he or his own parents could have been victims. At the same time he felt fear, he also experienced guilt. "I feel guilty because I'm a German . . . I'm not guilty as a Turk. Because Turks didn't do anything. But I'm guilty as a German and also as a human being." Then he added, "But the most important thing is that something like this does not happen again." His approach to the crime was both particular and universal, and the poignant sense of empathy was reaching out both to the victims and to the repentant perpetrators.

The newspaper story was superficial and turned Berat into a caricature but had a happy ending. Confronted with the reality of the Holocaust at Auschwitz, Berat learned how bad it is to make jokes about Jews, how far Germany has come since 1945, and what a democratic place Germany is now. He also learned to take responsibility for German history. Despite this happy ending, none of the online comments on the article expressed enthusiasm about Berat's integration into German Holocaust memory discourse. Instead, most commenters expressed irritation that the journalist had suggested that Berat had "no connection to the Holocaust" or Auschwitz in his family, implying that as a Turkish-background German, he bore less responsibility for it than did ethnic Germans.

The article had begun by asking a question of its assumed white German readers:

> Berat is a young German who has no relationship to the Holocaust. No grandfather who was in the army [*Wehrmacht*], no great uncle who was an SS officer. He is a German who has nothing to do with Auschwitz. Or does he?

The piece generated an intense discussion among the readers of the newspaper, with two hundred and ninety-eight readers writing up to five-hundred-word comments and readers responding to each other's comments in long nested threads. Although the unique names commentators choose on the *Die Zeit* website make it difficult to determine their ethnic background, the content of the comments make it clear that most of the commentators are well-educated white Germans. Some indicated that they or their children are half German. A handful of users who choose names such as Kanaka or Kielbasam wrote messages whose content gave the strong impression that they were immigrant-background Germans.

As from the first comments, readers reacted quite angrily at the statement that Berat had nothing to do with the Holocaust, complaining that it implied that as ethnic Germans they did have something to do with it, at least more to do with it than Berat. Over and over again, readers[7] declared that they were no more guilty of the Holocaust than Berat. "I'm also German and I have nothing to do with the Holocaust. It happened fifty years before I was born." Or, "If someone like me has ancestors who were part of the cruel regime, then they have a connection to the Holocaust and the features person 'Berat' doesn't? What nonsense! What can I do about my ancestors?" were most common.

Some readers reacted strongly against Berat's statement that if he had lived in Germany at that time, then as a German, he would also be a perpetrator. Here Berat was trying to identify with the perpetrator position and shoulder the burden of German history himself, as he was encouraged to do throughout the Muslims in Auschwitz education program. Many readers took this statement as an unfair and even outrageous accusation against all Germans during the Third Reich. They reminded him of how many Germans were also victims of the Nazi regime and thus could not be considered perpetrators. One reader in this opinion wrote: "It's actually not that simple. Even as a German, you could be a victim."

A number of readers approached the issue from the other side of the equation and disputed the innocence attributed to Berat in relation to the Holocaust.

They listed other crimes Berat might be genealogically implicated in, crimes such as the Armenian Genocide and some listed the Holocaust itself. Berat was just as guilty as they were, they argued: "Even as a foreigner you could be a perpetrator . . . Since we have a Turkish-born young man in front of us, he could also deal with the Armenians if he is interested in the participation of his biological ancestors." Other commentators point out that Berat was not innocent because he belongs to a nation that once helped the Third Reich.

Some chimed in with the argument that the danger of repetition of the past comes not from the Germans but from the Muslim minority, so now they are the potential perpetrators against Jews.

The article also prompted a large number of readers to express their desire to feel responsible for the Holocaust, but many emphasized that they would like to do so as citizens of the world and as their own personal choice, not as Germans who bear a special burden. They were claiming their right to the same kind of innocence as that accorded to Berat, their right to be appreciated for voluntarily shouldering responsibility for the Holocaust. I quote this reader's comment extensively, as the passionately written comment resonates with simultaneous desires to own and yet share, even offload, the guilt for the Holocaust.

> Namonym (comment #1.27): A big problem from the beginning was that the Germans were seen as the sole culprits. This released all countries (or the bulk of their populations) from all responsibility for the long term. But Germans, too, are just human, like any other person from any other country. Since we are all the same, and we all could have been guilty, we have a responsibility to ensure that this matter does not disappear into oblivion and potentially burden us with a "future guilt" (e.g., a repetition).
>
> This does not change anything retrospectively in relation to the "main guilt" of the Germans, who caused all this in part unknowingly, but it imposes the "future guilt" on all people the world over.
>
> Furthermore, I see guilt here in those countries that have placed all responsibility for this future guilt on the Germans. They have contributed significantly to the fact that only the Germans engage in this cult of remembrance, and [in so doing] they impose the potential for "future guilt" on the great mass of mankind.
>
> The same likely applies to the [Ottoman Turkish] Armenian Genocide.

By placing quotation marks around the phrase "main guilt," Namonym leaves the reader with a question about who the other guilty parties in the Holocaust might be and whether Germans are even mainly to blame. The second half of the sentence establishes that Germans "contributed" to an unnamed "all this" only "in part" and "unknowingly" and hence did not really carry out the mass crimes that constitute the Holocaust. No one should place too much blame on the shoulders of Germans for the parts of the crime they committed unknowingly, because Germans are only humans, and any human could have been guilty of such a crime. Hence, in Namonym's associative logic, which generalizes from the part to the whole, all humans are responsible for what happened, not just Germans. Despite this relative innocence of Germany, Namonym reasons, other nations have continued to unfairly accuse Germany of being the main culprit and have placed the burden of the cult of remembrance solely on its shoulders, charging them alone with a future guilt.

With the last sentence, Namonym makes sure not to extend the innocence he proposes for Germany to other peoples. Where Germans should be relieved of their guilt, Turks—and in the context of the article, Turkish Germans like Berat—should be required to carry the burden of their own past genocides. No mention is made of Germans feeling responsible as human beings for the Armenian Genocide. The newspaper article should have arrived at a different judgment, Namonym implies: Berat should be seen as guilty—partly for the Holocaust, as a human being, and completely for the Armenian Genocide, as a Turk. Germans, on the other hand, may feel responsible for the Holocaust if they choose, but only as human beings, not as Germans.

The comments written in the center-left-leaning, well-established weekly demonstrate that the official line about accepting full responsibility for the Holocaust is not embraced in its entirety, even by *Die Zeit's* educated, center-left-leaning readers. None of the commentators minded that the German Muslim minority wanted to learn about the Holocaust, but they were all quite sensitive to what such a non-German connection with public Holocaust memory discourse might mean for their own relationship as Germans to the past. Differing from the official ideology of German responsibility, the commenters longed to be as innocent of the Holocaust as any other world citizen.

Transforming Muslims in Auschwitz Transforms German Society

Auschwitz-Birkenau has been a powerful site of pilgrimage since its liberation at the end of World War II. Visitors from around the world come to this site of horror to see firsthand the disturbing remnants of unimaginable evil. So much power has been attributed to the place that many hope the act of stepping onto the site itself will cure dedicated Holocaust deniers, committed antisemites, and obstinate criminals whose crimes have nothing to do with what happened in Auschwitz. Projects such as Muslims in Auschwitz take Middle Eastern/Muslim-background German youth to this major crime site with the hopes that they will be fundamentally transformed in their disposition and learn to embrace post-war German civil values such as tolerance, empathy, and democracy.

The expectation of being transformed and of having a strong emotional reaction is so high that many visitors, but especially suspect visitors such as Muslim minority youth, feel anxious beforehand about not having the right kind of emotional reaction while there at the camp—not feeling empathetic enough, not being moved enough, not being able to cry. In all the organized tours to Auschwitz and Nazi camps in Germany that I participated in, Muslim-background youth came out of the sites having had very strong emotions and deep intersubjective connections with the Jewish victims. They reported having had the strongest feelings when they identified with the victims and likened them to their own family members, their own status as religious minorities, and their own feeling of being German but not accepted as German. Engaging with the Holocaust made them reflect on being German, but it did not always lead them to identify with the white German majority position.

Participants in the Muslims in Auschwitz project join the project not only to transform themselves through their encounter with the Holocaust. They also hope to demonstrate their engagement with the Holocaust to white Germans; they hope that white Germans, too, will be shocked and transformed when they see how readily and intensely minorities engage with the German past and learn its moral lessons. If we can take the readers' comments from *Die Zeit* on the Muslims in Auschwitz project as indicative of a strong response that resonates with a larger, well-educated, center-left-leaning German society, then it is clear that the Muslim minority is welcome to visit the German past and shoulder its burdens as long as they lighten the burden placed on German shoulders by spreading the guilt and admitting that they, too, are guilty of antisemitism and that their ancestors, too, collaborated with the Nazis. But this does not necessarily mean that they will be taken as full Germans and that differences in ethnic background will be forgotten.

CONCLUSION

Can Muslims Flip the Script of the German Memory Theater?

As I write this book, the strong sense of commitment to Holocaust memory that I found so impressive when I arrived in Germany in the early 2000s is being systematically chipped away by the far right. Alternative für Deutschland (AfD), a new right-wing populist political party represented in the Bundestag since 2013, explicitly calls for a change in German memory culture, which they believe focuses too much on the Nazis and does not take into consideration the positive aspects of German history (Alternative für Deutschland 2016). Alexander Gauland, one of the co-founders of AfD, dismissed Hitler and the Nazis as mere "bird shit" in the passage of over a thousand years of successful German history (Wiederwald 2018). Arguing that Germany needs to reclaim its history, he told a group of supporters, "If the French are rightly proud of their emperor, and the British of Nelson and Churchill, we have the right to be proud of the achievements of the German soldiers in two world wars" (Reuters in Berlin 2017). Bjorn Hoecke, the leader of the far-right faction of the AfD, called for a "one-hundred-and-eighty-degree change in German memory culture" that would focus history education on German achievements and the embrace of German victimhood during World War II (Höcke 2017). At the same event, Jens Maier, now a member of the Bundestag for the AfD, also gave a speech calling for an end to the "cult of guilt" (Ringelstein 2017).

The story I tell in this book, that of subcontracting the guilt of the Holocaust and antisemitism to Muslim-background immigrants, is a more subtle but more pervasively powerful way of chipping away at the official German postwar Holocaust narrative. During the seventy-fifth anniversary of the Holocaust, held on

January 23, 2020, Friedrich Merz, a candidate to fill the leadership position for the ruling Germany party Christian Democratic Union (CDU), was unapologetic in pointing his finger at Arab and Muslim refugees who had arrived in Germany in 2015 as importers of antisemitism into Germany. On Holocaust Commemoration Day, he tweeted, "75 years after liberation of #Auschwitz we experience again #Anti-Semitism—mostly from the right, but also due to immigration from 2015/16. Many bring hatred of Jews with them, which is preached in their home countries. There should be no tolerance for that either" (Merz 2020). His tweet suggested that right-wing antisemitism was not being tolerated in Germany, but Middle Eastern antisemitism was. Phillip Amthor from the CDU took Merz's position a step further by pointing his finger not only at the recent wave of refugees but at all Muslims as being responsible for antisemitism, stating that disciplining them was the most important task facing the country:

> One must not forget that anti-Semitism is particularly represented in Muslim cultures . . . Of course there are many concerns for the Jewish population in the context of the migration of recent years. And I can understand that too. German society rightly expects immigrants to adhere to our culture. Then it also means that anti-Semitism has no place with us. (n-tv 2020).

The trends of externalizing antisemitism from Germany and subcontracting the guilt as well as the responsibility for the Holocaust have expanded exponentially since I completed my field research in 2019 (Dekel and Ozyurek, forthcoming). Since then, not only have Arab- and Turkish-background Germans been accused of being antisemites or of promoting antisemitic sentiment, but also Jewish-background Germans and non-Germans, as well as white left-liberal Germans, a significant number of them women. These speakers have been denounced uniformly because they do not adhere to the exceptionalist rules of Holocaust memory. Their fault is that they compare the Holocaust to other genocides and do not espouse antisemitism as inherently distinct from other forms of racism.

Offloading the accusation of antisemitism and hence subcontracting the guilt of the Holocaust onto minority groups, outsiders, and women, both in Germany and worldwide, serves to fetter the extremely important and necessary discussion of antisemitism and racism precisely at a time when both are on the rise in Germany and in the world more broadly. This coincidence of accusations and political trends signals that the targeting of liberal and left-leaning intellectuals and institutions has become an important feature of the ritualized memory of National Socialism in Germany. In Germany, it is primarily well-educated white Christian Germans and a small number of Jews who are granted the right to frame the discussion or to appear on its fringes as critics. According to German Jewish sociologist Y. Michal Bodemann (1990), remembering the Holocaust is a topos of "ideological labor" for contemporary Germans that serves to reflect the benevolence and civility of the majority Christian society. Discussions about antisemitism in Germany are therefore always about the making of the majority society, and it is not a coincidence that minorities are excluded from it. As I have attempted to show in this book, in the last two decades minorities who have been excluded from remembering the Holocaust came to play a central role in how to remember National Socialism and hence both define and challenge the boundaries of what constitutes German society.

Muslim Minority Flips the Script in the German Memory Theater

Y. Michal Bodemann (1996b) developed the concept *Gedachtnistheater* to describe both the performative nature of collective acts of national commemoration and the Jewish role in staging the collective German memory in such national commemorations. Bodemann argues that the Jewish presence in postwar Germany fulfills the specific moral purpose of normalizing and redeeming Germany, and, as a result, lightening the Germans' burden of guilt and shame for the Holocaust. In the German "memory theater," Jews are given the role of witnessing white Germans as they come to terms with the past and redeem their guilt. Such a role is designed not to help Jews heal their traumas but rather to meet the needs of the majority German society in dealing with guilt and shame.

In his recent popular books, German Jewish poet, public intellectual, and political scientist Max Czollek (2018, 2020a, 2020b) builds on Bodemann's concept and contends that non-Jewish non-Germans also have set roles in the same memory theater that serve the needs of the majority German society. They can either function as "good" immigrants who assimilate and hence mark the superiority of German values or as "bad" immigrants who serve as Others who mark the limits of German/European society. Scholars of immigration have long noted that the German integration paradigm is such that only white Christian middle-class Germans may determine who has (properly) integrated and who has not (Terkessidis 2017), and that this process involves "migrantizing"—turning into migrants people who have been living in Germany for generations (El-Tayeb 2016).

Given the connected (Adelson 2000) but asymmetrical roles assigned to Jews and Muslims in the German national memory theater, German Jews may have some power to slightly unsettle the script by "dis-integrating themselves," as Czolleck (2018) suggests through acts of disidentification (Muñoz 1999) and identification with the Other through queering (El-Tayeb 2016), or Kanakization.[1] When we look at the kind of agency Muslims can employ in the national theater, the path Czolleck suggests for Jews is not available to the migrantized Muslims of Germany. The Muslim youth I met in the working-class neighborhoods of postindustrial Duisburg can unsettle the memory theater not by dis-integrating but rather by inserting themselves into the German memory theater as actors, and then by "flipping the script."

"Flipping the script" is a strategic practice, first named in African American subculture. In *Scripting Addiction*, anthropologist Summerson Carr explains this practice in the context of a drug and alcohol addiction program that homeless Black American addicts are required to attend to gain access to housing, food, and custody of their children. Clients perform the narrative they believe therapists want to hear. By convincing the therapists that they are on the path to recovery, drug users are able to access the resources they need in order to succeed and ultimately change, or "flip," their life trajectories. According to Carr, to understand how flipping the script works, we must conceive of scripts as texts whose "animator," the person who is voicing the script, is not its author (Goffman 1981). Goffman suggests that viewed in this light, it would be wrong to interpret the speech produced by the animator as either true or false; rather, it can only be evaluated as more or less successful, faithful, or believable (Carr 2011, 192). Carr also suggests that script flippers are adept at reading "contextualization cues," the communicative indexes that "let people know what is going on in any given situation and how they are expected to proceed" (193).

Cultural sociologist Jeffrey Alexander (2004) also argues that "cultural performance is the social process by which actors, individually or in concert, display for others the meaning of their social situation" (529). For him, the success of the performance does not lie in the fact that the actors adhere to meaning structures they display, but that they make others believe in them. "In order for their display to be effective, actors must offer a plausible performance, one that leads those to whom their actions and gestures are directed to accept their motives and explanations as a reasonable account" (529). Alexander argues that in order to understand cultural performances we can liken them to theater. Like the successful clients in the addiction program Carr studied, and the cultural actors Alexander discusses, the Turkish- and Arab-background youth I focus on here are highly adept at rendering the Holocaust memory script, or more precisely the script normally given to the white German role in the *Gedachtnistheater.* What is important is that they act it out in a successful, faithful, and believable way both because they have figured out how German memory culture works and because they do genuinely believe in the efficacy and transformative power of this culture. The Turkish- and Arab-background youth who perform the memory script of the repenting perpetrator in the way it was meant to be for white Germans are thus able to situate themselves within the fold of the German society and gain access to previously unavailable resources, including social recognition, access to funding for their youth work projects, and possibly a better social trajectory. The more faithfully their performance reproduces the white Christian German Holocaust memory discourse script, the more they are recognized and accepted into the mainstream German society narrative, and the easier it is for them to feel part of and act in ways that are acceptable to that society. More importantly, the more they are taken for granted in performing this script, the more they are able to flip it—that is, overturn it—as their seamless performance demonstrates that this transformative script is no longer only for white Christian background Germans but also for racialized and migrantized group members like themselves.

Recently there have been other, completely different immigrant engagements that outperform and by doing so challenge the public Holocaust memory discourse. On February 15, 2021, Afghan-background Mostahari Hilal and Indian-background Sinthujan Varatharajah engaged in the Instagram conversation "Capital and Racism, People with Nazi Germany." In their conversation the artists talked about how people with Nazi background still benefit financially from this background. The video started a public debate about the term Nazi background—*Nazihintergrund.* In an interview they gave to weekly *Die Zeit,*[2] Sinthujan commented:

> [The concept] is a reversal of the term "people with migration background." We use it to mark that part of society that otherwise and completely naturally marks others. The interest in where people come from—which actually expresses an interest in what they are, who they are and how they go where they are now—is often one-sided. We want to swap these roles and do an ethnographic analysis. The starting point of "people with Nazi-background" is not a purely geographical question, but a historical, economic, and ideological one that has to be located in the history of this country.

When asked about why they felt the need to talk about the subject, considering they are children of refugees, Moshtari responded by asking why they should not.

> We live in this country, its present affects us and it can only be understood by looking at history. In our conversation, however, we are also concerned with how this past is expressed not only ideologically but also materially, which capital relationships can be traced back to the present and how they also shape spaces in which we as artists move today. This critical examination is not new; it was mainly carried out by Jewish activists and artists. We therefore take up many aspects again and ask what that means for us.

In that sense, what Sinthujan and Moshtari do here is similar to what Muslims in Auschwitz does in that they take German history and National Socialism very seriously and as a personal matter. Both groups look closely into their lives to see if they have also residually benefitted from Nazi crimes. Sinthujan brings up the question of whether some of the goods they had at home as refugee families were leftovers from Jewish victims. Or they think about how art can come to terms with material gains from the Holocaust. This genuine critical engagement with the Nazi past, when done so seriously, authentically, and faithfully, opens space for talking about German society as a whole and a unique opportunity to legitimately critique it.

Looking at immigrant integration into Holocaust memory through metaphors of *Gedachtnistheater* and flipping the script work especially well, because role-plays and theater performances are central to Holocaust memory and antisemitism prevention projects designed for Muslims. Because the programs are Muslim-only, participants have no choice but to literally act out both the

Jewish and German roles—meaning victim and perpetrator—of these scripts themselves, finding occasional places to add Muslim/Arab roles as perpetrators. The original postwar social contract and the national theater that depicts it has not considered them. Muslim actors who write and act out these scripts sincerely hope that they will be able to flip the script and start a new social contract both for themselves and for the nation by flawlessly performing guilt, repentance, and responsibility. They are well aware that their part in the contract is partial and conditional with rules that are harsher for them than for white Germans. Nevertheless, they are determined to keep learning and thinking through National Socialism as a way to open up a genuine space for them to better understand how racism works and provide them with the strong motivation to stand against it. Whether or not this faithful act of remembering the Holocaust and genuine empathy with its Jewish victims will end in giving them onstage roles in the national German theater—and whether changing the actors will end in changing nationally the script itself—only time will tell.

NOTES

Preface and Acknowledgments

1. These experiences form the background of Marc David Baer's (2020) book, *German, Jew, Muslim, Gay: The Life and Times of Hugo Marcus.*

Introduction

1. As an example of this exclusionary German approach to Holocaust memory discourse, a common homework assignment at school on the topic of World War II asks students to talk with their grandparents about their memories of the war, effectively leaving at least a quarter of today's German schoolchildren out of this central nation-making narrative (Gün 2010).

2. Among the most extreme examples are a German woman, born in 1946, who claims that she is the reincarnation of a young Jewish man killed by the Nazis (Illig-Mooncie 2014), and Ernst Mueller, who falsely presented himself as a Jew and an Auschwitz survivor (Bodemann 2013).

3. The phrase "gifted child" was later popularized by German psychologist Alice Miller, who refers to children "gifted" with abuse and trauma and has a monocausal analysis of "the roots of violence" and "poisonous pedagogy" (a term she borrowed from Katharana Rutschky's 1977 book, *Schwarze Pedagogik*) in *For Your Own Good: Hidden Cruelty in Child-Rearing and the Roots of Violence* [1980] (1983). There, she explains the violence of Hitler and serial killer Jürgen Bartsch, the self-destructive drug addiction of Christiane F. and suppressed suffering of Sylvia Plath, the compliance of "good Germans" with Nazism and German terrorists in the 1960s and 1970s—all through an object relations take on childhood trauma inflicted by "poisonous pedagogy." While developing her ideas, Miller relied in part on the American psychologist Walter Langer's *The Mind of Adolf Hitler* in 1972, based on the 1944 report submitted to the US Office of Strategic Services. The book argues that Hitler's development as a leader was primarily due to the trauma of his strict and abusive upbringing.

4. For a critique of the *Sonderweg* theory in German historiography, which contended that Germany took a different path toward capitalism and democracy than the rest of Europe, see Blackbourn and Eley (1984).

5. In a different context, Peter van der Veer (2006) argues that in the Netherlands, the Dutch see Muslims as carrying the past selves the Dutch have long left behind—for example, erstwhile Dutch who adhered to strict morals—into the present. One can extend this discussion to include political morals developed after the Holocaust, which is framed in the Netherlands as tolerance culture.

6. Tiffany Florvil (2001) talks about how Black poets in Germany, such as May Ayim and Aurde Lorder, also engaged with the memory of the Holocaust in the 1990s and established links between antisemitism and anti-Black racism.

7. https://de.rt.com/inland/118667-cdu-politiker-keine-einbuergerung-bei-antisemitismus/.

8. For a detailed discussion of Muhammad Amin al-Hussaini's engagement with the Nazis, see Motadel (2014).

Chapter 1

1. All names of participants have been changed to ensure anonymity, except in a case such as Burak Yılmaz, whose public statements I have quoted.

2. I use the term "heroes" in the way that organizers and participants use it: referring both to the Heroes program (capitalized) and to the program's graduates, who aspire to act as heroes (lowercased) in their communities. See the Heroes website: https://www.heroes-net.de/.

3. Patricia Ehrkamp (2006), who did research in Marxloh at the end of the 1990s, notes that even at that time, Turkish and German identities were highly polarized in the neighborhood. The ethnic German residents accused Turkish-background residents of resisting integration into German society by holding fast to their language and their honor codes. The Turkish-background residents accused Germans of never approaching them or interacting with them. Her research revealed the acceptance and at times outright embrace by many Turkish-background residents of Marxloh of this representation of them as determinedly separate in German public discourse. They were proud to be different and questioned the Turkish identity loyalty of those who took German passports or dressed like Germans, dismissing them as *eingedeutscht* (Germanized) (1687).

4. Ahmed Mansour and Cem Özdemir also co-founded the "Initiative Säkulare Muslime" (Secular Muslims Initiative) ahead of a recent iteration of the German Muslim Conference in 2018. Abdel-Samad, Seyran Ates, and Necla Kelek were also part of this; http://www.euro-islam.info/2018/11/27/former-german-green-party-chairman-co-founds-initiative-secular-muslims-together-anti-islam-pundits/.

5. For a full listing of Mansour's awards, see his online CV at https://ahmad-mansour.de/#cv.

6. A curious detail that appears in both books is the shame with which Arabs

regard masturbation. This piece of information is presented first in *The Arab Mind*, based on a single 1954 survey of a small sample of Arab and American college students (Patai [1976] 2002, 144). Mansour repeats the claim without citing any evidence.

7. For how Alevi Muslims, an oppressed minority in Turkey, compete with Sunni Muslims for the role of the good Muslim, see Özyürek 2009.

8. https://www.heroes-net.de/presse/preise-f%C3%BCr-heroes.html.

9. See the Heroes program description here: https://www.heroes-net.de/heroes.html.

10. http://dref.de/en/research/student-numbers-in-germany/.

Chapter 2

1. This number puts Germany ahead of more than half of the other nations in the European Union. See Anti-Defamation League 2014. For a discussion of different studies whose findings were similar, see Bundesministerium des Innern 2011, 54–58.

2. http://archive.adl.org/anti_semitism/conference_vienna.html (accessed 24 September 2015).

3. Other scholars, including Brian Klug (2004) and Paul Silverstein (2008), have been critical of this discourse and pointed out the politically motivated aspects of this alarmism.

4. http://archive.adl.org/anti_semitism/conference_vienna.html (accessed 24 September 2015).

5. Ibid.

6. Ibid.

7. http://archive.adl.org/durban/durban_ngo.html (accessed 24 September 2015).

8. The conference, which ran an extra day, produced a compromise resolution written by the European and Arab states and facilitated by South Africa; it did not include anti-Israel language; http://archive.adl.org/durban/durban_ngo.html (accessed 24 September 2015).

9. https://www.osce.org/files/f/documents/b/2/37239.pdf.

10. Ibid.

11. www.european-forum-on-anti-Semitism.org/taskforce-education-on-anti-Semitism/overview/?fontsize=0%2Fcontact.php (accessed 24 September 2015).

12. *Entimon* is from the Greek, meaning "dignity" or "respect."

13. kiga-berlin.org/index.php?page=ueber-uns&hlsen_US (accessed 24 September 2015).

14. Amira-berlin.de/Aktuelles/35.html (accessed 24 September 2015). Both organizations develop model projects. They implement them a few times before

they publish their models. Staff from both groups complained that it was difficult to continually develop new models, especially when those they had previously developed had not become a permanent part of the curriculum—programs were tried out but not retained. People who work in the field explained to me that this was one of the difficulties facing multicultural education in Germany.

15. The predecessor to this program, called Entimon, operated from 2001 to 2006 with a yearly budget of 15 million euros and the motto, "Together against Violence and Right-Extremism." The shift in the focus of the program from "right-extremism," meaning eastern Germans, to one that includes migrants, meaning Muslims, is visible in the 2007 program. Beginning on January 1, 2011, this program was replaced by a parallel one with the same goals called *Toleranz Fördern—Kompetenz Stärken* (Promoting Tolerance—Boosting Competence) (Bundesprogram 2007).

16. Ibid.

17. Ibid.

18. https://global100.adl.org/map.

19. Although it has roots in the nineteenth century, Turkish-Islamic Synthesis is an ideology that became prominent after the 1980 military coup in Turkey, promoted by the junta to unite the nation against leftist ideologies (see Cetinkaya 1999; Toprak 1990).

20. For a fascinating account of artistic and political engagements of Palestinians with Germans and Israelis in Berlin, see Atshan and Galore 2020.

Chapter 3

1. See also Can et al. (2013), who write about these education programs.

2. The first German philosopher to engage with the concept of *Einfühlung* was the eighteenth-century Romantic Johann Gottfried Herder, who explored the connection between feeling and knowing (Edwards 2013). German philosopher Robert Vischer popularized the term in 1873 in his dissertation in the field of aesthetics and advanced the notion that, taken literally, the term denotes "feeling into" an art object (Vischer et al. 1993, 89–123). Yet a third German philosopher, Theodor Lipps (1903), introduced the concept to the field of psychology as the basic capacity to understand others as minded creatures. The word "empathy" appeared in the English language for the first time in 1909 in the United States, when Cornell University psychologist Edward Titchner translated the German word into English, defining it as Lipps had used it. The German-born American anthropologist Franz Boas relied on the concept of *Einfühlung* as developed by Herder to describe the basis of the anthropological method of ethnography (Edwards 2013; Bunzl 2004).

3. Douglas Hollan and Jason Throop (2008) also note that there is confusion

about the moral and social significance of the terms "sympathy" and "empathy" (386).

4. Other scholars have explored how hope has been seen as necessary for the reproduction of capitalism (Narotzky and Besnier 2014), political reform (Sukarieh 2012), and the development of management (Papazu 2016), and how hope is unevenly distributed in society (Hage 2003).

5. For a thorough review of phenomenological approaches in anthropology, see Desjarlais and Throop 2011.

6. Studies have demonstrated that different societies act on different assumptions about the accessibility of other minds. Joel Robbins and Alan Rumsey (2008) co-edited a special issue of *Anthropological Quarterly* dedicated to the widespread belief in the Pacific that it is extremely difficult to know other people's minds, which they termed "the doctrine of the opacity of other minds."

7. Nazmiye's perspective is similar to the perspectives of dozens of other women who took part in the project, whose experiences are documented in great detail by Michael Rothberg and Yasemin Yıldız (2011).

8. Established in 1994, Muslim Youth in Germany promotes a Muslim youth culture based on German identity and Islamic principles. For a long time, it was included on the watch list of the government agency responsible for protecting the constitution. It was only recently taken off the list.

9. Memory scholar Irit Dekel, who wrote about emotional performances in this memorial, argues that feelings of being lost and of sadness are most commonly displayed by white Germans (Dekel 2014, 74).

10. See Primo Levi's description of this figure (Levi 1959, 103).

11. See http://www.yadvashem.org/odot_pdf/Microsoft%20Word%20-%206474.pdf.

12. Irit Dekel (2014, 76) also notes that at the memorial to the Jewish victims of the Holocaust in Berlin, German students speak less about the Holocaust but are nevertheless expected to be, and to display being, touched by the memorial experience.

13. Those imprisoned in concentration or labor camps during the Third Reich for behaviors that did not conform to strict social norms were deemed "asocial" and their clothing was marked with a black triangle. This group included beggars and the homeless, alcoholics and addicts, prostitutes, pacifists, the nomadic Roma and Sinti peoples, and those with psychiatric disorders and intellectual disabilities.

Chapter 4

1. The British Mandate for Palestine was established in 1920 at the end of World War I when British military rule over parts of the defeated Ottoman

Empire was replaced by British colonial civil rule. The mandate formally came to an end in 1948 in the middle of the 1947–49 Israeli War for Independence / Palestinian Naqba following three years of Arab revolt, four years of Jewish insurgency, and implementation of the United Nations Partition Plan for Palestine.

2. Al-Quds Day is a day of protest against Israel's occupation of Jerusalem (*al-Quds* in Arabic), begun in 1979 by the Islamic Republic of Iran ostensibly as a counter to the Israeli holiday of Jerusalem Day, a day commemorating the capture of the Old City of Jerusalem during the Six-Day War in 1967. In recent years, Al-Quds Day protests have been staged in various cities and countries.

3. Ahmad Mansour is referring to Arab Jews who were pressured to leave their countries after the establishment of Israel in 1948. For critical analyses of how these people are defined as refugees, see Arkin 2018 and Zamkanei 2016.

4. How Hitler took inspiration from Kemal Ataturk along with Mussolini has been discussed by Stefan Ihrig (2014) in his book *Ataturk in the Nazi Imagination*. He argues that Hitler tried to imitate the way Ataturk radically remade a nation from the ashes of the Ottoman Empire.

5. https://taz.de/Streit-unter-Leipzigs-Antideutschen/!5517963/.

Chapter 5

1. According to the program website, "Since its inception in 1988, more than 260,000 alumni from 52 countries have marched down the same 3-kilometer path leading from Auschwitz to Birkenau on Holocaust Remembrance Day . . . as a tribute to all victims of the Holocaust." https://www.motl.org/about/.

2. https://www.psychiatry.org/patients-families/ect.

3. https://www.dw.com/en/muslim-world-leaders-visit-auschwitz-in-strong-signal-of-interfaith-support/a-52034131.

4. https://www.pbs.org/newshour/world/islamic-leaders-make-groundbreaking-visit-to-auschwitz.

5. Berlin artist Gunter Demnig has placed more than 75,000 *Stolpersteine* in commemoration of victims of National Socialism in over 1,200 cities and towns across Europe. See the project website: http://www.stolpersteine.eu/.

6. I do not think that being the first person in the group to burst into tears had anything to do with my political or personal views. I am easily brought to tears. I am an easy target for "tearjerker" films, even when I know the scenario does not make sense, and although I am a determined antinationalist, I get goose bumps when I hear a national anthem.

7. All online comments cited here are from Schrader (2018). Comments are cited by their username and comment number throughout.

Conclusion

1. Kanak is a slur used in Germany to denote people from the Middle East. The word is also used in a self-affirmative way.

2. https://www.zeit.de/zett/politik/2021-03/ns-familiengeschichte-instagram-diskussion-nazihintergrund-moshtari-hilal-sinthujan-varatharajah.

REFERENCES

Abdel-Samad, H. 2016 [2014]. *Islamic Fascism*. New York: Prometheus Books.

AfD Potsdam. 2017. Berlin: Erste Schwulen-Moschee eröffnet | Jouwatch. Posted June 16. www.facebook.com/afdpotsdam/posts/seyran-ates-vision-einer-liberalen-moschee-in-der-alle-muslime-gemeinsam-beten-k/1955453924480781/.

Adelson, Leslie. 2000. "Touching Tales of Turks, Germans, and Jews: Cultural Alterity, Historical Narrative, and Literary Riddles for the 1990s." *New German Critique* 80: 93–124.

Achcar, Gilbert. 2010. *Arabs and the Holocaust: The Arab-Israeli War of Narratives*. London: Saqi Books.

Adorno, Theodor W. 2005. "Education after Auschwitz." In *Critical Models: Interventions and Catchwords*, 191–204. New York: Columbia University Press.

Adorno, Theodor W., Else Frenkel-Brunswik, Daniel J. Levinson, and R. Nevitt Sanford. 1950. *The Authoritarian Personality*. New York: Harper and Row.

Agamben, Giorgio. 2002. *Remnants of Auschwitz: The Witness and the Archive*. Translated by Daniel Heller-Roazen. New York: Zone Books.

Akkad, Dania. 2022. "Is Germany Paying for the Surveillance of Palestinians and Their Supporters?" Middle East Eye, April 26. https://www.middleeasteye.net/news/germany-palestine-supporters-surveillance-paying-case-answer.

Alexander, Jeffrey. 2004. "Cultural Pragmatics: Social Performance between Ritual and Strategy." *Sociological Theory* 22(4): 527–73.

Allouche-Benayoun, J., and G. Jikeli. 2013. "Introduction." In *Perceptions of the Holocaust in Europe and Muslim Communities*, edited by G. Jikeli and J. Allaouche-Benayoun, 1–12. Dordrecht, Neth.: Springer.

Alternative für Deutschland. 2016. *Programm für Deutschland: Das Grundsatzprogramm der Alternative für Deutschland*. Stuttgart, June 27. https://www.afd.de/wp-content/uploads/sites/111/2017/01/2016-06-27_afd-grundsatzprogramm_web-version.pdf.

Amira—Anti-Semitismus im Kontext von Migration und Rassismus. 2009. "Anti-Semitismus in der Türkei: Hintergrunde-Informationen-Materialien."

Berlin. https://www.vielfalt-mediathek.de/material/antisemitismus-in-der-tuerkei-hintergruende-informationen-materialien.

Anti-Defamation League. 2003. "OSCE Conference on Anti-Semitism." June 19. https://web.archive.org/web/20160420234203/http://archive.adl.org/anti_semitism/conference_vienna.html.

Anti-Defamation League. 2004. "Contemporary Manifestations of Anti-Semitism in the OSCE Region." Excerpts from an address by the Anti-Defamation League to the Organization for Security and Cooperation in Europe's Conference on Anti-Semitism, Berlin, April 29. http://archive.adl.org/durban/durban_ngo.html.

Anti-Defamation League. 2022. "The ADL Global 100: An Index of Anti-Semitism." http://global100.adl.org/.

Arkin, Kimberly. 2018. "Historicity, Peoplehood, and Politics: Holocaust Talks in 21st Century France." *Comparative Studies in Society and History* 68(4): 468–97.

Artforum. 2022. "Documenta Art Space Hosting Palestinian Collective Vandalized." June 1. https://www.artforum.com/news/documenta-art-space-hosting-palestinian-collective-vandalized-88708.

Assmann, Jan. 2011. *Cultural Memory and Early Civilization: Writing, Remembrance, and Early Civilization.* New York: Columbia University Press.

Ateş, Seyran. 2003. *Große Reise ins Feuer: Die Geschichte einer deutschen Türkin.* Berlin: Rowohlt Verlag.

Ateş, Seyran. 2011. *Der Islam braucht eine sexuelle Revolution: Eine Streitschrift.* Berlin: Ullstein Buchverlage.

Ateş, Seyran. 2017. *Selam, Frau Imamin: Wie ich in Berlin eine liberale Moschee gründete.* Berlin: Ullstein Buchverlage.

Atshan, Sa'ed, and Katharina Galor. 2020. *The Moral Triangle: Germans, Israelis, Palestinians.* Durham, NC: Duke University Press.

Ayalon, Yoni, and Izhak Schnell. 2014. "German Youth Educational Travel to Israel." *Journal of Hospitality and Tourism Education* 26(4): 188–97.

Ayalon, Yoni, and Izhak Schnell. 2019. "The Impact of German Youth Tours on Attitudes toward the Israeli-Palestinian Conflict." *Palestine-Israel Journal* 24(3): 122–27.

Baer, Marc David. 2013a. "Turk and Jew in Berlin: The First Turkish Migration to Germany and the Shoah." *Comparative Studies in Society and History* 55(2): 330–55.

Baer, Marc David. 2013b. "An Enemy Old and New: The Dönme, Anti-Semitism, and Conspiracy Theories in the Ottoman Empire and Turkish Republic." *Jewish Quarterly Review* 103(4): 523–55.

Baer, Marc David. 2018. "Mistaken for Jews: Turkish PhD Students in Nazi Germany." *German Studies Review* 41(1): 19–39.

Baer, Marc David. 2020a. *German, Jew, Muslim, Gay: The Life and Times of Hugo Marcus*. New York: Columbia University Press.

Baer, Marc David. 2020b. *Sultanic Saviors and Tolerant Turks: Writing Ottoman Jewish History, Denying the Armenian Genocide*. Bloomington: Indiana University Press.

Balci, Güner Yasemin. 2008. *Arabboy: Eine Jugend in Deutschland oder Das kurze Leben des Rashid A.* [Arabboy: A youth in Germany or the short life of Rashid A.]. Frankfurt am Main: S. Fisher Verlag.

Bali, Rıfat. 1999. *Cumhuriyet Yıllarında Türkiye Yahudileri: Bir Türkleştirme Seruveni (1923–1945)*. Istanbul: İletişim.

Balkenhol, M. 2016. "Silence and the Politics of Compassion: Commemorating Slavery in the Netherlands." *Social Anthropology* 24(3): 278–93.

Ball, Karyn. 2009. *Disciplining the Holocaust*. Albany: State University of New York Press.

Barkey, Karen. 2008. *Empire of Difference: Ottomans in Comparative Perspective*. Cambridge: Cambridge University Press.

Bartov, Omer. 1998. "Defining Enemies, Making Victims: Germans, Jews, and the Holocaust." *American Historical Review* 103(3): 771–816. https://doi.org/10.2307/2650572.

Bashir, Bashir, and Amos Goldberg. 2018. *The Holocaust and the Naqba: A New Grammar of Trauma and History*. New York: Columbia University Press.

Benedict, Ruth. 2019 [1946]. *The Chrysanthemum and the Sword: Patterns of Japanese Culture*. New York: Houghton Mifflin.

Benz, Wolfgang. 2012. "Hetzer mit Parallelen." *Süddeutsche Zeitung*, March 21, sec. Antisemiten und Islamfeinde. https://www.sueddeutsche.de/politik/antisemiten-und-islamfeinde-hetzer-mit-parallelen-1.59486.

Berek, Mathias. 2018. "Antisemitism and Immigration in Western Europe Today: Is There a Connection? The Case of Germany." Report. Stiftung EVZ. Berlin. https://archive.jpr.org.uk/object-ger251.

Bergerson, Andrew Stuart. 1997. "In the Shadow of the Towers: An Ethnography of a German-Israeli Student Exchange Program." *New German Critique* 71(Spring–Summer): 141–76.

Berlant, Lauren, ed. 2004. *Compassion: The Culture and Politics of an Emotion*. London: Routledge.

Bennhold, Katrin. 2018. "One Legacy of Merkel? Angry East German Men Fueling the Far Right." *New York Times*, November 5.

Biess, Frank. 2006. *Homecomings: Returning POWs and the Legacies of Defeat in Postwar Germany*. Princeton, NJ: Princeton University Press.

Bishop Kendzia, Victoria. 2018. *Visitors to the House of Memory: Identity and Political Education at the Jewish Museum Berlin*. New York: Berghahn Books.

Blackbourn, David, and Geoff Eley. 1984. *The Peculiarities of German History: Bourgeois Society and Politics in Nineteenth-Century Germany.* Oxford: Oxford University Press.

Bodemann, Y. Michal. 1990. "The State in the Construction of Ethnicity and Ideological Labor: The Case of German Jewry." *Critical Sociology* 17(3): 35–46.

Bodemann, Y. Michal. 1996a. "Reconstructions of History: From Jewish Memory to Nationalized Commemoration of Kristallnacht in Germany." In *Jews, Germans, Memory: Reconstructions of Jewish Life in Germany*, edited by Y. Michal Bodemann, 179–226. Ann Arbor: University of Michigan Press.

Bodemann, Y. Michal. 1996b. *Gedächtnistheater: Die jüdische Gemeinschaft und ihre deutsche Erfindung.* Hamburg: Rotbuch.

Bodemann, Y. Michal. 2013. "Holocaust Memory or Holocaust Parody? The Tales of Ernst Müller." *Holocaust Studies* 19(1): 81–100.

Boersema, Jacob, and Noam Schimmel 2008. "Challenging Dutch Holocaust Education: Towards a Curriculum Based on Moral Choices and Empathetic Capacity." *Ethics and Education* 3(1): 57–74.

Borneman, John. 1993. "Uniting the German Nation: Law, Narrative, and Historicity." *American Ethnologist* 20(2): 288–311. https://doi.org/10.1525/ae.1993.20.2.02a00050.

Borneman, John, ed. 2004. *Death of the Father: An Anthropology of the End in Political Authority.* New York: Berghahn Books.

Borneman, John. 2015. *Cruel Attachments: The Ritual Rehab of Child Molesters in Germany.* Chicago: University of Chicago Press.

Borneman, John, and Stefan Senders. 2000. "Politics without a Head: Is the 'Love Parade' a New Form of Political Identification?" *Cultural Anthropology* 15(2): 294–317. https://doi.org/10.1525/can.2000.15.2.294.

Boum, Aomar, and Sarah Abrevaya Stein, eds. 2018. *The Holocaust and North Africa.* Stanford: Stanford University Press.

Breitbart London. 2017. "Germany Opening First Liberal Mosque Where Men, Women and Gays Pray Together." Breitbart, June 16. www.breitbart.com/europe/2017/06/16/germany-opening-first-liberal-mosque-where-men-women-and-gayspray-together/ (accessed 13 May 2020).

Brettfeld, Katrin, and Peter Wetzels 2007. *Muslime in Deutschland. Integration, Integrationsbarrieren, Religion sowie Einstellungen zu Demokratie, Rechtsstaat und politisch-religiös motivierter Gewalt. Ergebnisse von Befragungen im Rahmen einer multizentrischen Studie in städtischen Lebensräumen.* Hamburg: Bundesministerium des Innern.

Brink-Danan, Marcy. 2012. *Jewish Life in Twenty-First Century Turkey: The Other Side of Tolerance.* Bloomington: Indiana University Press.

Brumlik, Micha, and Tanya Lieske. 2020. "Solidaritätsbrief für Achille Mbembe—

'Vergleich bedeutet nicht Gleichsetzung.' " *Deutschlandfunk*, May 4, sec. Kultur heute. https://www.deutschlandfunk.de/solidaritaetsbrief-fuer-achille-mbembe-vergleich-bedeutet.691.de.html?dram:article_id=475977.

Bundesministerium des Innern. 2011. *Anti-Semitismus in Deutschland—Ercheininungsformen, Bedingungen, Präventionsätze. Bericht des unabhängigen Expertenkreises Anti-Semitismus.* Berlin: Bundesministerium des Innern. https://www.bmi.bund.de/SharedDocs/downloads/DE/publikationen/themen/heimat-integration/expertenkreis-antisemitismus/antisemitismus-in-deutschland-bericht.pdf?__blob=publicationFile&v=3.

Bundesministerium des Innern. 2017. *Anti-Semitismus in Deutschland—aktuelle Entwinklungen.* Berlin: Bundesministerium des Innern. http://www.bmi.bund.de/SharedDocs/downloads/DE/publikationen/themen/heimat-integration/expertenkreis-antisemitismus/expertenbericht-antisemitismus-in-deutschland.pdf?__blob=publicationFile&v=7

Bunderministerium des Innern. 2020. *Politisch motivierte Kriminalität im Jahr 2019 Bundesweite Fallzahlen.* https://www.bmi.bund.de/SharedDocs/downloads/DE/veroeffentlichungen/2020/pmk-2019.pdf;jsessionid=0A238B46C12E89E205055C49D1A0DBA7.1_cid364?__blob=publicationFile&v=6.

Bundesverband der Recherce- und Informationsstellen Antisemitismus e.V. 2022. *Bericht dokumentierter antisemitischer Vorfälle 2021. Antisemitism Report. report-antisemitism.de.*

Bunzl, Matti. 2004. "Boas, Foucault, and the Native Anthropologist: Notes towards a Neo-Boasian Anthropology." *American Anthropologist* 106(3): 435–42.

Bunzl, Matti. 2005. "Between Anti-Semitism and Islamophobia: Some Thoughts on the New Europe." *American Ethnologist.* 32(4): 499–508.

Can, M., K. Georg, and R. Hatlapa. 2013. "Challenges and Opportunities of Educational Concepts Concerning National Socialist Crimes in German Immigration Society." In *Perceptions of the Holocaust in Europe and Muslim Communities, edited by G. Jikeli and J.* Allaouche-Benayoun, 173–88. Dordrecht, Neth.: Springer.

Carr, E. Summerson. 2011. *Scripting Addiction: The Politics of Therapeutic Talk and American Sobriety.* Princeton, NJ: Princeton University Press.

Carrier, Peter, et al. 2015. *The International Status of Education about the Holocaust.* Fontenoy: UNESCO.

Chin, Rita. 2007. *The Guest Worker Question in Postwar Germany.* Cambridge: Cambridge University Press.

Chin, Rita. 2010. "Turkish Women, West German Feminists, and the Gendered Discourse on Muslim Cultural Difference." *Public Culture* 22(3): 557–81.

Cho, Daniel K. 2009. "Adorno on Education or, Can Critical Self-Reflection Prevent the Next Auschwitz?" *Historical Materialism* 17(1): 74–97.

Çileli, Serap. 2006. *Wir sind eure Töchter, nicht eure Ehre*. München: Blanvalet.

Çetinkaya, Gökhan. 1999. "Rethinking Nationalism and Islam: Some Preliminary Notes on the Roots of 'Turkish-Islamic Synthesis' in Modern Turkish Political Thought." *The Muslim World* 89(3/4): 350–76.

Clark, David. 2018. "Remembering National Socialism in the Federal Republic of Germany." In *A Companion to Nazi Germany*, edited by Shelley Baranowski, Armin Nolzen, and Claus-Christian W. Szejnmann, 599–613. New York: Wiley Blackwell.

Cohen, Mark. 2008. *Under the Crescent and the Cross: The Jews in the Middle Ages*. Princeton, NJ: Princeton University Press.

ConAct. 2010. *German-Israeli Youth Exchange in the Past and Present: A Short Overview for 2010*. Wittenberg: ConAct. https://www.conact-org.de/fileadmin/user_upload/pdf/1.oa_Short_Infomation_Youth_Exchange_2010.pdf.

Czollek, Max. 2018. *Desintegriert euch!* Munich: Carl Hanser Verlag.

Czollek, Max. 2020a. "Gegenwartsbewältigung / Overcoming the Present." Translated by Jon Cho-Polizzi. *TRANSIT* 12(2). https://escholarship.org/uc/item/82j1524z.

Czollek, Max. 2020b. *Gegenwartsbewältigung*. München: Carl Hanser Verlag.

Dabashi, Hamid. 2011. *Brown Skin, White Masks*. New York: Pluto Press.

Dantschke, Claudia. 2010. "Feinbild Juden: Zur Funktionalität der anti-Semitischen Gemeinschaftsideologie in muslimisch geprägten Milieus." In *Konstellationen des Anti-Semitismus: Anti-Semitismus Forschung und sozialpädagogische Praxis, edited by* Wolfram Stender, Guido Follert, and Mihri Ozdogan, 139–46. Wiesbaden: VS Verlag für Sozialwissenschaften.

Day, Matthew. 2009. "Poland Sends Prisoners to Auschwitz." *The Telegraph*, May. https://www.telegraph.co.uk/news/worldnews/europe/poland/5272983/Poland-sends-prisoners-to-Auschwitz.html.

Der Spiegel. 2016. "Duisburg-Marxloh versinkt im Chaos." https://www.spiegel.de/video/duisburg-marxloh-versinkt-im-chaos-video-1697245.html.

De Koning, Martin. 2015. "Muselmann—The Prisoners Who Became 'Muslims' in Auschwitz." *Closer*, May 4. https://religionresearch.org/closer/2015/05/04/muselmann-the-jews-who-became-muslims-in-auschwitz/ (accessed 1 May 2018).

Dekel, Irit. 2013. *Mediation at the Holocaust Memorial in Berlin*. London: Palgrave Macmillan.

Dekel, Irit. 2014. "Jews and Other Others at the Holocaust Memorial in Berlin." *Anthropological Journal of European Cultures* 23(2): 71–84.

Dekel, Irit. 2016. "Subjects of Memory? Holocaust Memory in Two German Historical Museums." *Dapim: Studies on the Holocaust* 30(3): 296–314.

Dekel, Irit, and Esra Özyürek. 2020a. "Perfides Ablenkungsmanöver." *Die Zeit*,

July 10. https://www.zeit.de/kultur/2020-07/antisemitismus-debatte-holocaust-deutschland-rassismus-kolonialismus-diskriminierung-10nach8.

Dekel, Irit, and Esra Özyürek. 2020b. “What Do We Talk about When We Talk about Antisemitism in Germany?” *Journal of Genocide Research* (December): 1–8. https://doi.org/10.1080/14623528.2020.1847859.

Dekel, Irit, and Esra Özyürek. (forthcoming). “The Expanding Logic of the Fight against Antisemitism in Germany in Three C ultural Shifts.” *Patterns of Prejudice*.

Demirel, Aycan, and Yasmin Kassar. 2011. “ ‘Persönliche Friedensprozesse’ initiieren und begleiten–Herausforderungen, Erfahrungen und Erkenntnisse einer Pädagogik im Spannungsfeld zwischen Anerkennung und Konfrontation.” In *Das globalisierte Klassenzimmer: Theorie und Praxis zeitgemäßer Bildungsarbeit*, edited by Mirko Niehoff and Emine Üstün, 142–54. Immenhausen bei Kassel: Verlag Barbara Budrich.

Desjarlais, Robert, and C. Jason Throop. 2011. “Phenomenological Approaches in Anthropology.” *Annual Review of Anthropology* 40(1): 87–102.

Deutsche Welle. 2013. “Roma Migrants Overwhelm Duisburg.” https://www.dw.com/en/roma-migrants-overwhelm-duisburg/a-17052814.

Deutsche Welle. 2020. “Germany Sees High Numbers of Femicide.” https://www.dw.com/en/germany-sees-high-numbers-in-femicide/a-55555702.

Dicks, Henry V. 1950. “Personality Traits and National Socialist Ideology: A War-Time Study of German Prisoners of War.” *Human Relations* 3(2): 111–54. https://doi.org/10.1177/001872675000300201.

Diner, Dan. 1986. “Negative Symbiose: Deutsche und Juden nach Auschwitz.” *Babylon* 1: 9–20.

Doughan, Sultan. 2013. “Deviation: The Present Orders.” *Fieldsights*, Member Voices, September 18. https://culanth.org/fieldsights/deviation-the-present-orders.

Doughan, Sultan. 2022. “A Secular Conversion to Protestant Morals?” In *Contending Modernities*. https://contendingmodernities.nd.edu/theorizing-modernities/a-secular-conversion-of-protestant-morals/.

Duranti, Alessandro. 2010. “Husserl, Intersubjectivity and Anthropology.” *Anthropological Theory* 10(1–2): 16–35. https://doi.org/10.1177/1463499610370517.

Dymond, R. F. 1949. “A Scale for the Measurement of Empathic Ability.” *Journal of Consulting Psychology* 13(2): 127–33. https://doi.org/10.1037/h0061728.

Eder, Jacob S. 2021. *Holocaust Angst: The Federal Republic of Germany and American Holocaust Memory since the 1970s*. New York: Oxford University Press.

Edwards, Laura Hyatt. 2013. “A Brief Conceptual History of Einfühlung: 18th-Century Germany to Post–World War II U.S. Psychology.” *History of Psychology* 16(4): 269–81. https://doi.org/10.1037/a0033634.

Ehrkamp, Patricia. 2006. " 'We Turks Are No Germans': Assimilation Discourses and the Dialectical Construction of Identities in Germany." *Environment and Planning A: Economy and Space* 38(9): 1673–92.

Eichengreen, Barry. 2018. *The Populist Temptation: Economic Grievance and Political Reaction in the Modern Era*. Oxford: Oxford University Press.

El-Tayeb, Fatima. 2008. " 'The Birth of a European Public': Migration, Postnationality, and Race in the Uniting of Europe." *American Quarterly* 60(3): 649–70.

El-Tayeb, Fatima. 2016. *Undeutsch: Die Konstruktion des Anderen in der postmigrantischen Gesellschaft*. Bielefeld: Transcript Verlag.

Eley, Geoff, ed. 2000. *The "Goldhagen Effect": History, Memory, Nazism—Facing the German Past*. Ann Arbor: University of Michigan Press.

Elger, Katrin, and Maik Grosskathöfer. 2021. "Umstrittene WDR-Moderatorin El-Hassan: Ich schäme mich für diese Zeit." *Der Spiegel*, September 16. https://www.spiegel.de/panorama/gesellschaft/ich-schaeme-mich-fuer-diese-zeit-a-8d08dc60-7bb3-4c70-94f7-1d63c6ec4922.

Elisha, Omri. 2008. "Moral Ambitions of Grace: The Paradox of Compassion and Accountability in Evangelical Faith-Based Activism." *Cultural Anthropology* 23(1): 154–89.

Erikson, Erik H. 1993 [1963]. *Childhood and Society*. 2nd ed. New York: W. W. Norton.

European Monitoring Centre on Racism and Xenophobia. 2003. *Manifestations of Antisemitism in the EU 2002–2003*. Vienna. https://fra.europa.eu/sites/default/files/fra_uploads/184-AS-Main-report.pdf.

Ewing, Katherine Pratt. 2008. *Stolen Honor: Stigmatizing Muslim Men in Berlin*. Stanford, CA: Stanford University Press.

Farris, Sara. 2017. *In the Name of Women's Rights: The Rise of Femonationalism*. Durham, NC: Duke University Press.

Fassin, Didier. 2005. "Compassion and Repression: The Moral Economy of Immigration Policies in France." *Cultural Anthropology* 20(3): 362–87.

Fassin, Didier. 2011. "Noli Me Tangere: The Moral Untouchability of Humanitarianism." In *Forces of Compassion: Humanitarianism between Ethics and Politics*, edited by Erica Bornstein and Peter Redfield, 35–52. Santa Fe, NM: School for Advanced Research.

Fassin, Didier, and Richard Rechtman. 2009. *Empire of Trauma: An Inquiry into the Condition of Victimhood*. Princeton, NJ: Princeton University Press.

Fava, Rosa. 2015. *Die Neuausrichtung der Erziehung nach Auschwitz in der Einwanderungsgesellschaft. Eine rassismuskritische Diskursanalyse*. Berlin: Metropol.

Fay, Jennifer. 2008. *Theaters of Occupation: Hollywood and the Reeducation of Postwar Germany*. Minneapolis: University of Minnesota Press.

Feldman, Jackie. 2008. *Above the Death Pits, Beneath the Flag: Youth Voyages to Poland and the Performance of Israeli National Identity*. New York: Berghahn Books.

Felman, Shoshana, and Dori Laub. 1992. *Testimony: Crises of Witnessing in Literature, Psychoanalysis, and History*. New York: Routledge.

Flanzbaum, Hilene, ed. 1999. *The Americanization of the Holocaust*. Baltimore, MD: Johns Hopkins University Press.

Florvil, Tiffany. 2001. "Queer Memory and Black Germans in New Fascism Syllabus." http://newfascismsyllabus.com/opinions/queer-memory-and-black-germans/.

Fox, Thomas C. 2001. *Stated Memory: East Germany and the Holocaust*. Rochester, NY: Camden House.

French, Robert, and Jem Thomas. 1999. "Maturity and Education, Citizenship and Enlightenment: An Introduction to Theodor Adorno and Helmut Becker, 'Education for Maturity and Responsibility.'" *History of the Human Sciences* 12(3): 1–19.

Freud, Sigmund. 2001 [1913]. *The Complete Psychological Works of Sigmund Freud: Totem and Taboo and Other Works*, vol. 13 (1913–1914). London: Vintage.

Freud, Sigmund. 2001 [1939]. *The Complete Psychological Works of Sigmund Freud: Moses and Monotheism, An Outline of Psychoanalysis, and Other Works*, vol. 23 (1937–1939). London: Vintage.

Frey, Arun. 2020. "Cologne Changed Everything: The Effects of Threatening Events on the Frequency and Distribution of Intergroup Conflict in Germany." *European Sociological Review* 36(5): 684–99.

Fulbrook, Mary. 1999. *German National Identity after the Holocaust*. Cambridge: Polity Press.

Georgi, Viola. 2003. *Entliehene Erinnerung: Geschichtsbilder Junger Migranten in Deutschland*. Hamburg: Hamburger Edition.

Glaeser, Andreas. 2000. *Divided in Unity: Identity, Germany, and the Berlin Police*. Chicago: University of Chicago Press.

Goffman, Erving. 1981. *Forms of Talk*. Philadelphia: University of Pennsylvania Press.

Göktürk, Deniz, David Gramling, and Anton Kaes, eds. 2007. *Germany in Transit: Nation and Migration 1955–2005*. Berkeley: University of California Press.

Goldberg, Amos. 2016. "Empathy, Ethics, and Politics in Holocaust Historiography." In *Empathy and Its Limits*, edited by Aleida Assmann and Ines Detmers, 52–76. London: Palgrave Macmillan.

Goldberg, Theo. 2006. "Racial Europeanization." *Ethnic and Racial Studies* 29(2): 331–64.

Goldhagen, Daniel. 1996. *Hitler's Willing Executioners: Ordinary Germans and the Holocaust*. New York: Alfred A. Knopf.

Göpffarth, Julian, and Esra Özyürek. 2020. "Spiritualizing Reason, Rationalizing Spirit: Muslim Public Intellectuals in the German Far Right." *Ethnicities*, June. https://doi.org/10.1177/1468796820932443.

Greuel, Frank. 2012. "Pädagogische Prävention von Ethnozentrismus und Anti-Semitismus bei Jugendlichen mit Migrationshintergrund." In *Ethnozentrismus und Anti-Semitismus bei Jugendlichen mit Migrationshintergrund. Erscheinungsformen und padagogische Praxis in der Einwanderungsgesellschaft*, edited by Frank Greuel and Michaela Glaser, 90–143. Halle: Deutsches Jugendinstitute, Deutsches Jugendinstitut.

Gryglewski, Elke. 2010. "Teaching about the Holocaust in Multicultural Societies: Appreciating the Learner." *Intercultural Education* 21(1): 41–49.

Gryglewski, Elke. 2013. *Anerkennung und Erinnerung: Zugänge arabisch-palästinensischer und türkischer Berliner Jugendlicher zum Holocaust*. Berlin: Metropol Verlag.

Gün, Gülay. 2010. "Gedenkstättenrezeption von Türkischstämmigen Deutschen—Ein Besuch in Der KZ-Gedenkstätte Bergen-Belsen." Bachelor's thesis, History, University of Bremen. https://www.academia.edu/9673737/Gedenkst%C3%A4ttenrezeption_von_t%C3%BCrkischst%C3%A4mmigen_Deutschen_Ein_Besuch_in_der_KZ_Gedenkst%C3%A4tte_Bergen_Belsen.

Guttstadt, Corry. 2013. *Turkey, the Jews, and the Holocaust*. Cambridge: Cambridge University Press.

Haaretz. 2015. "Netanyahu: Hitler Didn't Want to Exterminate the Jews." *Haaretz*, October 21, sec. Israel News. https://www.haaretz.com/israel-news/netanyahu-absolves-hitler-of-guilt-1.5411578.

Habermas, Jurgen. 1993 [1986]."A Kind of Settlement of Damages on Apologetic Tendencies in German History Writing." In *Forever in the Shadow of Hitler?*, edited by Ernst Piper. Atlantic Highlands, NJ: Humanities Press.

Hage, Ghassan. 2003. *Against Paranoid Nationalism: Searching for Hope in a Shrinking Society*. Annandale, VA: Pluto Press & Merlin.

Harris, Peter, Sue Nagy, and Nicholas Vardaxis, eds. 2014. "American Journal of Orthopsychiatry." In Mosby's Dictionary of Medicine, Nursing and Health Professions, 3rd ed.

Haug, Sonya, Stephanie Mussig, and Anja Stichs. 2009. *Muslimisches Leben in Deutschland: Im Auftrag der Deutschen Islam Konferenz*. Nuremberg: Bundesamt für Migration und Flüchtlinge.

Heni, Clemens. 2010. "Ein Nazi und sein Schüler: Karl Bosl und Wolfgang Benz." *Die Achse des Guten*, January 15, sec. Gastautor. https://www.achgut.com/artikel/ein_nazi_und_sein_schueler_karl_bosl_und_wolfgang_benz.

Hersh, Seymour M. 2004. "The Gray Zone." *The New Yorker*, May 16. https://www.newyorker.com/magazine/2004/05/24/the-gray-zone.

Herzog, Dagmar. 1998. "'Pleasure, Sex, and Politics Belong Together': Post-Holocaust Memory and the Sexual Revolution in West Germany." *Critical Inquiry* 24(2): 393–444.

Herzog, Dagmar. 2005. *Sex after Fascism: Memory and Morality in Twentieth-Century Germany.* Princeton, NJ: Princeton University Press.

Hillgruber, Andreas. 1986. *Zweierlei Untergang: Die Zerschlagung des Deutschen Reiches und das Ende des europäischen Judentums.* Cologne: Corso bei Siedler.

Hirsch, Marianne. 2012. *The Generation of Postmemory: Writing and Visual Culture after the Holocaust.* New York: Columbia University Press.

Hirsi Ali, Ayaan. 2006. *The Caged Virgin: An Emancipation Proclamation for Women and Islam.* New York: Atria.

Höcke, Björn. 2017. "17.01.2017: Dresdner Gespräche Mit Björn Höcke." Streamed live on January 17. YouTube video, COMPACTTV, 1:50:01. https://www.youtube.com/watch?v=sti51c8abaw.

Hollan, Douglas W., and C. Jason Throop, eds. 2011. *The Anthropology of Empathy: Experiencing the Lives of Others in Pacific Societies.* New York: Berghahn Books.

Holz, Klaus, and Michael Kiefer. 2010. "Islamistischer Anti-Semitismus Phänomen und Forschungsstand." In *Konstellationen des Anti-Semitismus: Anti-Semitismusforschung und sozialpädagogische Praxis*, edited by Wolfram Stender, Guido Follert, and Mihri Özdoğan, 109–38. Wiesbaden: Vs. Verlag für Sozialwissenschaft.

Horowitz, Sara. 1992. "Review: Rethinking Holocaust Testimony: The Making and Unmaking of the Witness." *Cardoza Studies in Law and Literature* 4(1): 45–68.

Huggan, Graham. 2001. *The Postcolonial Exotic: Marketing the Margins.* London: Routledge.

Husserl, Edmund. 1988 [1931]. *Cartesian Meditation: An Introduction to Phenomenology.* Translated by Dorion Cairns. London: Kluwer Academic.

Ihrig, Stefan. 2014. *Atatürk in the Nazi Imagination.* Cambridge, MA: Harvard University Press.

Ilan, Gur-Ze'ev. 2000. "Defeating the Enemy Within: Exploring the Link between Holocaust Education and the Arab/Israeli Conflict." *Religious Education* 95(4): 373–401.

Illig-Mooncie, Louise. 2014. *The Jewish Ghost: Being German—A Search for Meaning.* Hastings: Edgerton Publishing Services.

International Holocaust Remembrance Alliance. 2000. "Stockholm Declaration." IHRA, January 27. https://www.holocaustremembrance.com/about-us/stockholm-declaration.

International Holocaust Remembrance Alliance. 2016. "Working Definition of

Antisemitism." Press release. Bucharest: IHRA. https://www.holocaustremembrance.com/sites/default/files/press_release_document_antisemitism.pdf.

Israeli, Raphael. 2009. *Muslim Anti-Semitism in Christian Europe: Elemental and Residual Anti-Semitism.* New Brunswick, NJ: Transaction.

Jarausch, Konrad H. 2006. *After Hitler: Recivilizing Germans, 1945–1995.* Translated by Brandon Hunziker. Oxford: Oxford University Press.

Jaspers, Karl. 2001 [1947]. *The Question of German Guilt.* Translated by E. B. Ashton. 2nd ed. New York: Fordham University Press.

Jennings, Louise B. 2010. "Challenges and Possibilities of Holocaust Education and Critical Citizenship: An Ethnographic Study of a Fifth-Grade Bilingual Class Revisited." *Prospects: Quarterly Review of Comparative Education* 40(1): 35–56.

Jikeli, Günther, Robin Stoller, and Hann Thoma. 2007. "Proceedings: Strategies and Effective Practices for Fighting Antisemitism among People with a Muslim or Arab Background in Europe." Berlin: International Institute for Education and Research on Antisemitism. https://iibsa.org/proceedings-strategies-and-effective-practices-for-fighting-antisemitism-among-people-with-a-muslim-or-arab-background-in-europe/.

Jilovsky. Esther. 2017. *Remembering the Holocaust: Generations, Witnessing, and Place.* London: Bloomsbury.

Jones, Timothy. 2018. "Germany Sees Almost 1,000 Anti-Muslim Crimes in 2017." *Deutsche Welle,* March 3.

Juriet, Ulrike, and Christian Schneider. 2010. *Gefuehlte Opfer: Ilissionen der Vergangenheitsbewaeltigung.* Stuttgart: Klett-Cotta Verlag.

Kampe, Norbert. 1987. "Normalizing the Holocaust? The Recent Historians' Debate in the Federal Republic of Germany." *Holocaust and Genocide Studies* 2(1): 61–80.

Karr, Chadwick, and Frank Wesley. 1966. "Comparison of German and US Child-Rearing Practices." *Child Development* 37: 715–23.

Kelek, Necla. 2005. *Die fremde Braut: Ein Bericht aus dem Inneren des türkischen Lebens in Deutschland.* Köln: Verlag Kiepenheuer & Witsch.

Kelek, Necla. 2006. *Die verlorenen Söhne: Plädoyer für die Befreiung des türkisch-muslimischen Mannes.* Köln: Verlag Kiepenheuer & Witsch.

Kelek, Necla, Claus Christian Malzahn, and Anna Reimann. 2007. "German Integration Summit: 'We Really Have Nothing to Celebrate.' " *Spiegel Online International,* December 7. https://www.spiegel.de/international/germany/german-integration-summit-we-really-have-nothing-to-celebrate-a-493888.html (accessed 8 June 2019).

Kelly, Tobias. 2012. "Sympathy and Suspicion: Torture, Asylum, and Humanity." *Journal of the Royal Anthropological Institute* 18(4): 753–68.

KIgA. 2006. *Pädagogische Konzepte gegen Anti-Semitismus in der Einwanderungsgesselchaft.* Berlin: Kreuzberger Initiative gegen Anti-Semitismus.

KIgA. 2011. *Israel, Palästina und der Nahostkonflikt - Ein Bildungs- und Begegnungsprojekt mit muslimischen Jugendlichen im Spannungsfeld von Anerkennung und Konfrontation.* Berlin: Kreuzberger Initiative gegen Anti-Semitismus.

KIgA. 2013. *Widerspruchstoleranz—Ein Theorie-Praxis-Handbuch zu Anti-Semitismuskritik und Bildungsarbeit.* Berlin: Kreuzberger Initiative gegen Anti-Semitismus.

Klein, Naomi. 2007. *The Shock Doctrine: The Rise of Disaster Capitalism.* New York: Picador.

Klose, Bianca, and Verein für Demokratische Kultur in Berlin, eds. 2008. "Du Opfer!"—"Du Jude!" Anti-Semitismus und Jugendarbeit in Kreuzberg: Dokumentation der amira-Tagung am 16.09.2008 im Stadtteilzentrum Alte Feuerwache, Berlin-Kreuzberg. Berlin: Zentral- und Landesbibliothek Berlin ZLB. Senatsbibliothek, September 16. https://digital.zlb.de/viewer/resolver?urn=urn:nbn:de:kobv:109-opus-171694.

Klug, Nora. 2019. *Belonging: A German Reckons with History and Home.* New York: Scribner.

Konuk, Kader. 2007. "Taking on German and Turkish History: Emine Sevgi Özdamar's *Seltsame Sterne*." https://doi.org/10.1524/9783050062334.221.

Korteweg, Anna, and Gökçe Yurdakul. 2009. "Islam, Gender, and Immigrant Integration: Boundary Drawing in Discourses on Honor Killing in the Netherlands and Germany." *Ethnic and Racial Studies* 32(2): 218–38.

Koselleck, Reinhard. 2018. *Sediments of Time: On Possible Histories.* Stanford, CA: Stanford University Press.

Kouparanis, Panagiotis. 2008. "Guided Tours for Muslims in Berlin's Jewish Museum: Discovering a Different Belief." *Qantara*, September 3. http://en.qantara.de/content/guided-tours-for-muslims-in-berlins-jewish-museum-discovering-a-different-belief (accessed 1 May 2018).

Kundnani, Hans. 2009. *Utopia or Auschwitz: Germany's 1968 Generation and the Holocaust.* London: C. Hurst.

Küntzel, Matthias. 2009. *Jihad and Jew-Hatred: Islamism, Nazism and the Roots of 9/11.* New York: Telos Press.

Lacan, Jacques. 2015 [1956]. *On the Names of the Father.* New York: Polity Press.

Langer, Walter. 1972. *The Mind of Adolf Hitler.* New York: Basic Books.

Lehrer, Erica. 2013. *Jewish Poland Revisited. Heritage Tourism in Unquiet Places.* Bloomington: Indiana University Press.

Levi, Primo. 1991 [1947]. *If This Is a Man*. London: Abacus.

Levi-Strauss, Claude. 1969 [1949]. *The Elementary Structures of Kinship*. Revised ed. Boston: Beacon Press.

Lipps, Theodor. 1979 [1903]. "Einfühlung, Innere Nachahmung und Organempfindung." *Archiv fu¨r Gesamte Psychologie* 1: 465–519. Translated as "Empathy, Inner Imitation and Sense-Feelings." In *A Modern Book of Esthetics: An Anthology*, edited by M. M. Radar, 374–82. New York: Holt, Rinehart and Winston.

Ludwig, Emil. 1943. *How to Treat the Germans*. New York: Hutchinson.

Lueter, Albert, and Albert Bergert. 2015. *Gewaltprävention in einer pluralen Stadt. Drei Projektevaluationen*. Berlin: Arbeitsstelle Jugendgewaltprävdention im Auftrag der Landeskommission Berlin gegen Gewalt.

Luo, Zhida. 2017. "Motivating Empathy: The Problem of Bodily Similarity in Husserl's Theory of Empathy." *Husserl Studies* 33(1): 45–61.

Lustick, Ian S. 2017. "The Holocaust in Israeli Political Culture: Four Constructions and Their Consequences." *Contemporary Jewry* 37(1): 125–70. https://doi.org/10.1007/s12397-017-9208-7.

Mandel, Ruth. 2008. *Cosmopolitan Anxieties: Turkish Challenges to Citizenship and Belonging in Germany*. Durham, NC: Duke University Press.

Mansel, Jürgen, and Viktoria Spaiser. 2013. *Ausgrenzungsdynamiken: In welchen Lebenslagen Jugendliche Fremdgruppen abwerten*. Weinheim: Beltz Juventa.

Mansour, Ahmad. 2014. *Generation Allah: Warum wir im kampf gegen religioesen Extremismus umdenken muessen*. Berlin: S. Fisher Verlag.

Maran, Rita. 2002. "A Report from the UN World Conference against Racism, Racial Discrimination, Xenophobia and Related Intolerance, Durban, South Africa, 2001." *Social Justice* 29(1–2): 177–85.

Margalit, Gilad. 2009. "On Being Other in Post-Holocaust Germany: German Turkish Intellectuals and the German Past." In *Juden und Muslime in Deutschland: Recht, Religion, Identitat, edited by J. Bruner and S. Lavi*. Tel Aviv: Wallstein Verlag.

Margalit, Gilad. 2010. *Guilt, Suffering and Memory: Germany Remembers Its Dead of World War II*. Translated by Haim Watzman. Bloomington: Indiana University Press.

Mariotti, Shannon L. 2016. *Adorno and Democracy: The American Years*. Lexington: University Press of Kentucky.

Markovits, Andrei S. 2006. "A New (or Perhaps Revived) 'Uninhibitedness' toward Jews in Germany." *Jewish Political Studies Review* 18: 1–2.

McGlothlin, Erin. 2006. *Second-Generation Holocaust Literature: Legacies of Survival and Perpetration*. Rochester, NY: Camden House.

Merz, Friedrich @_FriedrichMerz. 2020. "75 Jahre nach der Befreiung von #Auschwitz erleben wir erneut #Antisemitismus—überwiegend von rechts, aber auch durch die Einwanderung von 2015/16. Viele bringen Judenhass mit, der in ihren Heimatländern gepredigt wird. Auch dafür darf es keine Toleranz geben. (tm) #WeRemember." Twitter. @_FriedrichMerz (blog). January 27. https://twitter.com/_FriedrichMerz/status/1221872528014135297.

Meseth, Wolfgang. 2012. "Education after Auschwitz in a Unified Germany." *European Education* 44(3): 13–38.

Meseth, Wolfgang, and Matthias Proske. 2010. "Mind the Gap: Holocaust Education in Germany, between Pedagogical Intentions and Classroom Interactions." *Prospects* 40: 201–22.

Miller, Alice. 1987 [1980]. *For Your Own Good: Hidden Cruelty in Child-Rearing and the Roots of Violence.* Translated by Hildegarde and Hunter Hannum. London: Virago Press.

Mills, Charles. 1997. *The Racial Contract.* Ithaca, NY: Cornell University Press.

Mitscherlich, Alexander, and Margerete Mitscherlich. 1975. *The Inability to Mourn: Principles of Collective Behavior.* Translated by Beverly Placzek. New York: Grove Press.

Moeller, Robert G. 1996. "War Stories: The Search for a Usable Past in the Federal Republic of Germany." *American Historical Review* 101(4): 1008–48.

Moeller, Robert G. 2006. "Germans as Victims? Thoughts on a Post-Cold-War History of World War IIs Legacies." *History and Memory* 17(1–2): 145–94.

Moghadham, Assaf, and Michel Wyss. 2018. "Of Anti-Zionists and Antideutsche: The Post-War German Left and Its Relatiosnhip with Israel." *Democracy and Security* 15(1): 49–74.

Moses, Dirk. 2001. "Coming to Terms with Genocidal Pasts in Comparative Perspective: Germany and Australia." *Aboriginal History* 25: 91–115.

Moses, Dirk. 2021. "German Cathecism." *Geschichte der Gegenwart.*

Motadel, David. 2014. *Islam and Nazi Germany's War.* Boston: Harvard University Press. https://geschichtedergegenwart.ch/the-german-catechism/

Muehlebach, Andrea. 2011. "On Affective Labor in Post-Fordist Italy." *Cultural Anthropology* 26(1): 59–82.

Müller, Jan-Werner. 2000. *Another Country: German Intellectuals, Unification, and National Identity.* New Haven, CT: Yale University Press.

Müller, Jochen. 2007. "Islamism, Pan-Arabism, and Anti-Semitism." In *Proceedings: Strategies and Effective Practices for Fighting Anti-Semitism among People with a Muslim or Arab Background in Europe, edited by G.* Jikeli, R. Stoller, and H. Thoma, 35–37. Berlin: International Institute for Education and Research on Antisemitism.

Müller, Jochen. 2009. "Islamophobie und Anti-Semitismus—Kritische Annerkenungen zu einem fragwurdigen Vergleich." In *"Die Juden sind Schuld": Anti-Semitismus in der Einwanderungsgesellschaft am Beispiel muslimisch sozialisierter Milieus. Beispiele, Erfahrungen, und Handlungsoptionen aus der pädagogischen und kommunalen Arbeit*, edited by Claudia Dantschke, 24–29. Berlin: Amadeu Antonio Stiftung.

Muñoz, José Esteban. 1999. *Disidentifications: Queers of Color and the Performance of Politics*. Minneapolis: University of Minnesota Press.

Naimark, Norman M. 1995. *The Russians in Germany: A History of the Soviet Zone of Occupation, 1945–1949*. Cambridge, MA: Belknap.

Nandy, Ashis. 2009. *The Intimate Enemy: Loss and Recovery of Self under Colonialism*. Delhi: Oxford University Press.

Narotzky, Susana, and Niko Besnier. 2014. "Crisis, Value, and Hope: Rethinking the Economy." *Current Anthropology* 55(Suppl. 9): S4–S16.

Neiman, Susan. 2019. *Learning from the Germans: Race and the Memory of Evil*. New York: Farrar, Straus and Giroux.

Niven, Bill, ed. 2006. *Germans as Victims: Remembering the Past in Contemporary Germany*. Basingstoke, UK: Palgrave Macmillan.

Nolte, Ernst. 1986. "Die Vergangenheit, die nicht vergehen will. Eine Rede, die geschrieben, aber nicht gehalten werden konnte." *Frankfurter Allgemeine Zeitung*, June 6. Archived from the original at the Internet Archive on February 19, 2014. https://web.archive.org/web/20140219012727/http://www.hdg.de/lemo/html/dokumente/NeueHerausforderungen_redeNolte1986/.

Norman, Ralph D., and Waldemar C. Leiding. 1956. "The Relationship between Measures of Individual and Mass Empathy." *Journal of Consulting Psychology* 20(1): 79–82.

n-tv. 2020. "Kritik an Antisemitismus in 'muslimischen Kreisen.' " Nachrichten, January 27. https://www.n-tv.de/politik/Kritik-an-Antisemitismus-in-muslimischen-Kreisen-article21535706.html.

Olick, Jeffrey. 2007. *The Politics of Regret: On Collective Memory and Historical Responsibility*. London: Routledge.

OSCE (Organization for Security and Co-Operation in Europe). 2003. Press release, June 20.

OSCE. 2004. *Berlin Declaration*. Bulgarian Chairmanship, the Chairman-in-Office. Helsinki: Organization for Security and Co-operation in Europe. https://www.osce.org/files/f/documents/9/8/31432.pdf (accessed 24 September 2015).

Özyürek, Esra. 2009. " 'The Light of Alevi Fire Was Lit in Germany and Then Spread to Turkey': The Debate about the Relationship between Alevism and Islam." *International Journal of Turkish Studies* 10(2): 233–53.

Özyürek, Esra. 2014. *Being German, Becoming Muslim: Race, Religion, and Conversion in the New Europe*. Princeton, NJ: Princeton University Press.

Özyürek, Esra. 2016. "Export-Import Theory and Racialization of Antisemitism:

Turkish and Arab-Only Prevention Programs in Germany." *Comparative Studies in Society and History* 58(1): 40–65.

Özyürek, Esra. 2022. "Muslim Minorities as Germany's Past Future: Islam Critics, Holocaust Memory, and Immigrant Integration." *Memory Studies* 15(1).

Papazu, Irina. 2016. "Management through Hope: An Ethnography of Denmark's Renewable Energy Island." *Journal of Organizational Ethnography* 5(2): 184–200.

Paragi, Beata. 2017. "Contemporary Gifts: Solidarity, Compassion, Equality, Sacrifice, and Reciprocity from an NGO Perspective." *Current Anthropology* 58(3): 317–39.

Parkinson, Anna. 2015. *An Emotional State: The Politics of Emotion in Postwar West German Culture*. Ann Arbor: University of Michigan Press.

Partridge, Damani James. 2008. "We Were Dancing in the Club, Not on the Berlin Wall: Black Bodies, Street Bureaucrats, and Exclusionary Incorporation into the New Europe." *Cultural Anthropology* 23(4): 660–87.

Partridge, Damani J. 2010. "Holocaust Mahnmal (Memorial): Monumental Memory amidst Contemporary Race." *Comparative Studies in Society and History* 52(4): 820–50.

Patai, Raphael. 2002 [1973]. *The Arab Mind*. Rev. ed. New York: W. W. Norton.

Pateman, Carole. 1988. *The Sexual Contract*. London: Polity Press.

Pettitt, Joanne. 2019. "Introduction: New Perspectives on Auschwitz." *kugel* 27(1): 1–11.

Poiger, Uta G. 2000. *Jazz, Rock and Rebels: Cold War Politics and American Culture in a Divided Germany*. Berkeley: University of California Press.

Policy Matters. 2020. *Die Haltung der Deutschen zum Nationalsozialismus, Januar 2020, im Auftrag von Die Zeit: Ergebnisse einer repräsentativen Erhebung*. Berlin: Policy Matters, Gesellschaft für Politikforschung und PolitikBahadi rung mbH. https://www.policy-matters.de/site/assets/files/1400/20200128_zeit_ns-zeit_final_v2.pdf.

Press Association. 2018. "Chelsea to Send Racist Fans on Auschwitz Trips Instead of Banning Them." *The Guardian*, October 11, sec. Football. http://www.theguardian.com/football/2018/oct/11/chelsea-to-send-racist-fans-auschwitz-instead-banning-orders-antisemitism.

Puar, Jasbir. 2008. *Terrorist Assemblages: Homonationalism in Queer Times*. Durham, NC: Duke University Press.

Reich, Wilhelm. 1970 [1933]. *The Mass Psychology of Fascism*. Translated by Vincent R. Carfagno. New York: Farrar, Straus and Giroux.

Reichert, Markus. 2011. *Mit Muslimischen Jugendlichen Israel bereisen*. Documentary. DVD, 30 mins. Redaktion, Kamera, and Schnitt: Markus Reichert.

Rensmann, Lars, and Julius H. Schoeps. 2010. "Politics and Resentment: Examining Antisemitism and Counter-Cosmopolitanism in the European Union and Beyond." In *Politics and Resentment: Antisemitism and Counter-Cosmopolitanism in the European Union*, edited by Lars Rensmann and Julius H. Schoeps, 1–79. Leiden: Brill Academic. https://brill.com/view/book/edcoll/9789004190474/B9789004190474_002.xml.

Reuters in Berlin. 2017. "AfD Co-Founder Says Germans Should Be Proud of Its Second World War Soldiers." *The Guardian*, September 14. http://www.theguardian.com/world/2017/sep/14/afd-co-founder-alexander-gauland-says-germany-needs-to-reclaim-its-history.

Ringelstein, Ronja. 2017. "Vorredner von Björn Höcke: Der Richter von Der AfD: Ein Demagoge in Robe." *Der Tagesspiegel*, January 24, sec. Politik. https://www.tagesspiegel.de/politik/vorredner-von-bjoern-hoecke-der-richter-von-der-afd-ein-demagoge-in-robe/19295504.html.

Rhue, Morton. 1993 [1981]. *The Wave*. New York: Laurel Leaf Library.

Robbins, Joel, and Alan Rumsey. 2008. "Introduction: Cultural and Linguistic Anthropology and the Opacity of Other Minds." *Anthropological Quarterly* 81(2): 407–20.

Romeyn, Esther. 2020. "(Anti) 'New Antisemitism' as a Transnational Field of Racial Governance." *Patterns of Prejudice* 54(1–2): 199–214.

Rosenfeld, Alan. 2020. "Pork Chop Anti-Semitism." *Tablet Magazine*, May 4. https://www.tabletmag.com/sections/news/articles/pork-chop-anti-semitism.

Rothberg, Michael. 2009. *Multidirectional Memory: Remembering Holocaust at the Age of Decolonization*. Stanford, CA: Stanford University Press.

Rothberg, Michael, and Yasemin Yıldız. 2011. "Memory Citizenship: Migrant Archives of Holocaust Remembrance in Contemporary Germany." *Parallax* 17(4): 32–48.

Said, Edward. 2003. *Orientalism*. London: Penguin.

Sayre-McCord, G. 2013. "Hume and Smith on Sympathy, Appropriation and Moral Judgement." *Social Philosophy and Policy* 30(1–2): 208–36.

Schaffner, Bertram. 1948. *Father Land: A Study of Authoritarianism in the German Family*. New York: Columbia University Press.

Schein, Seth L. 1984. *The Mortal Hero: An Introduction to Homer's Iliad*. Berkeley: University of California Press.

Schissler, Hanna. 2001. *The Miracle Years: A Cultural History of West Germany, 1949–1968*. Princeton, NJ: Princeton University Press.

Schmidt, Christoph. 2010. "The Israel of the Spirit: The German Student Movement of the 1960s and Its Attitude to the Holocaust." *Dapim: Studies on the Holocaust*. 24(1): 269–318.

Schmidt, Thomas. 2021. "Der Holocaust war kein Kolonialverbrechen." *Die Zeit*, April 11. https://www.zeit.de/2021/15/erinnerungskultur-holocaust-kolonialismus-menschheitsverbrechen-vergleichbarkeit-michael-rothberg-juergen-zimmerer?utm_referrer=https%3A%2F%2Fwww.google.com%2F.

Schneider, Michael, and Jamie Owen Daniel. 1984. "Fathers and Sons, Retrospectively: The Damaged Relationship between Two Generations." *New German Critique* 31: 3–51.

Schrader, Hannes. 2018. "Holocaust: Bahadir fährt nach Auschwitz." *Die Zeit*, July 9. https://www.zeit.de/campus/2018-06/holocaust-deutsche-identitaet-muslime-tuerken-antisemitismus.

Schrire, Dani. 2010. "Raphael Patai, Jewish Folklore, Comparative Folkloristics, and American Anthropology." *Journal of Folklore Research* 47(1/2): 7–43.

Schwab, Gabriele. 2010. *Haunting Legacies: Violent Histories and Transnational Trauma*. New York: Columbia University Press.

Seidel, Claudius. 2021. "War der Holocaust eine koloniale Tat?" *Frankfurter Allgemeine Zeitung*, March 1. https://www.faz.net/aktuell/feuilleton/streit-um-gedenkkultur-war-der-holocaust-eine-koloniale-tat-17217645.html.

Şenocak, Zafer, and Bülent Tülay. 2000. "Germany-Home for Turks?" In Zafer Şenocak, *Atlas of a Tropical Germany: Essays on Politics and Culture, 1990–1998*. Translated and edited by Leslie Adelson. Lincoln: University of Nebraska Press.

Sheramy, Rona. 2007. "From Auschwitz to Jerusalem: Re-enacting Jewish History on the March of the Living." In *Polin 19*, edited by Mieczslaw B. Biskupski and Antony Polonsky, 307–26. Oxford: Littman Library for Jewish Civilization.

Shooman, Yasemin. 2014 *". . . weil ihre Kultur so ist": Narrative des antimuslimischen Rassismus*. Bielefeld: Transcript Verlag.

Shoshan, Nitzan. 2017. *The Management of Hate: Nation, Affect, and the Governance of Right-Wing Extremism in Germany*. Princeton, NJ: Princeton University Press.

Sieg, Katrin. 2010. "Black Virgins: Sexuality and the Democratic Body in Europe." *New German Critique* 109: 147–85.

Silverstein, Paul. 2008. "The Context of Anti-Semitism and Islamophobia in France." *Patterns of Prejudice* 42(1): 1–26.

Smale, Alison. 2015. "Memo from Europe: Teaching the Holocaust to Muslim Germans, or Not." *New York Times*, June 17. https://www.nytimes.com/2015/06/18/world/europe/teaching-the-holocaust-to-muslim-germans-or-not.html (accessed 9 June 2018).

Spielhaus, Riem. 2011. *Wer is hier Muslim? Die entwicklung eines islamischen Bewustseins in Deutchland zwischen Selbstidentifikation und Fremdzuschriebung*. Wuerzburg: Ergon Verlag.

Spierings, Niels, and Andrej Zaslove, 2015. "Gendering the Vote for Populist Radical Right Parties." *Patterns of Prejudice* 49(1–2): 135–62.

Staas, Christian. 2020. "Das Ende der Selbstgewissheit." *Die Zeit*, April 28. https://www.zeit.de/2020/19/erinnerungskultur-nationalsozialismus-aufarbeitung-deutschland-rechtsextremismus-umfrage?utm_referrer=https%3A%2F%2Fwww.google.com%2F.

Stewart, Lizzie. 2017. "Postmigrant Theatre: The Ballhaus Naunynstraße Takes on Sexual Nationalism." *Journal of Aesthetics & Culture* 9(2): 56–68.

Stoler, Ann Laura. 1989. "Rethinking Colonial Categories: European Communities and the Boundaries of Rule." *Comparative Studies in Society and History* 31(1): 134–61.

Sukarieh, Mayssoun. 2012. "The Hope Crusades: Culturalism and Reform in the Arab World." *Political and Legal Anthropology Review* 35(1): 115–34.

Taguieff, Pierre-Andre. 2004. *Rising from the Muck: The New Anti-Semitism in Europe*. Translated by Patrick Camiller. Chicago: Ivan R. Dee.

Terkessidis, Mark. 2017. *Nach der Flucht: Neue Ideen für die Einwanderungsgesellschaft*. Ditzingen: Reclam.

Thiel, Thomas. 2019. "Der Kurswechsel wird zum Kraftakt." *Frankfurter Allgemeine Zeitung*, December 17. https://www.faz.net/1.6538869.

Throop, C. Jason. 2008. "On the Problem of Empathy: The Case of Yap, Federated States of Micronesia." *Ethos* 36(4): 402–26.

Throop, C. Jason. 2012. "On the Varieties of Empathic Experience: Tactility, Mental Opacity, and Pain in Yap." *Medical Anthropology Quarterly* 26(3): 408–30.

Ticktin, Miriam. 2011. *Casualties of Care: Immigration and the Politics of Humanitarianism in France. Berkeley: University of California Press.*

Tietze, Nikola. 2006. "Gemeinschaftsnarrationen in der Einwanderungsgesellschaft: Eine Fallstudie uber Palastinenser in Berlin." In *Neue Judenfeindschaft? Perspektiven fur den padagogischen Umgang mit dem globalisierten Anti-Semitismus: Jahrbuch zur Geschichte und Wirking des Holocaust*, edited by Bernd Fehler, Fritz Bauer Institute, and Jugenbegegnungs stätte Anne Frank, 80–102. Frankfurt a.M: Campus.

Toprak, Binnaz. 1990. "Religion as State Ideology in a Secular Setting: The Turkish-Islamic Synthesis." In *Aspects of Religion in Secular Turkey*, edited by Malcolm Wagstaff, 10–15. Durham: Center for Islamic and Middle Eastern Studies, University of Durham.

Turner, Victor. 1973. *The Forest of Symbols: Aspects of Ndembu Ritual*. Ithaca, NY: Cornell University Press.

United States Holocaust Memorial Museum. 2019. "Rationale and Learning Objectives." https://www.ushmm.org/teach/fundamentals/rationale-learning-objectives.

van der Veer, Peter. 2006. "Pim Fortuyn, Theo van Gogh, and the Politics of Tolerance in the Netherlands." *Public Culture* 18(1): 111–24. https://doi.org/10.1215/08992363-18-1-111.

van Rahden, Till. 2011. "Clumsy Democrats: Moral Passions in the Federal Republic." *German History* 29(3): 485–504.

van Rahden, Till. 2019. *Demokratie: Eine gefährdete Lebensform*. Frankfurt: Campus Verlag GmbH.

Virtue, Rob. 2018. "Horror on Streets of Germany: State of Emergency Declared as 80 Men Brawl with MACHETES." *Express*, March 29. https://www.express.co.uk/news/uk/938824/Germany-news-duisburg-state-of-emergency-fight-riot-machetes.

Vischer, Robert, Conrad Fiedler, Heinrich Wolfflin, Adolf Goller, Adolf Hildebrand, and August Schmarsow. 1993. *Empathy, Form, and Space: Problems in German Aesthetics, 1873–1893*. Translated by Harry Francis Mallgrave and Eleftherios Ikonomou. Santa Monica, CA: Getty Center for the History of Art and the Humanities.

von Bieberstein, Alice. 2016. "Not a German Past to Be Reckoned With: Negotiating Migrant Subjectivities between *Vergangenheitsbewältigung* and the Nationalization of History." *Journal of the Royal Anthropological Institute* 22(4): 902–19.

Welch, Stephen, and Ruth Wittlinger. 2011. "The Resilience of the Nation State: Cosmopolitanism, Holocaust Memory, and the Nation State." *German Politics and Society* 29(3): 38–54.

Whine, Michael. 2004. "International Organizations Combating Anti-Semitism in Europe." *Jewish Political Studies Review* 16: 3–4.

Whitaker, Brian. 2004. " 'Its Best Use Is as a Doorstop.' " *The Guardian*, May 24, sec. World News. http://www.theguardian.com/world/2004/may/24/worlddispatch.usa.

Wiederwald, Rupert. 2018. "Gauland bezeichnet NS-Zeit als 'Vogelschiss in der Geschichte.' " *Deutsche Welle*, February 6. https://www.dw.com/de/gauland-bezeichnet-ns-zeit-als-vogelschiss-in-der-geschichte/a-44054219.

Wilds, Karl. 2013. "Cultural Memories of German Suffering during the Second World War: An Inability *Not* to Mourn?" In *The Use and Abuse of Memory: Interpreting World War II in Contemporary European Politics*, edited by C. Karner and B. Mertens, 81–100. Piscataway, NJ: Transaction Books.

Wolfgram, Mark A. 2010. *"Getting History Right": East and West German Collective Memories of the Holocaust and War*. Lewisburg, PA: Bucknell University Press.

Wolf-Graaf, Anke, and Jarek Presnück. 2015. *Junge Muslime in Auschwitz.* Documentary. 27 mins.

Wüllenweber, Walter. 2018. "In Deutschland gibt es No-Go-Areas, behaupten Populisten." *Die Stern.* https://www.stern.de/politik/deutschland/deutschland--no-go-areas--ortsbesuch-in-duisburg-marxloh-und-neukoelln-8206968.html

Wüstenberg, Jenny. 2017. *Civil Society and Memory in Postwar Germany.* Cambridge: Cambridge University Press.

Yıldız, Yasemin. 2011. "Governing European Subjects: Tolerance and Guilt in the Discourse of 'Muslim Women.'" *Cultural Critique* 77(1): 70–101.

Yılmaz, Burak. 2016. "Judenhass als Teil der Erziehung." Blog, July 3. Diekolumnisten.de/2016/06/03/judenhass-als-teil-der-erziehung/.

Yılmaz, Burak. 2018. "Blog." *Burak Yilmaz* (blog), January 14. http://burak-yilmaz.de/hallo-welt/.

Yılmaz, Burak. 2021. *Ehrensache: Kämpfen gegen Judenhass.* Berlin: Suhrkamp Taschenbuch.

Younes, Anna. 2020. "Fighting Anti-Semitism in Contemporary Germany." *Islamophobia Studies Journal* 5(2): 249–66.

Yurdakul, Gökçe, and Y. Michal Bodemann. 2006. " 'We Don't Want to Be the Jews of Tomorrow': Jews and Turks in Germany after 9/11." *German Politics and Society* 24(2/79): 44–67.

Zahavi, Dan. 2003. *Husserl's Phenomenology.* Stanford, CA: Stanford University Press.

Zahavi, Dan. 2014. *Self and Other: Exploring Subjectivity, Empathy, and Shame.* Oxford: Oxford University Press.

Zamkanei, Shayna. 2016. "Justice for Jews from Arab Countries and the Remembrance of the Jewish Refugee." *International Journal of Middle East Studies* 48(3): 511–30.

Zick, Andreas, and Beate Küpper. 2011. *Antisemitische Mentalitäten. Bericht über Ergebnisse des Forschungsprojektes Gruppenbezogene Menschenfeindlichkeit in Deutschland und Europa. Expertise für den Expertenkreis Antisemitismus.* Report. Bielefeld: Expertenkreis Antisemitismus und Bundesministerium des Inneren.

Zick, Andreas, Daniela Krause, Wilhelm Berghan, and Beate Küpper. 2016. "Gruppenbezogene Menschenfeindlichkeit in Deutschland 2002–2016." In *Gespaltene Mitte—Feindselige Zustände: Rechtsextreme Einstellungen in Deutschland 2016*, edited by Daniela Krause, Andreas Zick, and Beate Küpper, 33–81. Bonn: Verlag J. H. W. Dietz Nachf.

Zimmerer, Jürgen. 2011. *Von Windhuk nach Auschwitz?: Beiträge zum Verhältnis von Koloniasmus und Holocaust.* Münster: LIT Verlag.

INDEX

Endnotes are referenced with "n" followed by the endnote number.